SELECTED DICKINSON LECTURES IN ACCOUNTING 1936-1952

This is a volume in the Arno Press collection

THE DEVELOPMENT OF CONTEMPORARY ACCOUNTING THOUGHT

See last pages of this volume for a complete list of titles.

SELECTED DICKINSON LECTURES IN ACCOUNTING 1936-1952

Edited by
Stephen A. Zeff

With an Introduction

ARNO PRESS
A New York Times Company
New York • 1978

Publisher's Note: This book has been reproduced from the best available copies.

Editorial Supervision: LUCILLE MAIORCA

Reprint Edition 1978 by Arno Press Inc.

THE DEVELOPMENT OF CONTEMPORARY ACCOUNTING THOUGHT
ISBN for complete set: 0-405-10891-5
See last pages of this volume for titles.

Manufactured in the United States of America

Library of Congress Cataloging in Publication Data

Main entry under title:

Selected Dickinson lectures in accounting, 1936-1952.

(The Development of contemporary accounting thought)
Reprint of selected lectures published 1942-1952.
CONTENTS: May, G. O. Improvement in financial accounts.--Paton, W. A. Recent and prospective developments in accounting theory.--Staub, W. A. Auditing developments during the present century. [etc.]
1. Accounting--Addresses, essays, lectures.
2. Financial statements--Addresses, essays, lectures.
I. Zeff, Stephen A. II. Series.
HF5629.S44 657 77-87323
ISBN 0-405-10935-0

ACKNOWLEDGMENTS

Reprinted by permission of the *Harvard Business Review*; "Problems in Reporting Corporate Income, "by George D. Bailey, September, 1948. Copyright © 1948 by the President and Fellows of Harvard College; all rights reserved.

Reprinted by permission of the Harvard Business Review; "Concepts of Income," by George D. Bailey, November, 1948. Copyright © 1948 by the President and Fellows of Harvard College; all rights reserved.

Reprinted by permission of the Harvard Business Review; "Cost Factors in Price-Making," by Howard Clark Greer, July/August, 1952. Copyright © 1952 by the President and Fellows of Harvard College; all rights reserved.

"Improvement in Financial Accounts" and "Recent and Prospective Developments in Accounting Theory" were reprinted by permission of the publishers from *Dickenson Lectures in Accounting*, 1936-1940, George O. May, and others, Cambridge, Mass.: Harvard University Press, Copyright © 1943, 1971 by the President and Fellows of Harvard College.

Reprinted by permission of the publishers from *Auditing Developments During the Present Century* by Walter A. Staub, Cambridge, Mass.: Harvard University Press, Copyright © 1942, 1970 by the President and Fellows of Harvard College.

Reprinted by permission of the publishers from *Surplus and Dividends* by Henry Rand Hatfield, Cambridge, Mass.: Harvard University Press, Copyright © 1943, 1971 by the President and Fellows of Harvard College.

By Stephen A. Zeff

The Dickinson Lectures in Accounting were given at the Graduate School of Business Administration of Harvard University between 1936-1937 and 1954-1955. The Arthur Lowes Dickinson Fund had been established in January, 1929, by the public accounting firm of Price, Waterhouse & Co. "in recognition of the debt due by the accounting profession in general, and particularly by this firm, to a former partner, Sir Arthur Lowes Dickinson."

Initially, the income from this fund was used exclusively to support accounting research, but in 1936, a year after the death of Sir Arthur, the terms of the Fund were modified to provide that "in addition there may from time to time be appointed, for one year, a man outstanding in Accounting who shall deliver at the Graduate School of Business Administration one or more lectures, and shall be designated as Dickinson Lecturer."[1]

The Dickinson Lectures were apparently the first endowed lecture series in accounting in the United States. Each Lecture

---

[1]The historical background of the Dickinson Lectures is taken from the Foreword in Dickinson Lectures in Accounting (George O. May, Sir Laurence Halsey, William A. Paton) (Cambridge, Mass.: Harvard University Press, 1943), p. vii. For a biographical article on Dickinson, see Mary E. Murphy, "Arthur Lowes Dickinson: Pioneer in American Professional Accountancy," Bulletin of the Business Historical Society, 21 (April, 1947), pp. 27-38.

was published by the Harvard University Press or appeared as a pair of articles in the Harvard Business Review. The complete list of the 15 Lectures appears below:

1936-1937 Improvement in Financial Accounts, George O. May

1937-1938 The Position of the Public Accountant in Relation to Business and Government in Great Britain, Sir Laurence Halsey

1939-1940 Recent and Prospective Developments in Accounting Theory, William A. Paton

1940-1941 Auditing Developments During the Present Century, Walter A. Staub

1941-1942 Surplus and Dividends, Henry Rand Hatfield

1942-1943 Accounting in the Administration of Large Business Enterprises, Charles A. Heiss

1946-1947 The Comptroller: His Functions and Organization, J. Hugh Jackson

1947-1948 Problems in Reporting Corporation Income; Concepts of Income, George D. Bailey

1948-1949 Depreciation and 1949 Price Levels; Two Concepts of Accounting, Thomas H. Sanders

1949-1950 Accounting for Pensions, Arthur H. Dean

1950-1951 The Path of Accounting - Past and Future, Percival F. Brundage

1951-1952 Prices and Costs in a Free Economy; Prices and Costs under Government Regulation, Howard C. Greer

1952-1953 Accounting and the Accountant in Management, Harry Elmer Humphreys, Jr.

1953-1954 Wanted: More Owners of American Business, G. Keith Funston

1954-1955 Public Accounting Practice and Accounting Education, Donald P. Perry

The Lecturers were six partners in public accounting firms, four university academics, three corporation executives, a Wall Street lawyer, and the President of the New York Stock Exchange.

In this collection, we reprint six of the Lectures which, in the editor's opinion, possess enduring value. The editor joins Arno Press Inc. in expressing gratitude to the Harvard University Press and the *Harvard Business Review* for their permission to reproduce these essays.

George O. May, in the first Dickinson Lecture, touches upon the theme, so often found in his writings, that the financial accounts "must always be largely a matter of convention, judgment, and opinion" and are "necessarily tentative and approximate." In such a circumstance, consistency and fair disclosure are "supreme virtues." May cautions that the accounts "cannot rise higher in the scale of certainty than the events which they reflect." This Lecture provides a succinct statement of May's views at a pivotal moment in the development of enunciated accounting principles in the United States.

Three years later, William A. Paton echoes the commonplace assertion of the 1930s, also to be found in May's Lecture, that the income statement had superseded the balance sheet as the more important financial statement. Paton contrasts different views of the accounting entity and proceeds to examine the controversies surrounding the accounting recognition of revenue and expense. Several of the Patonian peeves--classification of purchase discounts as revenue, the inclusion in plant cost of the interest implicit in lump-sum debt payments to be made in future years, cost ranking, and "self-insurance"--are exposed to critical review. Paton's recommendations on asset revaluation are much affected by his view, evidently formulated in the early 1930s, that "the accountant is inevitably coerced in considerable measure by the legal framework." Historical cost possesses legal standing, a brutal fact which the accountant may not safely ignore. Paton therefore urges "compromise procedures" and supplementary disclosures in order that current values and general price-level effects might be communicated to readers without obliterating historical costs. This is a good summary of Paton _circa_ 1939, replete with the beguiling metaphors for which the author is well known.

From 1914 until his death in 1945, Walter A. Staub was a partner in the New York office of the public accounting firm of Lybrand, Ross Bros. & Montgomery (as it was then known). When his Lecture was given, he was a member of the Committee on Accounting Procedure of the American Institute of Accountants. (May, Paton, and George D. Bailey were also prominent members of the Committee.) His Lecture is as much a review of accounting as of auditing developments, and perhaps the most valuable portion is Part III, in which he discusses the evolution of the auditor's report. Staub quotes from numerous important documents, including some to which access today would be quite difficult.

Of particular interest is his discussion of the influence of the tax law on accounting practice beginning with the abruptly higher tax rates in 1917-1918. Staub's Lecture was given shortly after the Securities and Exchange Commission had completed its lengthy investigation into the colossal fraud at McKesson & Robbins, Inc., and the reforms in auditing practice brought about by the scandal and the resulting shock waves are recounted with especial immediacy.

"Surplus and Dividends" was Henry Rand Hatfield's last major work. The Lecture is characteristically Hatfieldian, as it knits together the threads of an unraveled literature. Hatfield is tolerant of others' views, but he is not reluctant to prick the balloons of assertion and bluster. Of particular interest are 14 pages of comment on the accounting recognition of asset appreciation. Inconsistencies and illogic are exposed with relish, and one can almost see the glint in Hatfield's eye as he gently compares the Paton of 1918 to the Paton of the 1930s. Hatfield is not to be read for proclamations or pronunciamentos. One reads Hatfield for insights into the writings of others. That he was more an annotator than an advocate is everywhere evident in his Dickinson Lecture.

The latter 1940s were a period of strain for the American accounting profession. Corporate profits were being widely attacked as excessive at a time when accountants could not agree on how to account for the effects of inflation. Moreover, the

SEC and the Institute's Committee on Accounting Procedure were at odds over the treatment of unusual and nonrecurring items. George D. Bailey, who was one of the founders of the firm then known as Touche, Niven, Bailey & Smart, served as chairman of the Institute's Committee on Accounting Procedure from 1944 to 1947. It should not be surprising, therefore, that Bailey would place heavy emphasis on "a sharp determination of earnings." Bailey's explanation of the historical background of the controversy over the "all-inclusive vs. current operating performance" notions of the income statement is especially instructive.

In the final essay, Howard Clark Greer, a financial executive who has also toiled in the groves of acadème, discusses the reciprocal relation between costs and prices. "The fact is," writes Greer, "that prices and costs are in a continuous process of becoming adjusted to each other, with neither in absolute control." Greer offers a pragmatic guide to the interrelations between (and among) cost, price, and volume in both unregulated and regulated industries.

CONTENTS

IMPROVEMENT IN FINANCIAL ACCOUNTS

By GEORGE O. MAY
Partner; Price, Waterhouse & Co., New York

I. HISTORICAL

IT GIVES ME special pleasure to be lecturing here and on this Foundation, because the first Dean of the School and the man in whose honor this lectureship is founded were the two who most influenced my adult life. My first words must be a recognition of my debt to them and an expression of my gratitude. My next should, perhaps, express my satisfaction that after twenty-seven years I have been invited to reappear as a lecturer at the School.

Improvement in financial accounts seems to be the inevitable choice as the subject for the lectures which the faculty of the Business School has done me the honor of asking me to deliver. It lies in the field of accounting with which I have been mainly concerned and regarding which I am best qualified to speak; it is also the field in which the accountant in whose honor this Foundation was established was preeminent. It is a subject which possesses importance not only to those of you whose main preoccupation after you have completed your course will be with accounts, but to all who expect to be interested in any active phase of American business. It is one that lends itself to discussion outside the carefully arranged courses in accounting which form a part of your education here. Moreover, it is a subject of great public importance, the interest in which has increased notably in the last decade.

Developments under the Securities Acts have already influenced practice in the field of financial accounting, and I believe that important changes in the form of presentation of such accounts are likely to occur in the coming years. These changes will be made in an attempt to meet more fully the needs of business and of investors. All of you, therefore, will have an interest in them and some of you may be able to exercise an influence upon their character. So in these lectures I am going to try to discuss in a broad rather than a technical way some considerations relating to financial accounts and their presentation. I shall discuss the question in relation to corporations, because it is the financial accounts of corporations which are of the greatest importance, and because such accounts present substantially all the problems which are involved in financial accounts of unincorporated businesses, with some added complexities due to the law of corporations.

By financial accounts I mean those kept for the purpose of affording guidance in regard to the financial position and results of an enterprise — to either the management, the stockholders, or others. Those accounts which are kept to record amounts due to creditors or by debtors, or to afford guidance to those in charge of operations, do not come within the scope of this discussion although naturally the figures shown by them are reflected in the financial statements. I am concerned, rather, with the balance sheet, the income and profit and loss accounts, and the general accounts which underlie them. At the outset I should like to warn you that the terminology of accountancy is somewhat loose and vague, and particularly I would draw your attention to two usages which are so common that I may quite probably fall into them myself. When you hear a reference made to an accounting "principle" you may find that in reality it is nothing more exalted than a convention or a rule of convenience. In the same way, when reference is made to a "valuation," you will be well advised to stop to consider whether what is referred to is really a valuation or whether it is not merely a determination by a process other than valuation of the figure at which an asset or a liability is to be stated.

The accounting profession is so frequently reproached with the looseness of its use of the terms "value" and "valuation" that it will welcome the recent publication of Professor Bonbright's treatise on the subject,[1] which aptly begins with the quotation of Humpty Dumpty's classic dictum that when he used a word it meant exactly what he chose it to mean, neither

[1] J. C. Bonbright, *The Valuation of Property* (New York, McGraw-Hill Book Company, 1937).

more nor less; and proceeds to demonstrate conclusively in what Humpty Dumptian language the law and decisions on valuation are written.

Ten years ago I should have thought it necessary to begin any discussion of this subject by explaining at some length why financial accounts are always in some measure (and in the case of a complex business, perhaps in a very large measure) based on conventions, estimates, and opinion. Today, I think, this fact may be taken for granted, and recognition of it and of the implications from it is a prerequisite of any solution of the problem of improving the financial reports of corporations. If any of you do not fully understand why this should be so, you can secure enlightenment from the admirable report made in 1934 by Professor T. H. Sanders for a committee of which Mr. Walter S. Gifford was chairman, and which has been published by the Department of Commerce under the title *Reports to Stockholders*; or in a report which was made by a committee of the American Institute of Accountants to the New York Stock Exchange in 1932.

The field of financial accounting is not one in which guidance is to be found wholly in fixed principles — it is a field of shadowy outlines in which the discovery of a correct course depends upon the possession also of an ability to recognize the essential facts and to appreciate their true significance (distinguishing where necessary between form and substance); upon informed and wise judgment; and upon objectiveness and honesty of purpose. It will be observed that these are not qualities which can be insured by regulation. When the committee of the American Institute of Accountants to which I have referred undertook to lay down some of the basic principles of modern accounting, it found itself unable to suggest more than half a dozen which could be regarded as generally acceptable, and even those were rules rather than principles, and were, moreover, admittedly subject to exception.

Some may question what I have just said and ask whether the distinction between capital and income, for instance, is not a fundamental principle of accounting. As a practical matter, no doubt it is; though the distinction in accounting today between capital expenditure and income expenditure does not rest on any such essential difference in the nature of the property acquired as that between land and other property which is sometimes made in the field of economics. It rests, rather, upon the relation between the length of the useful life of the property acquired and the length of the accounting period for which income is being determined. A capital expenditure is one, the usefulness of which is expected to extend over several accounting periods. If the accounting period were increased from the customary year to a decade, most of what is now treated as capital expenditure would become chargeable to income; while if the period were reduced to a day, much of what is now treated as current maintenance would become capital expenditure.

I shall not dwell on these considerations, because I am sure that the point which I am trying to make has been impressed on you in the course of your work, since to the businessman it is the most vital single fact in relation to accounts. All accounts, if I may restate the point, are necessarily tentative and approximate; in many cases alternative methods of accounting which will produce materially different results may be equally permissible; and therefore the weight to be attached to any accounts can only be determined upon consideration of the bases on which they have been prepared (which may legitimately vary according to the purpose for which they are intended) and of the competence and integrity of those by whom they have been prepared. While it is necessary to make this point clear as a foundation for any discussion of the subject, recognition of the limitations on the significance of accounts should not be allowed to obscure their great value — indeed, despite their inevitable limitations, they are an indispensable part of the equipment of modern business. In this, as in almost every field of endeavor, we have to operate on the basis of working hypotheses and approximations which, though not completely valid for all purposes, are nevertheless practically effective for the ordinary purposes of daily life.

The fact that accounts may properly differ according to the purposes for which they are prepared requires some further notice. Much heated argument, particularly in the field of cost accounts, has arisen from a failure to recognize this. The cost accountant rightly insists that in any comparative figures of cost designed to show the relative profitability of different products regard should be had to the difference in the amount of capital employed and the resulting difference in the capital cost as well as to the relative amount of labor employed and the resulting difference in labor cost. He concludes, therefore, that interest should be included in cost. The financial accountant (equally rightly, as I think) insists that to treat interest as a part of cost in financial accounts is to anticipate a profit, which is contrary to one of the most generally accepted rules of financial accounting. To my mind, it is not so much a matter of one accountant being right and the other wrong, as of accounts being made up for entirely different purposes. The real difficulty arises when accounts are required for different purposes and the question has to be decided whether entirely separate accounts shall be prepared for each, whether accounts prepared for the major purpose shall be adjusted roughly to fit any other purposes, or whether a compromise method of accounting shall be adopted which will meet with a reasonable degree of satisfaction all the purposes for which they are required. Railroad and public utility accounts which are required for the purpose of an annual report, of a prospectus, and of supplying information needed by the regulatory bodies are a case in point.

It is gratifying to note a growing recognition outside the profession of the fact that the form of accounts is quite legitimately influenced by the purpose for which they are required. Indeed, Professor Bonbright turns the tables and asks for wider recognition of it within the profession:

It is to be hoped that the accounting profession will give far more attention than it has heretofore given to the effect on the "proper" balance sheet and earnings statement of the specific purposes for which these financial documents are customarily used. A good beginning could be made by assuming, first, that no use will be made of the company's reports except by buyers and sellers of the corporate stock. In the light of this single assumed objective, all of the alternative procedures of accounting, such as the valuation of fixed assets at original cost versus replacement cost, the use of straight-line versus sinking-fund methods of depreciation, the booking of current assets at cost versus the lower of cost or market, and so forth, might be subjected to a critical rating of their relative merits. This task having been accomplished, the accountant might then forget the stockholder and assume that an "ideal" set of financial reports is such a set as will best fit the needs of the credit department of a commercial bank. Still other objects, such as that of the company management in the determination of its price-making policies, or such as that of the management in its decisions as to whether to increase this line of business and to drop that line, would be taken up in turn. The result of this inquiry would be the creation of standards for "single-purpose" balance sheets and earnings statements. Further research would consider the question whether a workable multiple-purpose scheme of accounts might not be so devised that, by the aid of pencil and paper, a reader could reconstruct the accounts to fit his own requirements.

Already some work of this nature has been done; for the progressive-minded accountants have abandoned the traditional notion that a balance sheet can be said to be right or wrong by reference to any universal standards of correctness; and they are thinking in terms of the special functions that the accounts are supposed to serve, as guides to business conduct. But until this task has been pursued with far more vigor than has yet been the case, there will remain countless unsettled questions as to the extent to which the earnings reported by a company, even after approval by reputable auditors, are acceptable evidence of the capital value of the property.[2]

Now, this fact as to the form of accounts has an important bearing on the question what direction improvements in present practice in corporation reports ought to take. In order to make its importance clearer, it seems worth while to trace briefly the history of the development of corporations and corporate accounts. For this purpose, we may divide business history into three periods according to the relative importance

[2] *Op. cit.*, pp. 253 f.

therein of three different forms of business organization: (a) the individual venture or partnership; (b) the corporation with limited liability, which is owned and managed by a relatively small group of stockholders, and for whose securities there is no public market; (c) the corporation owned by relatively large numbers of stockholders, the management of which may be largely divorced from beneficial ownership and the securities of which are bought and sold freely on an established securities market. We are apt to forget how recently the change to these second and third forms of organization took place in our country. As Judge Learned Hand, in his foreword to the fiftieth volume of the *Harvard Law Review* (1936–1937), has recently pointed out: ". . . it was during the last half century that the practice became common, by means of the private corporation, to conduct industry without personal liability"; and the records show that forty years ago only thirty industrial stocks were listed on the New York Stock Exchange. Even in England, from which our accounting thought was in earlier days largely derived, general limited liability legislation was not enacted until after the middle of the nineteenth century.

Now, so long as the individual proprietorship and the partnership were the typical, if not the only, forms in which business was conducted, the only restriction on the right of the owners to adopt such accounting methods as they thought fit was the obligation to do nothing that might be fraudulent as against creditors, and the fact that the owners of the business were personally liable for all its debts was a substantial assurance against this restriction being widely ignored.

The introduction of the principle of limited liability made the protection of creditors more important. The legal capital of such companies was regarded as the main protection of creditors. This view is characteristically reflected in the lines of W. S. Gilbert's *Utopia, Ltd.:*

> Some seven men form an Association
> (If possible, all Peers and Baronets),

> They start off with a public declaration
> To what extent they mean to pay their debts.
> That's called their Capital.

Stringent rules were made to safeguard creditors against any reduction of the legal capital otherwise than in the manner contemplated by law — which involved notice to creditors and an opportunity for them to be heard before a reduction could be made effective. Thus a question was raised which has been before courts and legislatures many times and in many forms. Should the capital (which may not be paid out except in a proceeding for the reduction of capital) be deemed to be the property paid in for capital stock or the money value of that property at the time when it was paid in? If, for instance, a corporation acquires a mine of the supposed value of $1,000,000 by the issue of capital stock of a par value of a million dollars, is the capital which must not be impaired the mine or the million dollars? Is the position different if the corporation sells stock for a million dollars and pays the million dollars in cash for the mine? If, later, the corporation sells a half interest in the mine for a million dollars, is that million dollars capital or income? Conversely, if the value of the mine shrinks to half a million, must the other half million be made good out of income before any dividends can be declared?

So varied, important, and difficult are the problems resulting from the choice of either horn of this dilemma that the American Institute of Accountants some years ago offered $10,000 in prizes for the best discussion of the subject, without, however, securing any notable contribution toward the solution of the difficulty. It is, I think, true to say also that the basic questions involved have never yet been satisfactorily settled by either legislatures or courts.

Except for the important change in the matter of the protection necessary for creditors, the position of what is still called in England the private company presented, from the accounting standpoint, few differences from the earlier partnership; it was still permissible for stockholders to adopt such accounting methods for the determination of profits and of the amounts divisible by way of dividends as they might see fit, so long as they did not impair the just rights of creditors.

The English rule is laconic; it reads: "No dividend shall be paid otherwise than out of profits." Even this is not a rule of law, but a standard provision which is commonly adopted. The law contents itself with saying how capital may be reduced and leaves the rest to inference. Buckley, discussing the question, mentions the many cases that have been decided and the difficulty of reconciling the decisions; he then refers to the rule that dividends must not be paid out of capital and goes on to say that, subject to this proviso:

> . . . such questions as how the profit and loss account shall be made out, whether profits have been earned, and if so whether they shall be divided, are primarily business questions for the directors or shareholders to determine in accordance with the company's regulations, and provided they act honestly, and in accordance with such regulations in coming to such determination, they discharge all the obligations imposed upon them by the Act.
>
> But the application of even such a plain abstract proposition as that dividends must not be paid out of capital may in practice raise questions of the utmost difficulty in their solution, and the question what are profits and what is capital may be a difficult and sometimes an almost impossible problem to solve. The House of Lords in *Dovey* v. *Cory* accordingly, whilst expressing the view that no great difficulty would arise in dealing with any particular case on its own facts and circumstances, declined to attempt to treat these questions in the abstract or to do that which Parliament has refrained from doing, namely to formulate precise rules for the guidance or embarrassment of business men in the conduct of business affairs.[3]

The introduction of the notion of free transferability, in theory and practice, of shares of capital stock of corporations, however, clearly introduced a new consideration. If stocks were to be held, bought, and sold by persons who were not in the councils of the enterprise, then obviously accounts ought

[3] *The Law and Practice under the Companies Acts*, 11th Ed. (London, Stevens, Stevens & Sons, Ltd., 1930), p. 756, the edition which followed the passage of the Acts of 1928 and 1929, the last important revision of the English company law.

to be so framed as not consciously to mislead to their detriment those who were buying or selling these stocks. Financial accounts of corporations became called upon to serve a double purpose — their traditional purpose of a purely historical report by the management to the proprietors, and a new purpose of affording an indication to potential buyers as well as to potential sellers of the value of the shares of stock in the corporation. The points of view and the interests of the permanent investor and the speculative operator in stocks are by no means identical, and much of the difficulty in the problem of deciding on the form of corporate reports is due to this diversity of interests.

The value of a share of stock is dependent on what it may be expected to produce in the future. Reports dealing with the past are valuable to the extent that they throw light on this probability. The corporate official preparing a report has today to consider, therefore, not only its import as a historical record, but also the implications for the future which it may suggest. In a complex business and in times when conditions are changing rapidly, this is often a task of no mean difficulty.

The first evidence of recognition on any considerable scale of an obligation to give to stockholders who were not in the councils of the corporation a substantial amount of information in regard to their investment may be said to have come about in the first days of the present century. All authorities will probably agree that the first full report of the United States Steel Corporation, which was for the year ending December 31, 1902, was a landmark in the history of this development. The great importance of the Corporation and the public discussion which its report evoked gave wide influence to its example. In the course of the next twenty years, while there were some conspicuous exceptions, corporations whose securities were listed on the public market tended to give more and more information to stockholders and the public, and at the beginning of the Stock Exchange boom in the twenties the information that was currently being given by the great majority of listed companies was, I believe, reasonably satisfactory, if judged on the basis of a comparison with the highest standards observed in other parts of the world.

The time had come when pressure was clearly needed to compel those corporations whose standards were still unsatisfactory to improve their practice. In 1926, two events happened which tended to accelerate this movement: the New York Stock Exchange decided to take an active part in it and selected for that purpose an Executive Assistant to the Committee on Stock List, who carried on a persistent and effective campaign to bring about such an improvement. At the same time, a recognition of other unhealthy developments in corporate practice had aroused concern, and critics of these practices found in the glaring deficiencies of some corporate reports a source of reinforcement of their attack on corporate abuses and a ground for demanding some form of regulation which would at least bring the practice of all up to the highest standard then being observed. Their strictures may have indicated a lack of understanding of the problem and of its difficulties, their criticisms may have been in numerous instances gravely unjust, but at least public attention was drawn in a vivid way to a question of very real importance.

A few years later came the depression, in the course of which heavy losses in corporate securities were sustained by persons in all walks of life. It was inevitable that the same thing should then happen as had happened on numerous similar occasions in the past and which is admirably described in language contained in a pamphlet (published under a pseudonym but attributed by some authorities to Lord Overstone) which was written in 1849. For reference to this pamphlet, I am indebted to a former member of the Harvard Economics Faculty:

> Whenever the fingers are burned, a cure is always lustily called for by those who have been burned the most severely, and their object in this, as in the diversion that has hurt them is always the same — they call for the appointment of a government officer, who shall from time to time regulate how they shall hold their hands to the fire without being burned.

Whether this special interference shall be crowned with success by keeping down the heat of the fire, or by increasing the distance at which the venturesome hand shall be allowed to approach it, is a perplexing difficulty which has not yet been solved. When duly considered, that difficulty must be held to be not a little perplexing; for evidently, if the heat of the fire should be kept so low, or the distance from it so great, as that no hands can be burned, why then there will be no fun in the thing, and the government officer will enjoy a sinecure.[4]

When with the passage of time it shall become possible to review dispassionately the history of the depression, it will, I think, be found that inadequate or misleading reports of established businesses played but a relatively unimportant part in causing the catastrophic losses that were sustained. The speculative fever which produced also the Florida land boom (in which corporate reports played no part whatever), the pyramiding of holding corporations, unsound treatment of stock dividends, and belief in a new economic order encouraged by persons high in the political and economic world were far more potent influences. However, the temper of the times demanded control of the dealings in corporate securities, and of corporate reports, and it was felt, with reason, that confidence would not be restored until a drastic measure designed to create this control had been enacted. Time was pressing, and it may well have been thought impracticable to defer action until a carefully considered measure could be framed and a body competent to administer it satisfactorily created.

The Securities Act of 1933 had the appearance of an attempt to combine two inconsistent policies: one, of laying down specific requirements, to be administered according to rules which were to be outlined in greater detail by the regulating body; the other, of imposing an obligation, under penalties which were extremely, if not extravagantly, heavy, to disclose all information (whether prescribed or not) which was material. The task of administering the law was entrusted to the Federal Trade Commission, a body in many ways ill-suited to the task.

[4] Cf. B. C. Hunt, *The Development of the Business Corporation in England, 1800–1867* (Cambridge, Harvard University Press, 1936), p. 115.

In 1934, control of exchanges and of annual reports was established, and the opportunity was taken to modify some of the more extreme provisions of the Act of 1933 and to transfer the control from the Federal Trade Commission to a newly created Securities and Exchange Commission, of which a distinguished member of the Harvard law faculty became first a member and later chairman. The Commission was, fortunately, in the position of starting anew, and of being able to benefit without being bound by anything which the Federal Trade Commission had done. It wisely permitted temporary registration of existing securities on easy terms while it studied the question of requirements for permanent registration. This study could not fail to bring home to it that the problem with which it had to deal in the matter of corporate reports was far from being (as many, if not most, people had thought) one of requiring facts to be assembled and disclosed, or of sifting truth from falsehood; it was not a task of calling for "instantaneous photographs," in the vivid but somewhat misleading language of Professor Ripley — it was a far more difficult and delicate task, the general nature of which I propose to consider in some detail.

One of the major accomplishments of the Commission up to the present time has been that it has created in the minds of many people, including bankers, businessmen, and accountants, a much clearer understanding of what is practicable and what is impossible in the way of informing investors than existed previously even among those supposed to be most conversant with financial problems. As I have previously indicated, something had been accomplished by bodies such as the New York Stock Exchange and the American Institute of Accountants, but the Commission was obviously in a position of far greater influence and authority, and certainly in this respect it has used its powers to great advantage.

It seems desirable to conclude this rapid historical summary with a statement which may help you to preserve a just perspective. I do not wish for a moment to minimize or to excuse the extent to which some of our corporate officials have in the past heedlessly or wilfully made statements which the facts did not fully warrant or which were bound and perhaps in some cases designed to create expectations that were not likely to be realized. Nevertheless, I feel that even prior to 1934 the reports made by corporations whose securities were widely distributed were, in general, certainly more complete and, in so far as I am in a position to judge, not less fair than those in any other commercial country. This is not to say that the standard was completely satisfactory; on the contrary, it should and I think will be improved, but it was not and is not a case of raising a standard deplorably low.

The ideal set in the present law of statements that are believed by those making them, after due inquiry, to be true, and from which nothing is omitted which is necessary to prevent misinterpretations of them, is a worthy one. Undeniably, it is an exacting one, and it will not be surprising if it is not always attained. Indeed, not all the advocates of the reform are themselves free from criticism for the very defects which they condemn. One misstatement has been so freely made in support of the new laws that it can be criticized without any suggestion that one is being personal — it is, that the law of 1933 was in general character and scope similar to the corresponding portion of the English Companies Acts — an argument that carried great weight with many persons. I was extremely glad to hear Commissioner Landis, at the meeting of the American Management Association in 1935, expressly disclaim any such similarity, which obviously does not exist.

When we turn to consideration of the record of investigations into the financial practices of corporations by Congressional committees and commissions, the failure to attain the standard of fairness preached becomes even more conspicuous.

It is perhaps natural, but none the less regrettable, that some investigators who have studied a few cases in which practices clearly objectionable were followed should have been led to generalize unwarrantably from these experiences and give expression publicly to intemperate and indiscriminate abuse of corporate officials. My own experience, while it has brought to my attention many cases of corporate abuse, convinces me that no wholesale criticism of corporate officials is warranted. Few of us, of course, are so entirely objective in our attitude that our conclusions are altogether unaffected by our desires. The more whole-hearted the devotion of an individual to an enterprise, the more he is likely to be impressed by the importance of the object he seeks to attain and to overlook possible objections to the method which is being employed. I think this explains many of those corporate acts which have seemed open to criticism, just as I have regarded it as the explanation, for instance, of the not uncommon phenomenon of the executives of educational and charitable institutions deliberately understating their income or resources in order to strengthen appeals for new contributions or endowments.

Even the Securities law itself seems to violate the rules of conduct it seeks to establish when, in Section 13 of the Act of 1934, it provides for the filing by corporations of information, documents, and reports which will "insure fair dealing in the security." If such language occurred in a registration statement filed under the Act, can anyone doubt that the Commission would immediately require its elimination on the ground that it is manifestly impossible to insure fair dealing in the securities of a corporation by any set of reports or documents which the corporation could conceivably be required to file?

That reformers and legislators, animated by the best of motives, should thus fall below the high standards they would set for others should, perhaps, make us less harsh in our judgment of the conduct and motives of corporate officers, as well as humbly watchful for evidence of our own infirmities.

Since I have offered criticisms of others, I should add that I have no desire to extenuate the deficiencies of the accounting profession. The criticism which I would most readily concede to be just is that it too has at times exaggerated what could be done for business and investors. It has talked in terms of certainty and complete assurance where only an informed judgment and a substantial additional safeguard could, in fact, be provided. This is the more regrettable because the great value of the service which the profession has rendered, and can continue to render, is undeniable. But, as I have insisted, financial accounts must always be largely a matter of convention, judgment, and opinion — not a matter of certainty. Whoever claims more for them is doing a disservice to the investor, the businessman, and to the profession itself. Certainty would be very welcome in this field just as security in life would be, but it is unattainable and it is mischievous to encourage a belief that it has been or can be achieved.

II. THE PROBLEM OF UNIFORMITY

In my previous lecture, I undertook to discuss the question with which we are concerned mainly in its historical aspects. On this occasion, I propose to outline the problem as it exists today. In order to keep the discussion within reasonable limits, I am going to confine it mainly to the determination of income, which is now generally recognized as the most important single problem in the field of financial accounting.

Fortunately, it will not be necessary for us to enter upon a consideration of the senses in which the word "income" is used in the world of economics. The income with which we are concerned is a practical business concept. Nevertheless, the term has never been defined in any precise way that has met with universal acceptance even in the business world. In England, for instance, the law and practice definitely contemplate such a phenomenon as the gradual conversion of capital into income. There, the proceeds of mining before deduction for depletion, and the gross yield of an annuity, are income, while capital gains are not. With us, the opposite is true in each case.

The question "when is income" offers even greater difficulty than the question "what is income," especially when we are concerned with the income of a modern business, which is a net product from a variety of transactions linked in continuous series. As I pointed out in the first lecture, also, an income account may be designed to show what income has been realized in a given period or what was the earning capacity of the business under the conditions existing during the period — and is, more frequently, something in the nature of a compromise between the two. In some cases, also, what is required to be determined is the income of the enterprise which is being carried on, while in others it is the income of the particular corporation which is carrying on that enterprise. For instance, the requirement recently sustained by the Supreme Court that utilities shall record property on the basis of cost to the first owner employing it in the public service is based on the idea that it is the enterprise that is being regulated and that the rights of the public are not affected by any changes of ownership that may have occurred. A depreciation charge based on such cost may be proper from the standpoint of regulation, but is clearly inadequate from the standpoint of a particular corporation which has acquired the property at a time when costs were materially higher than when the property was first put into service.

At the threshold of any inquiry such as we are undertaking we encounter the question of uniformity, and it is one upon which there is much misconception. Because this is so, and because discussion of the question will throw light on the broad questions of accounting policy which are of importance to executives and investors as well as to accountants, I propose to devote this afternoon largely to its consideration.

Uniformity in the treatment in operating accounts of routine transactions is undoubtedly of great value for a number of administrative purposes — such, for instance, as those served by the notable series of studies of comparative costs in a variety of industries which the Harvard Business School has undertaken. However, this uniformity relates largely to subdivisions of general classifications which are not subdivided at all in the financial statements with which we are concerned, and it hardly touches our problem except in relation, perhaps, to the two questions of depreciation and inventories. The complaints which are heard today of lack of uniformity in corporate accounts relate sometimes to the treatment of these two questions of depreciation and inventories, but more frequently are concerned either with charges and credits which cannot be allocated to the years to which they strictly apply because not then ascertained or ascertainable, or with charges and credits arising from changes in conditions or policies.

It may be helpful at this stage to indicate some of the specific questions which are apt to arise. Among the more important are the following:

(1) Shall the accounting in respect of fixed assets be historical in character and based on cost, or shall it attempt in any way to reflect changes in value other than those due to exhaustion of useful life? Subsidiary to this is the question — shall the charge for property exhaustion commonly spoken of as "depreciation" be based on original cost, the present replacement value, or probable replacement cost of the property that is being exhausted?

(2) On what basis shall inventories be stated — cost, cost or market whichever is lower, basic cost, normal cost, so-called standard cost, etc.?

(3) How shall the premature termination of useful life be dealt with?

(4) How shall corrections of estimates of charges or credits properly relating to the accounts of previous periods be dealt with?

It will, I hope, be apparent to you that the questions here raised are of an entirely different character from those involved in preparing a uniform classification of operating expenses. As I shall show later, no invariable rules for their treatment are laid down in what are commonly called "uniform classifications," such as those of the Interstate Commerce Commission. Failure to appreciate these facts is responsible for much unwarranted criticism of an alleged lack in industrial accounts of a uniformity which is supposed to be, but is not, attained in regulated fields of activity. By way of making my point perfectly clear, let me say that I believe that there is today a closer approach to uniformity in the published accounts of the large steel companies than in those of the large railroads, though the former are not and the latter are subject to a uniform classification.

The difficulty of attaining uniformity is largely due to two facts: one, that income accounts are designed to serve more than one purpose, and the other, that accounting for income is based on more than one concept. I have already discussed the first of these facts; and while the second fact is probably well-known to you, it may not be amiss to discuss briefly various bases commonly used for determining charges or credits to income.

A. The most theoretically correct concept of the income account is that charges or credits to it accrue from day to day, and this concept is applied wherever it is practicable to do so — as in the case of rent or interest.

B. In many more cases, however, its application is impracticable, and the income charge or credit is deemed to arise at the moment when a transaction takes place — for instance, the profit on a sale is taken up when the sale is made, though obviously it is not the product of the moment of time when this occurs.

C. In some cases, the purpose for which an expenditure is made controls the accounting treatment thereof, but there are obvious dangers in basing accounts too largely upon motivation, seeing that the motives of an executive or a group of executives are not always clearly defined. Business prudence, therefore, qualifies the application of this principle by insisting that due weight be given to the probability of the purpose being actually achieved. Thus, while it is customary to capitalize charges for machinery on the ground that the expenditure is intended to result, and may be reasonably expected to result, in benefits extending over a period in the future, it is equally customary to write off to income expenditures for research, even though the research is undertaken with a view to benefits in the future — not in the year in which the expenditures are made.

D. Again, expenditures are often made with more than one object. In some such cases, an apportionment of the charge in respect of the expenditure is made in the accounts; in many other cases, practical wisdom dictates that the whole expense shall be charged against income, though in principle some part might be charged to capital. Salaries of officials engaged partly in construction, though mainly in operating, and advertising of new products are cases in point.

E. In some cases, credits or charges are known either to have arisen or to be accruing, but the amounts involved are not accurately or even approximately known, and in such cases provisional charges or credits are made with the intent that the necessary adjustments shall be effected when more accurate figures shall become available. Depreciation is an outstanding illustration under this head.

Now, even in an income accounting designed for a single purpose, such as the determination of what amount is available as a return on capital employed or what amount can properly be taxed, it is sufficiently difficult to lay down uniform rules to govern and harmonize the application of these different concepts. When, however, the income account is required to serve a variety of purposes, and particularly when those purposes include any attempt to measure earning capacity as a step toward a determination of capital value, uniformity becomes impossible if only for the simple reason that the relative importance as well as the character of the charge or credit involved must affect its proper treatment.

The conclusion thus derived from a study of the nature of the problem is reinforced by experience. It may be instructive to observe how far and in what way the specific questions which I have listed have been dealt with by the Bureau of Internal Revenue and in the regulations of a body such as the Interstate Commerce Commission.

The income tax law has long frankly recognized that complete uniformity of accounting is neither desirable nor attainable. You will recall that our first income tax was levied in 1913; and a provision which was written into the law of 1918 and which has remained substantially unchanged until the present time is very significant and important. If you turn to Part IV of the present income tax law, which deals with accounting periods and methods of accounting, you will find that Section 41 lays down a general rule beginning as follows:

> The net income shall be computed upon the basis of the taxpayer's annual accounting period (fiscal year or calendar year, as the case may be) in accordance with the method of accounting regularly employed in keeping the books of such taxpayer; but if no such method of accounting has been so employed, or if the method employed does not clearly reflect the income, the computation shall be made in accordance with such method as in the opinion of the Commissioner does clearly reflect the income.

It is true that the Bureau of Internal Revenue has established uniform rules to govern certain classes of transactions, but it is also true that in other cases it has specifically allowed optional procedures.

Both the Bureau of Internal Revenue and the Interstate Commerce Commission have dealt with the question of fixed assets (which was the first of those which I have listed) on the basis of historical cost, and it is difficult to see how any other method could as a practical matter be successfully employed. I think all accountants will agree that, in general, this method must be followed, though it must be realized that it involves the definite abandonment of the notion that a balance sheet will, in respect of such assets, reflect current values, and I am afraid there are today a great many people who not only think that a balance sheet ought to reflect the current value of all assets but assume that it does so. I can only trust that you are not among that number.

Even if the historical basis is followed in general, cases arise in which the disparity between cost and present or prospective value becomes so marked as to demand a reconsideration of the question. Take, for instance, the case of a corporation which during the war, or in the immediate postwar boom, has bought a steamship for $5,000,000. It has been charging off depreciation at the rate of $250,000 a year. Five years later an equally or perhaps even more efficient vessel can be bought for $2,000,000, and the corporation's vessel is able to earn a return which, while it would provide for depreciation and some profit on an investment of $2,000,000, will not even provide for depreciation on a cost of $5,000,000. From a practical standpoint, what has happened is that the corporation has suffered a capital shrinkage and now has a reduced income. If the corporation has no debts, is there any public interest which requires that it shall painfully restore the shrinkage of capital over a period of fifteen or twenty years without making any distribution to its stockholders in the meantime? It could, of course, reorganize into a new corporation with a reduced capital and thereafter base its charge for depreciation upon the present replacement value of the ship. This, however, would entail very considerable expense, and is there any reason of public policy why the unfortunate stockholders should be put to this expense for a purely formal purpose?

The correspondence which grew out of the report of the American Institute of Accountants to the New York Stock Exchange, to which I have referred, seems to indicate a very general feeling among accountants and corporate officers that this expensive procedure was unnecessary. The Institute's committee suggested and the Exchange endorsed the following rule:

> Capital surplus, however created, should not be used to relieve the income account of the current or future years of charges which would otherwise fall to be made thereagainst. This rule might be subject to the exception that where, upon reorganization, a reorganized company would be relieved of charges which would require to be made against income if the existing corporation were continued, it might be regarded as permissible to accomplish the same result without reorganization provided the facts were as fully revealed to and the action as formally approved by the shareholders as in reorganization.

It should be noted, however, that a corporation availing itself of this rule must accept the logical consequences, one of which is that it cannot, after such a readjustment of property values, have an earned surplus any more than a newly created corporation could have one. I have never been able to feel any sympathy with those who have sought to get the benefit of reduced depreciation charges, as if the corporation were a new one, and also to retain an earned surplus on the ground that, actually, it is still the old one. I should add that such readjustments should not be lightly undertaken and that I am wholly opposed to the idea of writing property accounts up and down at frequent intervals as costs of replacement fluctuate.

Turning to the much discussed question of depreciation, nothing could indicate more clearly the difficulty of the questions that arise in laying down rules for the treatment of depreciation than reference to the history of the Interstate Commerce Commission's relation to the subject. A mere recital of dates in the history of the Commission is in itself instructive:

Created, 1887 — which, incidentally, is the year in which the first accounting body (the American Association of Accountants) was organized
Prescribed first classification of accounts, 1907
Introduced the principle of depreciation (in relation to equipment only), 1914
Authorized and directed by Congress to deal with the whole question comprehensively, 1920
Initiated a study of and hearings upon the subject, 1924
Handed down decision, 1926
Decided to reconsider, 1929
Handed down new and different decision, 1931
Suspended effectiveness of new regulations, 1932
Suspension still in effect

To make the story complete, it should be added that the Supreme Court has indicated disagreement with the principles proposed by the Commission.

This recital of dates is not intended to imply criticism of the Commission. The difficulties of the question are enormous, as you will perceive if you undertake to read the proceedings before the Commission or even its decisions. I do not propose to consider the question further. If you are interested in my views you will find some discussion of them in a collection of papers and articles which I have written.

The income tax law has for many years allowed as a deduction from gross income in determining taxable income "a reasonable allowance for the exhaustion, wear, and tear of property used in the trade or business, including a reasonable allowance for obsolescence." The present regulations lay down no rigid rule but provide that: "The capital sum to be recovered shall be charged off over the useful life of the property, either in equal annual installments or in accordance with any other recognized trade practice, such as an apportionment of the capital sum over units of production."

In point of fact, industrial practice in the matter of depreciation approaches much more nearly to uniformity and is, incidentally, much more conservative than railroad or public utility practice. Straight-line depreciation charges are practically universal in the accounting of the larger industrial companies, and the differences in rates used in respect of similar properties are much narrower than in the regulated fields mentioned.

Our second problem was the carrying figure for inventories. We can get no light on this question from the regulations of the Interstate Commerce Commission, for the companies subject to its jurisdiction have practically no stocks of goods for sale and their inventories consist substantially of supplies which can properly be valued at cost, subject to a deduction for obsolescence, since no question of salability arises. I am glad, however, of an opportunity to cite a regulation of the Bureau of Internal Revenue on the subject, which has remained substantially unchanged since 1918, which, I think, shows the Bureau at its best, and which has a very direct bearing on the problem we are now discussing. It reads:

In order clearly to reflect income, the inventory practice of a taxpayer should be consistent from year to year, and greater weight is to be given to consistency than to any particular method of inventorying or basis of valuation so long as the method or basis used is substantially in accord with these regulations.

In industrial practice today, the statement of inventories at cost or market whichever is lower, is, I believe, by far the most generally accepted rule. Its merit lies obviously not in its logic but in its conservatism; and even though its acceptability for balance sheet purposes may be conceded, questions may fairly be raised as to how the difference between cost and market should be dealt with for the purposes of the income account. This is, I think, a case in which further study and development of practice are clearly called for and in which it would be most unwise to crystallize too hastily the existing practice through uniform regulations. In the interests of candor, I should perhaps add that there is considerable variety in the way in which the principle of "cost or market whichever is lower" is actually applied, and that the degree of uniformity now attained is therefore by no means as great as those unfamiliar with the actual workings of the system might suppose.

Our third group of difficult cases comprises those arising from premature termination of useful life. The common case is that of property which becomes obsolete substantially before the end of the period over which its cost is being written off under a depreciation scheme. It may not be amiss, however, to point out that similar problems may arise in respect of liabilities — indeed, the fall of interest rates has created many such cases. A bond issue, made on a basis that seemed at the time advantageous, is now burdensome. It is replaced by a more economical issue. How shall the unamortized discount on the old issue be treated?

Very little consideration of this general class of questions is necessary to bring home the realization of the difficulty of accounting problems and the impossibility of laying down fixed rules. I have referred to two concepts employed in determining income — one, of a completed transaction, and the other, of a continuous accrual, the two being illustrated by the completion of a sale and the accruing of interest. The premature termination of useful life does not fall into either of these categories. When a life ceases to be useful is, at best, a difficult qucstion of judgment. We can beg the question by doing nothing until the termination of usefulness is evidenced by action such as the discarding or sale of the property. Even then, the loss that has not been provided for by depreciation charges remains to be dealt with. Obviously, it is, properly speaking, a charge against the income over the years of the useful life which has now come to an end. Since the accounts of those years are closed and done with, the loss must be dealt with in some other way; and the question arises, shall its character as a charge against income control, and the loss be charged against income account even though it is in the wrong year, or shall its relationship to the past determine the treatment, and the loss be charged against the accumulated undistributed income?

It does not seem to me that it is possible to lay down any rule to be universally applied. In the case of a business employing a large number of property units, where such occurrences may be frequent, it may well be that the most appropriate disposition of the charge is to make it against current income. Where the unit retired is a relatively large proportion of the total investment, such a charge would obviously result in a distorted income account.

Under the Interstate Commerce Commission's classification, the normal procedure is to charge such losses against operating expense as the property is replaced, or against profit and loss if it is not replaced — a difference the logic of which is not very clear; but in either case, alternative forms of treatment, such as charging the loss against future income, are permitted where such a treatment would create a deficit or a distorted income account.

For income tax purposes, such losses are a charge against the year in which premature retirement takes place. This, of course, is logical, since the taxing authority takes annually its full share of the income of each year, as determined under its rules, and leaves in respect of its share of the income nothing corresponding to the undistributed profits which are left by stockholders to provide for just such contingencies as we are discussing. This fact is sometimes overlooked by persons who regard as obviously vicious any treatment of a loss or expense in the annual accounts of the corporation which is different from the treatment given to it in the corporation's income tax return.

The problem of dealing with corrections of estimates and of treatment of items relating to the past which are either not discovered or not determined until later, is of the same general character as that we have just considered. Some would urge that ordinarily they should be charged against accumulated undistributed income and not against the income account of the year, on the ground that they have nothing to do with the operations of the year. A grave objection to this procedure is that it offers a constant temptation to any executive who desires to produce a favorable income account to ignore or forget items of charge which, though not yet definitely ascertained, are likely to arise in respect of the operations of the year with which he is concerned. If he can improve his current income account only at the expense of the income account of a future year, he is much less likely to yield to the temptation. For this reason, and because the objective of bringing into each year all the items which strictly relate to its operation seems to me to be praiseworthy but unattainable, I am inclined to the alternative view that normally such items should be reflected in the income account of the year in which they are discovered. I think the wise course, since absolute accuracy is unattainable, is for managements consciously to err somewhat (but not unduly) on the side of conservatism; and it will always be an encouragement to them to do so, if they know that the benefit of any excess of caution will be reflected in the income account of a later year.

There are bound sometimes to be cases in which such a

charge against the income of a particular year would grossly distort it. Therefore, any scheme of accounting must permit of some alternative treatment. The rules of the Interstate Commerce Commission do so. The income tax regulations throw little light on the question because to the Bureau, as I have indicated, the distinction between charges against accumulated income and charges against current income has no significance.

You will see that in respect of the four types of questions we have considered there is no absolute uniformity even under a classification such as that of the Interstate Commerce Commission, and that both that body and the Bureau of Internal Revenue allow alternative methods of treatment in certain cases. It would be easy to cite other illustrations of optional methods under the regulations of these bodies, but I hope that what I have already said is sufficient to demonstrate that both reason and experience indicate the unwisdom of any attempt to enforce rigid uniformity in accounting. Obviously, where there is no paramount public interest involved and accounts are required for a variety of purposes, the case for latitude is far stronger. Routine transactions offer no difficulty, but transactions which are out of the ordinary will often require exceptional treatment. If each corporation is to determine for itself when the ordinary practice is to be varied, then uniformity becomes illusory. A demand for uniformity therefore implies a demand for an external authority to determine when and what variations from standard procedure shall be permitted.

Any system which provides for such uniformity, so enforced, seems to me to tend to put an end to progress and to exalt form at the expense of substance. In the case of corporations engaged in rendering service under a scheme of regulation, the problems are much less complex than in the industrial world. This consideration, together with the paramount public interest, may justify the creation of such a uniform system in relation to these corporations, although the undesirable consequences which flow from existing regulation should not be ignored. Among these consequences are the creation in the minds of the public of a belief in a degree of uniformity and comparability between the accounts of the different corporations subject to the same regulation which is not, and cannot be, warranted by the facts; and the steady tendency toward less conservative practice which results from the fact that authority cannot insist on conservatism, but only on minimum standards.

At this point, two extracts from the annual report of the Interstate Commerce Commission for 1934 (which were brought into juxtaposition in an editorial comment in *The Journal of Accountancy* for December, 1935) are pertinent. They seem to call for no comment except that where the expression "predepression" is used, the word "inadequate" would have been equally appropriate; and that the term "profit and loss" as used in railroad accounts means surplus:

> As has been stated in previous reports, this bureau was created to enable us effectively to regulate, and by periodical field investigations, supervise and police the accounts of carriers subject to the act in order that uniformity in accounting, as an essential regulatory requirement as well as a factor otherwise in the interest of the public, could be assured.[5]
>
> . . . . .
>
> Although depreciation charges continue on a predepression basis, we have permitted extensive retirements during 1933 and 1934 to be charged to profit and loss instead of to operating expenses, and also, some repairs, carried out with the aid of Public Works Administration loans, have been with our permission, in part charged to profit and loss instead of to operating expenses. Beginning with 1935 depreciation of equipment will be charged to operating expenses on a standardized basis.[6]

Admittedly, any current determination of corporate income for a year, or shorter period, is at best an approximation; but the further question — an approximation to what? — would be answered somewhat differently by different classes of persons, such as executives, investors, stock speculators, financial statisticians or investment counselors, bank creditors or bond-

[5] Page 35.

[6] Page 2.

holders, economists, accounting theorists, etc. As is so clearly recognized by Professor Bonbright in the passage which I quoted in my first lecture, no account will serve equally well the purposes of each of these classes, so that the practical question to be faced is how far the form is to be determined by their respective needs or desires. The accounting theorist would probably urge uniformity of treatment and suggest that, if for any particular purpose an exceptional transaction may call for special treatment, the party interested should make his own adjustment if he deems it worth while. This, however, seems to me an extremely theoretical solution of what is an intensely practical question.

It is apparent, first, that the interest of some groups is more direct and substantial than that of others, and, secondly, that some groups are better able than others to adjust accounts to fit their own requirements. In general, the individual stockholder has the most direct interest and is least qualified to make adjustments, and I feel strongly that he is entitled to the benefit of the judgment of the executive and the auditor on the question how, in all the circumstances, the special situation should be dealt with. True, the judgment of the executive may not always be entirely objective, nor the auditor always as independent in fact as in theory; but these are merely phases of the risks which the investor must always run when he entrusts his investment to a management or relies upon an audit. If the special treatment is fully disclosed, those who think the risk of dishonesty in the judgment outweighs the advantage of fuller knowledge in its formation, and prefer to adhere to immutable rules, may be left to make necessary adjustments for themselves.

In saying this, I do not wish to be understood as accepting the view that disclosure is all-sufficient and that no criticism can justly be made where the facts are disclosed, even though the form of disclosure is unsatisfactory. On the contrary, I believe not only that investors are entitled to an honest judgment by the executives upon both form and substance, but that they are also entitled to demand that auditors shall use their influence to make effective the views which they honestly hold on either point and shall be frank and explicit in expressing any material dissent from the form or content of an income account prepared by the executives.

I am convinced that under existing law investors have less to fear in the matter of financial accounts from dishonest managements or complaisant auditors than from efforts to create a system of rigid rules, departure from which would be permissible only upon the approval of an external authority having no interest in nor any responsibility to the investor and quite unlikely to be permanently free from influences affecting its rulings which would have their foundations elsewhere than in the theory and practice of accounting.

III. PRACTICAL LINES OF IMPROVEMENT

Our task today is to sum up the discussion of the last two days, and to suggest the direction which efforts to improve financial accounts should take. First, what is our objective? In the case of the Interstate Commerce Commission and the Bureau of Internal Revenue, to which I referred in my last lecture, the objectives are clear — in the one case, it is to secure healthy development of the railway transportation system and maintenance of rates that will be compensatory to the carriers and not unduly burdensome on the commerce of the country. In the case of the Bureau of Internal Revenue, it might be said to be to secure the collection of the revenue with such degree of justice to the taxpayer as seems to it to be compatible with that object.

What is the exact character of the public interest in the question of financial reports and accounts which should influence future developments in this field? I have pointed out that in England the general theory of law even today, when large publicly owned corporations exist there as here, is that in the absence of fraud, and subject to proper protection of creditors, corporations should be allowed to manage their own affairs, and particularly to determine the amount of profits available for distribution in dividends, in accordance with their own articles of association, which constitute the contract between their shareholders and are a matter of public record.

Obviously, the day has passed when any such *laissez-faire* policy could be regarded as acceptable in our country. However, in any procedure we may propose we should at least have some clear idea of the nature of the public interest which calls for limitations on such freedom of action on the part of stockholders and of the directors elected by them. I stress this point because it seems to have been frequently lost to sight in the extensive discussions of the last few years of the subject with which we are dealing. Criticisms have often been based on the fact that methods have differed, without regard to the question whether in a particular case the method followed was prejudicial to any legitimate interest. These criticisms have resulted in many footnotes to published accounts — footnotes not always lucid, and the gradual accumulation of which has undoubtedly tended to the confusion of stockholders and investors. Preoccupation with the importance of not misleading investors has obscured the desirability of enlightening them.

You will have gathered from the preceding lecture that while I recognize the value of a certain degree of uniformity, I do not believe complete standardization of accounting in the industrial field to be either desirable or attainable at this time, if ever. You will have observed, also, that it has not been attained in the past, even under so-called uniform classifications. In these days of wishful thinking, however, the idea that standardization can, and should, be achieved persists, especially outside the accounting profession. This is not surprising; we are all inclined to underrate the difficulties of other people's problems. I recall that at the last annual meeting of the American Institute of Accountants a distinguished practitioner proposed that the Institute should undertake to formulate a model Federal income tax law, and expressed the belief that it could be made short and simple; I assume he also contemplated that it should be reasonably equitable. We can hardly complain if others display a similar blithe optimism regarding our problems.

The usefulness of financial accounts may be increased by improvements in either their substance or their form. Let me first summarize the position regarding changes in substance which I discussed in my last lecture and then turn to the question of form, which I think presents both less difficulty and greater possibilities.

As I have said, I see no escape from the conclusion that continuity in accounting must be preserved, and that accounting in respect of fixed assets must necessarily be in general based on cost. I realize that from the standpoint of the new investor this is not altogether satisfactory, but it is obviously impossible to take cognizance in accounts of the fact that different stockholders acquired their stock interests at different times. Acceptance of cost as the basis for property accounts implies that in computing income depreciation will in general be based on cost rather than on present value. As indicated in my second lecture, I believe that it should be permissible, and that it is in the general interest that where the value of depreciable property has, in fact, fallen far below original cost, and the fall seems likely to be permanent, the downward adjustment of the property account should be facilitated. I think, however, it is undesirable and not wholly accurate to state, as some corporate officials have stated in recommending such readjustments of book values, that they imply no real loss to the stockholder. Even if the readjustments do not themselves imply a loss, the declaration of dividends out of earnings based on the reduced charge for depreciation in subsequent periods carries that implication; for the original stockholder is receiving as income in such a dividend part of that which was originally his capital and which prior to the adjustment had to be maintained out of income before any dividend distribution could be made.

The question may arise whether in the reverse situation capital values should be written up. Logic may suggest that they should be, but personally I should wish to be very fully assured of the reality and probable permanence of an increase in value before I should favor reflecting it in the books of the corporation. It will do no harm to reiterate that I am wholly opposed to the idea of writing property up and down at more or less frequent intervals as costs of replacing it fluctuate. I would also draw your attention to another practice sometimes adopted of placing depreciating property on the books at a very low or even nominal figure and making in the income account only a small provision, if any, for depreciation of this property. Clearly this practice, while having a specious appearance of conservatism in the balance sheet, results in an overstatement of income and is indefensible.

A step which I should regard with satisfaction would be the general acceptance of the practice of excluding from the income account capital gains and losses realized otherwise than in the ordinary course of a company's business — indeed, I believe that even in the case of investment trusts, in which capital gains and losses might be said to be normal incidents of the business, it is preferable to exclude them from the ordinary income account. My reason for these views I have set out on other occasions. It should also be recognized that to a corporation its own capital stock can neither be an asset nor produce income.

A legitimate question may be raised whether the illogical, if conservative, practice of taking inventories at cost or market, whichever is lower, is appropriate in the preparation of an income account which is designed, at least in part, as an indication of earning capacity. There is a substantial argument in favor of taking the inventory for the purposes of the income account uniformly on the basis of cost, making any adjustment to market value which may be necessary for the purposes of a statement of quick assets or a balance sheet, through another account. This procedure is, however, open to the objection that it permits the operating manager to improve his income statement by the production of goods for which there is no ready or certain market.

In regard to the question of premature retirements, correctness of estimates, and delayed items which I discussed yesterday, I confess I see no choice but to sanction alternative treatment according to the facts of the individual case. In this matter investors cannot secure protection through a uniformity which is likely to be superficial rather than real; they must rely on the honesty and competency of those responsible for the preparation and audit of the accounts.

Before leaving this branch of the question I should emphasize, first, the importance of consistency in accounting from year to year, and, secondly, the desirability of disclosing any exceptional items in such a way that those who may deem appropriate some treatment of an item other than that adopted in the accounts may be enabled to make their own adjustments. If you read the correspondence between the New York Stock Exchange and the American Institute of Accountants, or the report of the Gifford Committee, to which I referred in my first lecture, you will note the growing emphasis on the importance of consistency in accounting, which has been stressed in the regulations under the income tax law since 1918. No better rule could be laid down to cover general accounting methods than that laid down by the Bureau of Internal Revenue in relation to inventories, which I quoted in the preceding lecture, and which with the slight changes necessary would read as follows:

> In order clearly to reflect income the accounting practice of a registrant should be consistent from year to year, and greater weight is to be given to consistency than to any particular method of accounting, so long as the method used is in accord with the broad principles of accounting practice.

Separate disclosure of items in regard to the treatment of which there is room for legitimate difference of opinion will go far to meet the criticism of those who may disagree with the method actually adopted. In general, anyone competent to express agreement or disagreement on such a question is qualified to make any restatement of the accounts which may be necessary to meet his own point of view.

Turning now to questions of form: If we stop to consider what the investor is really interested in, the paramount importance of the income account and of statements of quick assets and liabilities at once becomes apparent, this importance resting on the simple ground that earning capacity and solvency are the most essential elements in commercial prosperity. I was sorry to see Sir Josiah Stamp emphasizing, recently, the importance of the balance sheet, because to my mind in England the balance sheet has been used by the secretive company director as the red herring to distract public attention from the income account, which I am sure Sir Josiah would agree is even more important.

I have on other occasions drawn attention to the fact that the English law until as lately as 1928 contained no statutory requirement for the submission to stockholders of anything in the nature of an income account, but required only a balance sheet. This has seemed to me the more surprising because a clear appreciation of the relative importance of the two statements is indicated in the language of the model form of articles of association which was attached to the Companies Act of 1862 and known as Table A. It is worth while to quote some of the articles of that table which, it should be pointed out, were suggestive and not compulsory:

> Art. 79. Once at least in every year the directors shall lay before the company in general meeting a statement of the income and expenditure for the past year, made up to a date not more than three months before such meeting.
>
> Art. 80. The statements so made shall show, arranged under the most convenient heads, the amount of gross income, distinguishing the several sources from which it has been derived, and the amount of gross expenditure, distinguishing the expense of the establishment, salaries, and other like matters: every item of expenditure fairly chargeable against the year's income shall be brought into account, so that a just balance of profit and loss may be laid before the meeting; and in cases where any item of expenditure which may in fairness be distributed over several years has been incurred in any one year the whole amount of such item shall be stated, with the addition of the reasons why only a portion of such expenditure is charged against the income of the year.
>
> Art. 81. A balance sheet shall be made out in every year, and laid before the company in general meeting, and such balance sheet shall contain a summary of the property and liabilities of the company arranged under the heads appearing in the form annexed to this table, or as near thereto as circumstances admit.

I think we should today accord to the income account the priority in importance which is given to it in these articles.

The Securities and Exchange Commission has in its regulations added to the standard set of major financial statements an account of the changes in reserves during the period for which the report is made. Such a statement throws a valuable light on the income account and is, I think, an addition to the sum of financial information which is of great importance and upon which the Commission is to be warmly congratulated.

Another valuable form of statement which might well be more generally adopted is the summary of resources and their disposition, such as the United States Steel Corporation has for many years published.

In my first lecture, I drew attention to the new importance which the income account has acquired as an index of earning capacity and hence of capital value, in addition to its former importance as a guide to the amount of profit available for distribution in dividends. Recognition of this new purpose, coupled with the demand for reports covering periods even shorter than a year, has led more and more to the use in the income account of accruals, estimates, and budgetary provisions in lieu of amounts actually received or expended, as the basis for the charge or credit in the particular period covered by the statement. Obviously this practice, while in some respects advantageous, has its own dangers in that it tends to make an income account a statement of averages rather than of current events. Even if it may have made the income account more useful from the standpoint of the person who is considering buying or selling stock in the corporation, which is arguable, it has rather distracted attention from the fact that a sound dividend policy permits the declaration of a dividend only when the company possesses cash resources which justify its payment as well as a surplus or undivided profits account available for appropriation. The statement of resources and their disposition answers the vital question — what has become of the cash? — and affords a useful corrective to views formed on the basis of an income account which perhaps unduly emphasizes net earning capacity as distinguished from net current receipts of income.

I should perhaps explain that in speaking of dividends I have in mind true cash dividends, and am not concerned with any of the mongrel types of distribution which were common during the boom period and which, although regarded by many stockholders as dividends, were in reality more in the nature of split-ups; nor with the new type of dividends resulting from the passage of the undistributed profits tax law, some of which are scarcely more than certificates of undistributed profits.

If the investor were given:

(1) a reasonably full and fair income account,
(2) a statement of quick assets and liabilities,
(3) a summary of changes in reserves, and
(4) a summary of resources and their disposition,

the balance sheet would then become of secondary importance to him, and the fact that in the balance sheet assets and liabilities, if those headings are to be retained, are stated on various conventional bases and not on any uniform theory of values would become of minor importance. It might, however, still be desirable to classify the assets and liabilities therein according to the different bases on which they are stated, or at least to make clear in each case the basis employed.

A minor change in accounting practice which I should like to see made effective is the elimination of the word "earnings" except in the case of companies engaged in rendering service. I think the term "undivided profits" is distinctly preferable to the term "earned surplus," which often includes credits which cannot be said to have been earned in any legitimate sense of that word.

Another change which, I think, is clearly called for is the separate disclosure of the figure at which goodwill and intangible values are carried by the corporation, and the same is true of land. I favor this proposal on a ground which is perhaps different from the position usually taken. I do not suggest that the value of intangible assets is any less real than that of tangible assets, and I would not even undertake to demonstrate that from the standpoint of value the two can be accurately separated — indeed, the validity of any separation of values is doubtful, if the premise be accepted, as I think it must be, that the value of capital assets depends primarily on earning capacity. My view is, rather, that while the value of the capital assets depends on the earning capacity, the amount of the net profits shown in turn depends, in a measure, on the provisions charged against income for exhaustion of property (commonly called depreciation), and these provisions in turn depend upon the figure at which the capital assets are carried on the books. Hence it is, I think, of material importance to the investor to know how much of the book figure of capital assets represents sums in respect of which depreciation is being charged and how far it represents items, such as intangible values or land, on account of which no depreciation charge is being made or is customarily regarded as necessary.

In the ways which I have suggested and in similar ways I think improvements can be made in respect of the form in which annual accounts are presented which would be extremely valuable to the investor. Substantial agreement as to the changes that are desirable could, I think, be reached without great difficulty, and the changes could be made effective at an early date without causing any disturbance to existing reporting methods, except the minor inconveniences of restating the accounts for a year or two in the past to facilitate comparison.

I hope that the Securities and Exchange Commission will seek improvement in financial accounts through sympathetic and patient encouragement of progress along these general lines and that it will not attempt to lay down rigid rules of accounting as it has sometimes been suggested that it should do.

One consideration alone seems sufficient to demonstrate the unwisdom of the latter course. For many years we have had accounting rules laid down by at least two governmental bodies — the Interstate Commerce Commission and the Bureau of Internal Revenue — and new regulating bodies are creating further classifications. I believe anyone familiar with the facts will agree that, in general, industrial accounting is today more conservative than the accounting that is prescribed by the Interstate Commerce Commission, or that permitted by the Bureau of Internal Revenue. If, therefore, the Securities and Exchange Commission should undertake to lay down a new set of rules, it would be facing an extremely embarrassing dilemma — it would either have to lower the standards of conservatism already in effect in the commercial world or establish rules on a higher standard of conservatism than those established by other governmental bodies which have been dealing with the subject for many years. Clearly, in such a situation it would not be doing its full duty to investors unless it should elect the second alternative. Equally clearly, however, this would create awkward situations, and its course might easily fail to find support in the courts, since it would be difficult to show upon what ground it could justly make mandatory procedures which were not required or even sanctioned by another governmental body. I am convinced that the Commission would do well to avoid such a dilemma, if possible, and I am convinced, also, that there is no reason of public policy today which imposes on it an obligation to face that dilemma.

I have considered up to this point the question of financial accounts required for the purpose of annual reports of established companies; and I should like to make it clear that in referring to the effects of the Securities Acts I have been considering only the case of companies of that character, that being the field of accounting in which I have some familiarity. The regulation of new and speculative promotions presents entirely different problems of which I cannot claim to have any special knowledge. I do not propose to discuss at length the question of accounts required for a prospectus, but it seems desirable to make a brief reference to that question and particularly to emphasize the difference between such accounts and accounts required for the ordinary purposes of an annual report.

The nature of a prospectus is clear and single — it is a representation made in connection with an offer to sell. The reader of it is concerned only with the future. Accounts covering a past period are of value to him in so far as they throw light on the probabilities of the future. In so far as they are purely historical they are devoid of any interest to him. As I have indicated, I believe that an annual report should be regarded as primarily a historical report to stockholders. The distinction which I have here suggested seems to me to have been obscured in the Securities Act of 1933, and practically ignored in the Act of 1934. Under Section 18 of that Act, executives of a corporation who have issued a report which is found to be misleading, within the terms of the section, are subjected to a potential liability to those who have bought or sold stock in the corporation. This section seems to me to be open to criticism — because it treats a periodical report too much as if it were a new edition of a prospectus instead of a historical report, and because it assumes a much closer relation between market transactions in stock of a corporation and periodical reports than the facts warrant. On the first point, it is, I think, regrettable that the Act should thus encourage, if it does not compel, the corporate executive to keep his eye on the stock market when he is preparing his report, and to prepare it with the trader in the stock of his company rather than the permanent investor in mind. On the second point, I think all the evidence tends to show that purchases of stocks are, in general, based far more largely on expectations for the future than on records of the past, and upon hopes of capital appreciation than on prospects of income yield. Some of you may perhaps have read the brilliant and entertaining discussion of this question which is contained in Keynes's recent book.[7]

The form of accounts presented in a prospectus should be determined by the purpose of that document. To accomplish this result it is necessary to recognize frankly that the statement which is appropriate for a purely historical report on the past is not always the right statement for guidance for the future, especially if changes in capitalization, property valu-

[7] John Maynard Keynes, *The General Theory of Employment, Interest and Money* (New York, Harcourt, Brace & Company, 1936), Chap. XII, *passim*.

ation, or other essential elements of the situation have been or are being effected. In so far as the accounts deal with past years in respect of which annual accounts have already been issued, not only should it be permissible, but it is desirable, that those accounts should be reconsidered and, if necessary, adjusted in the light of any additional information which has become available since they were prepared. At the present time the customary method of presenting financial information in prospectuses is admittedly unsatisfactory. Too often the investor is given a mass of information and explanations from which he is left to draw his own conclusions. Even those possessing technical qualifications have difficulty in interpreting the income account, followed by pages of footnotes, which is frequently found in the prospectus of today. This, I hope and believe, is merely a passing phase, though wholehearted and sympathetic cooperation between executives, lawyers, accountants, and the Commission will be needed to evolve a method of presentation which will be really enlightening to the investor and afford proper protection to those concerned in the issue of the prospectus against the liabilities which they may incur under the existing law.

In the narrower field of financial accounting as in the broader field of regulation of security issues and annual reports as a whole, we are clearly today at a tentative stage, and it would be in the highest degree unwise to attempt to stabilize the law and practice in either field at the point which we have now reached. In recent years the trend in both fields has been given a new impetus and a new and wiser direction. In respect of fullness and fairness of disclosure, I believe our standard is today among the highest in the world; what is needed, now, is the elimination of superfluous detail, greater simplicity, and clearer cut statements of honest and informed opinion on material questions. It would be interesting to pursue this question further, but to do so would carry us far from our original topic.

In conclusion, may I express my concern that you should take away from these lectures a just appreciation of both the usefulness of accounts, on the one hand, and the necessary limitations on their significance, on the other. They are accounts of happenings in a world of business which is subject to constant and sometimes violent change and full of uncertainties; naturally, they cannot rise higher in the scale of certainty than the events which they reflect. Necessarily, also, they involve the use of conventions and estimates, and the supreme virtues in them are consistency and fair disclosure. It is because I believe that recent years have brought a far wider recognition of these essential characteristics of accounts than previously existed that I look hopefully for improvement in the future. Not that the record of development in the past has been unsatisfactory — indeed, considering that the modern corporation and the profession of accounting have both been in existence for only a half century or so, I think the fact is otherwise.

Comparison has been sometimes made between the progress achieved in establishing standards in the accounting and in the engineering world, respectively, but it is obvious that the engineer, in computing his standards of construction, is dealing with the physical world, while in financial accounts the accountant is dealing with things metaphysical. Since accounting is a tool of business, and since courts have laid down the rule that what is good accounting should be determined by the best practices of businessmen, a fairer comparison is between the development of corporate accounting and that of commercial law. In any such comparison it must be remembered that the lawyers have the inestimable advantage that there is always a court composed of members of their own craft which is in a position to lay down rules that will be binding not only on members of the craft but on all others, and also that legislative bodies usually consist more largely of lawyers than of any other class. Bearing in mind this difference, and considering the unsatisfactory state of the law of valuation to which I have referred, and which you will find more fully set forth in Professor Bonbright's work; or considering the history of, let us say, the development of the law of negotiable instruments from the decisions of Lord Mansfield which began the process of coordination in the third quarter of the eighteenth century [8] to the formulation of a proposed uniform law in our country in the last years of the nineteenth century [9] and its gradual acceptance by the States and Territories over a period of thirty years thereafter, I do not think the accounting profession in America has any reason for dissatisfaction at what has been accomplished in the field of corporate accounting during the half century or less of its existence.

[8] "In *Heylyn* v. *Adamson* (1758) Lord Mansfield brought order out of chaos." C. H. S. Fifoot, *Lord Mansfield* (London, Oxford University Press, 1936), p. 91.

[9] The Uniform Negotiable Instruments law was proposed by the Commissioners on Uniform State Laws in 1896, and its adoption became complete in 1930.

RECENT AND PROSPECTIVE DEVELOPMENTS IN ACCOUNTING THEORY

By WILLIAM A. PATON
Professor of Accounting, University of Michigan

I. PRELIMINARY CONSIDERATIONS

THE SUBJECT selected for these talks is broad enough to furnish a speaker a wide area in which to range. Even so, I am not sure I shall be able to stick to the announced topic, under any reasonable interpretation of its scope. What I have to say might perhaps better be labeled "A Survey of Accounting Theory" or, merely, "Some Observations on Accounting Theory." Particularly with regard to "prospective developments" do I fear that any suggestions I have to offer will be more in the nature of wishful thinking than well-founded prediction. In any complex situation it is not difficult to see evidences which seem to point in the direction in which one desires to see things move. Not long ago I heard a trained investigator in the physical sciences admit that even in laboratory research serious blunders are sometimes made in sifting data because of an eagerness — of which the student may not be fully aware — to find materials which lend support to a particular hypothesis. In the dynamic field of business — an extraordinarily involved cross section of human affairs — there is still greater danger of questionable analysis and unsound conclusion.

At the outset it seems necessary for me to raise for brief comment a number of very general questions. First, what is accounting, in the broadest sense of the term? A possible answer is that accounting is a synthesis of concepts, rules, and techniques designed to facilitate understanding and control of economic activity. This may sound a bit pretentious, but I am not implying that accounting is the only instrument of this character. Accounting is in close partnership with general economics, law, and engineering. Accounting strives to *measure* economic forces in financial terms and *to communicate* the results of such measurement to interested parties. It is concerned with technical efficiency, as is engineering; it is vitally concerned with human rights and relationships, as is the law.

Next, what do we mean by accounting theory? In attempting to make a suggestion on this point, I shall ignore the fact that such terms as "theory," "principle," "logic," and "science" have become somewhat hackneyed and unsatisfactory as a result of too wide and too persistent use. Accounting theory is the core of the propositions, doctrines, and policies distilled from an appraisal of the purposes of accounting, an examination of the milieu in which accounting has its being, and a critical analysis of the nature of accounting practice. In particular, it should be recognized that theory and practice are not in opposition, as is so often assumed; they are integrated parts of a whole. Theory is both an analysis of practice and a framework for practice. Theory is in large measure the product of practice and at the same time the post to which practice is tethered (although sometimes by a very long rope). Thus the study of accounting theory is likewise the study of accounting practice in its most essential and significant aspects.

A word should be said with respect to the hallmarks of good theory, in any field. Theory should be characterized by clarity and orderliness; it should be schematic, have pattern. Rambling, hit-or-miss thinking is not good theory and cannot be expected to lead to good practice. It is a safe assumption, in other words, that logic and expediency are seldom at odds. Secondly, theory should be in harmony with observable, objective factors and conditions in their basic relations; daydreams are not theory. This is true of building bridges; it is equally true of preparing financial statements. A third and closely related criterion is the flavor of impartiality. In theory there should be no personal bias, no axe to grind, no playing of favorites. The theorist must show a measure of consistency; the playing-field fence should not be shifted every time a new man comes to bat. Finally, in a purposive field like accounting there should be in theory just a tincture of forward-looking, a trace of policy-forming, a bit of leaven for the loaf of practice.

In the last few years, as most of you know, there has been a marked revival of interest in accounting theory. A flood of articles on the subject has appeared in *The Journal of Accountancy*, in *The Accounting Review*, and in other periodicals. Accountants have been becoming increasingly conscious of the uncertainties and variations of their procedures, of the lack of an accepted body of principles or standards of wide applicability. An important influence in this connection is found in the development of the Securities and Exchange Commission — an influence which to date has probably been wholesome in its net effect. The principal professional organization, the American Institute of Accountants, and the academic group, the American Accounting Association, have taken an active part in this effort to re-examine accounting theory, with special reference to the preparation of corporate financial statements. Something over a year ago the Institute launched a department of research, under the direction of Professor Sanders, of the Harvard Business School, and this department has been giving serious attention to accounting principles in relation to a large number of practical problems facing the profession.

In the light of these conditions the discussion of developments in accounting theory at this time is not altogether inappropriate.

I have organized my survey of the subject around the following interrelated heads:

The Focus of Accounting
Measurement of Performance
The Period of Reckoning
Costs and Values

II. THE FOCUS OF ACCOUNTING

A FIRST STEP in the development of a "philosophy of accounts" is the taking of a position, the adoption of a point of view, the recognition of a focus or center of attention. There are, of course, a number of significant units or entities to be discerned in the economic fabric. Important examples are the natural person, the family, the business, the community, the industry, and the state. Accounting, as we all know, has flowered in the field of business operation, and has come to be regarded as peculiarly the tool of private-business enterprise. In recent decades, moreover, business accounting has taken on a noticeably institutional flavor. In an earlier period, accounting was largely represented by the record-keeping of the particular individual or proprietor, and little effort was made to draw a sharp line between business activity and personal or home activity. With the growth of corporate organization, and the sharpening of the line separating production from consumption, accounts have become more impersonal, statistical, institutional. The older account books were often a combination of personal or family history, financial data, and informal comment on the times. Present-day accounts are perhaps less interesting, but they are certainly more businesslike.

I have always been a supporter of the business-entity conception of accounting and have no desire to "change my tune" at this late date. In particular, this conception has been useful as a means of fostering the development of the managerial point of view, and thus encouraging progress in the field of cost accounting. In this area there has been a truly remarkable advance, and it is difficult to see how this could have been accomplished without a shift from the narrow limits of proprietary reckoning to the broader field of enterprise accounting. Another important result of using the enterprise as the focus of attention has been the development of the going-concern assumption, with derivative stressing of the interpretation of business operation as a continuing stream of activity. The increasing consideration being given to income measurement and reporting is presumably a manifestation of the influence of the business-enterprise, managerial point of view.

At the present time, however, it may be advisable to give some attention to the limitations of the enterprise conception and to speculate on the trend of thought in the future. Defined in terms of the specific corporation, the business entity as a center of accounting interest sometimes seems a bit legalistic and artificial. The branch, division, department, or other operating unit may have more vitality and significance in certain connections than the company viewed as a whole. All accountants are familiar with the fact that a clash of opinion often arises between department heads, or between the particular head and the general management, but thus far we have not been very successful in accommodating accounting theory and procedure to the proper needs of the various interested parties. Service departments, in particular, present a problem. With no revenues of their own the managers of such departments feel handicapped in their efforts to make a showing for their respective units. Perhaps more attention should be given to the possibility, in internal accounting, of accruing and apportioning budgeted enterprise revenue in terms of the various sections of operating activity, including so-called "nonproductive" areas. Or perhaps hypothetical revenues, based upon careful consideration of all available data as to costs and prices, should be set up for the service departments so that their performance may be measured in conventional two-sided fashion. A development in this direction, it may be added, would not necessarily require the inclusion in the periodic income statement of the corporate entity of unrealized income or loss.

Perhaps some lessons may be drawn from governmental accounting, where emphasis upon cross sections in the form of funds is traditional.

Granting that further attention may well be given to departmental reckonings, the dangers incident to any such movement should not be overlooked. Cost and revenue assignments at the best ignore many threads of connection and must not be taken too seriously. Particularly questionable are imputations by which earning power is attributed to the individual machine or other specific factor in production. It should also be remembered that there is no available means of making a convincing allocation of burdens which fall on the legal entity as such, of which the outstanding example is income taxes.

A modern development in the direction of an extension of the limits of the entity is reflected in the wide use of consolidated statements. In this connection I wish to make only two comments. First, the trend toward combined reporting need not be viewed as opposed to the trend toward departmentalizing. In departmental accounting an attempt is being made to present the data of a particular section of activity and management; in consolidated accounts, likewise, the desire is to present information relative to an area of business operation dominated by one ownership and administration. Secondly, there is a danger that the process of aggregation, like that of subdivision, will result in an obscuring of significant facts and hence be more misleading than helpful.

An important matter associated with the use of the corporate form of organization, of considerable interest to the accountant, is the relationship between the stockholder and his affairs and the corporate entity and its affairs. What is the proper conception of this relationship? Is the corporation merely an association of individuals having a common purpose, a glorified partnership, or is the corporation a vital business entity in its own right? In general, the dominant view in law has tended to justify the independent-enterprise conception and accounting has leaned heavily upon this interpretation. At the present time, however, the question seems to be very much unsettled, with some drift toward the association position. The efforts to treat stock dividends as income and to levy taxes on undistributed profits are indications of this condition. It would be a blessing if the atmosphere might be cleared. Either of the major positions represents a workable approach to corporate administration, from both public and private standpoints, but the attempt to apply both theories at once is somewhat unfortunate. I see no overwhelming objection to a treatment of the corporation for tax purposes as the steward of the stockholders. Under such treatment the corporation, like the partnership, would not be subject to income tax (except in so far as a tax on the right to do business as a corporation might be based on income) and the stockholders would be taxed individually on their distributive shares. As a matter of fact, this plan was applied to so-called "personal-service" corporations and their members for a few years. But there is nothing clear-cut or equitable about any scheme which taxes the corporation on undistributed profits or taxes the stockholder on stock dividends. Under the partnership conception the process of earning by the corporation is the decisive criterion of the accrual of income to the stockholder; under the independent-entity view it is the actual distribution of profit funds which is decisive.

Acceptance of the association theory in accounting would modify our procedure at a number of important points. On the stockholders' books it would then be proper for income to be accrued as reported earned by the corporation (as is now sometimes recommended for the corporate stockholder owning a majority interest). On the corporation's books profits would then be immediately assignable to stockholders' accounts, and surplus accounting — with its array of complexities — would tend to disappear.

In commenting on developments relating to the accounting entity, I should not neglect to refer to the growing conception of the organized business enterprise, particularly the corporation, as a semipublic institution — an institution in which immediate management, stockholders, creditors, employees, customers, and government have a stake. This conception, long a commonplace in the public utility field, is in process of being applied to industrial corporations. The following excerpt from a recent report of Swift & Company indicates that some corporate managements clearly recognize the trend:

> In addition to the responsibilities which the company has toward retailers, consumers, livestock producers, and employees as separate groups, it recognizes also a responsibility toward all these groups collectively — a responsibility to the public and the public interest.
>
> This responsibility is one of the most important of all. Every operation in which the company is engaged must be carried on in harmony with the rules laid down by the public in the form of law. And there is a vast network of laws to be respected and obeyed. There are pure food laws, anti-discrimination laws, laws against agreements in restraint of trade, laws with regard to taxes, and various other types. Moreover, the company is subject to the ordinances of thousands of towns and cities, to the laws of forty-eight states, the laws of the federal government, and the laws of every foreign country in which it does business. . . .

To the accountant, especially the public accountant, this development is important in that it requires an appraisal of accounting principles and procedures from a broad point of view; it requires careful consideration of each contemplated procedure in the light of the proper needs of all parties at interest.

One of the New Deal agencies whose activities are particularly related to accounting is the Securities and Exchange Commission. With protection of investors as its keynote, the Commission has been making a serious effort to mold corporate reporting to this end. As noted earlier, the work of the Commission in this direction, on balance, seems to be definitely on the constructive side. It should not be assumed, however, that losses to investors are caused primarily by inadequate or misleading accounts and statements. Losses of long-term investors are largely the result of business conditions, and the effect of accounting on such conditions is generally not very great. Losses of speculators are compounded of fluctuating business prospects, real and fancied, the nature of the mechanism employed, and speculative temperament. Accounting plays some part in this area in furnishing much of the data for the "dope sheet," but here too it is easy to exaggerate the possibility of improving the situation through better accounting. Given a condition of business fluctuation and development, people who wish to speculate, and machinery through which speculation is possible, it is hard to see how governmental supervision of accounting reports can be a control factor of major importance.

I believe every effort should be made to place corporate reporting on the highest possible level with respect to completeness, accuracy, and intelligibility, but nothing is gained by overemphasizing the importance of reform in this field. Assuming ideal accounting there remains the difficulty of securing attention and understanding on the part of investors. Where accounts are concerned the rank and file of stockholders are usually both indifferent and ignorant.

In my classes in accounting years ago, I was fond of raising the question of how the field would be affected if private business gave way to a socialist economic regime. At that time I considered the question to be purely academic — a topic with virtually no practical implications. Today the problem is perhaps less theoretic. With the amazingly rapid strides toward complete government control of business which we have been making in recent years, the young man looking at accounting as a possible profession might well attempt to see what can be expected to happen in this area if the private enterprise ceases to be the dominant entity in business. In this connection I shall attempt nothing more than a suggestion. In a broad sense the volume of accounting activity would probably increase under a socialistic organization of industry. With no system of more or less competitive market prices to refer to for guidance there would presumably be a great emphasis on operating records, especially cost compilations. At the same time there would doubtless be little left of many of the interesting and controversial questions now associated with the measurement of the capital, profits, and surplus of the private enterprise. In other words, there would probably be more busywork and less "spice." The mass of routine reports which government now requires of business is a taste of what might be expected.

In the following discussion I am taking the liberty of assuming — notwithstanding the danger signs — that the obliteration of the essential character of the private business institution is not imminent.

III. MEASUREMENT OF PERFORMANCE

AT AN EARLY meeting of the recently enlarged committee on accounting procedure of the American Institute of Accountants the vice-chairman of the committee, George O. May, proposed as a sort of guiding "golden text" the following statement: "A fair determination of income for successive accounting periods is the most important single purpose of the general accounting reports of a corporation." This statement, which was adopted by the committee, is in line with the shift in emphasis which is the most important development in accounting in recent years. Formerly preoccupied with the balance sheet, the statement of financial position, and the point of view of the commercial creditor, the accountant is coming to see that the more important accounting report is the income statement, prepared so as to give special attention to the needs of the investor. In other words, the accountant is beginning to recognize that the business enterprise should be conceived as a continuing stream of activity, rather than a series of positions, and that his primary task is to prepare reports of the course of this stream, in appropriate time sections. With the adoption of this conception the balance sheet becomes a reconciling, complementary exhibit, connecting the successive reports of performance.

The gauging of enterprise performance is essentially a process of matching two subdivisions of the stream of activity, revenues and costs. With respect to the revenue side of the picture there has been relatively little controversy. Accountants are generally agreed that revenue — the lifeblood of the enterprise — is measured by the volume of sales. The delivered sale, in most lines of business, is the culmination of the process of production. On the occasion of sale, there is a physical severing of product from the enterprise as well as a transfer of ownership; on the occasion of sale, the vendor enterprise generally comes into possession of new liquid resources in the form of cash or receivables (cash in process). As a rule, therefore, the sales amount constitutes a very satisfactory yardstick of realized revenue.

This does not mean that revenue may be assumed to be *earned* by the act of sale. The only reasonable view is that revenue results from the entire process of production as expressed by the applicable costs; there is no warrant for the opinion that there is something peculiarly productive about the act of selling as such as compared with other steps in the operation of the business. It may be proper to say that revenue is *realized* by sale, but it does not at all follow that revenue is produced by sale. The point is important in the analysis of departmental data and in geographical allocations of income.

Notwithstanding the agreement regarding the nature of revenue it may be permissible to point out that the sales basis of measurement has serious limitations in special circumstances, and should be critically tested from time to time from the standpoint of fitness to meet the needs of effective income reporting.

Accountants concede that in the construction field, where months or even years may be required to complete the particular job, modification of the sales basis of measurement is not without justification. The procedure usually recommended is the accruing of income in terms of the progress of production — percentage of completion. There is, however, another way of dealing with the difficulty. Why not solve the problem by shifting from the period of time to the project or job in reckoning income? Suppose, for example, that a contractor is building a dam for the government which will take five years to complete. In this situation is there any excuse for an attempt to report profit or loss before the work is finished? Would it not be better to confine interim reports to progress statements of costs incurred and advances received, with no matching of estimated earned revenue and costs? Here would seem to be a case where we should not insist on a determination of income every time the earth completes its journey around the sun.

There is likewise something to be said for recognition of revenue prior to sale in enterprises in which natural increase or accretion is an important factor, especially if such increase is in the form of current resources, readily marketable. In farm accounting, for example, it is considered legitimate practice to include the amount of natural increase in the inventory. Where the period of growth is long, there is again the alternative of recognizing revenue and matching revenues and costs in terms of projects rather than periods.

On the whole, more of a case can be made for moving the line of revenue recognition forward than can be made for moving the line backward. Very often the sale is an inconclusive transaction. Sales returns are common; uncollectible accounts, unfortunately, are no rarity. There is also the fact that "after-costs," such as billing and collection costs and charges arising out of product guaranties, are often substantial. Aside from these complications there is no escaping the fact that liabilities cannot be met or dividends paid with accounts receivable. (This point would be less important if there were adequate facilities for discounting book accounts.) With these conditions it is somewhat surprising that only in the field of installment sales has there been much agitation for the use of the cash basis of revenue measurement.

I should like to submit that the booking of revenues in terms of collections from customers rather than sales is a reasonable procedure, worthy of careful consideration. The procedure has never been adequately developed by accountants; the typical treatment of installment sales represents only a half-hearted application of the collections basis. It is not feasible here to discuss the question in detail, but the main features of a proper cash revenue procedure can be readily indicated. In the first place, a gross revenue account should be opened which is credited with the total amount received from customers, the same amount being concurrently charged to cash. Second, accounts receivable should be handled through a self-balancing ledger not tied into the general books. Third, goods consigned to customers should be charged at cost to a special account allied to inventory, and this account should be closed to cost of sales as invoices are collected. Fourth, all unassigned costs of administration and selling should be charged to expenses with due regard to their relation to the stream of collections. This last suggestion, it should be added, presents no more difficulty than is found under the conventional sales basis of reckoning. That is, selling costs and the fringe of general costs can be applied to collections in a reasonable manner just as readily as they can be applied to sales. At present such costs are usually dumped into expenses in the year in which incurred, without regard to their intrinsic relation to revenue. With this crude treatment in effect, the substitution of collections for sales as the measure of revenues would presumably not make matters worse.

It is important to understand that the substitution of collections for sales as the gauge of periodic revenue would not imply abandonment of the accrual system of accounting. The essence of this system is the assignment of costs in terms of revenues. If collections from customers rather than sales are accepted as the revenue yardstick, the absorption of costs should be modified accordingly, but there would be no less need for careful analysis and apportionment of charges.

Adoption of the collections basis of revenue measurement would have the advantage of squaring with the instinctive and not unreasonable feeling of many people associated with business that income is effectively realized only when received in cash.

One of the annoying aspects of existing procedure with respect to revenue measurement is found in the persistent treatment of purchase discounts and related cost corrections as realized income. Such treatment implies that revenue may be accrued in terms of the initial stage of cost incurring, at the very outset of the process of production. This position is absurd, especially in view of general agreement in manufacturing and trading fields to the effect that revenue recognition should be postponed until sale is effected. If invoices were regularly written in terms of net prices, with a penalty charge added for delay in making payment, the improper interpretation would probably disappear overnight. Even with the traditional method of bill writing, the net-price method is much more convenient than the gross-price procedure, as a goodly number of concerns have discovered.

Even where there is reason for holding that costs have been incurred on an exceptionally favorable basis — which is not at all true of cases involving acceptance of conventional discounts — it would be unwise to adopt the view that the saving in cost is a revenue. If costs are low, the effect will be registered soon enough in a matching of realized revenue and applicable charges. To hold otherwise is a step in the direction of abandoning cost incurred as a starting point in the reckoning of business expense, in favor of pure estimates. It is very likely true that costs incurred often fail to express fair market values with precision, but the fact remains that in all but the most extraordinary circumstances the price agreed upon by the two parties to the transaction is the most reliable evidence of value which is available. The assumption that the buyer has outsmarted the seller, or vice versa, cannot be regularly adopted for accounting purposes. Occasionally, no doubt, a case of the "lucky buy" actually occurs, but even so there is no warrant for immediate recognition of revenue.

Turning more definitely to the cost side of the picture of performance, we find that it is in this area that there is a large grist of unsettled problems. As a preliminary to commenting on some of these problems I wish to make a suggestion with respect to the relation between costs and assets. Emphasis on the income statement and the conception of the enterprise as a flow of activity is tending to modify — and in a desirable direction — the interpretation of assets. In the past there has been a reluctance to recognize as an asset any charge which was not clearly assignable to specific elements of tangible property. The emphasis has been upon physical character and transferability rather than economic incidence in a progressing stream of operation. Deferred charges have been viewed as nothing more than a necessary evil at the best. One of our very prominent professional accountants has suggested that the asset side of the balance sheet be labeled "assets, etc." But now there are some signs that we are on the verge of a more discriminating view of the situation. There are two main kinds of assets, and when this is clearly recognized a long step will have been taken in the direction of reconciling conflicting opinions regarding both periodic cost assignment and financial reporting. One class of assets consists of money resources, cash or near-cash in the form of receivables and marketable securities. The money resources, net of current bills, represent that portion of the capital of the enterprise which is relatively flexible, which awaits final commitment or utilization. The other main class consists of a pool of cost factors, costs incurred. Here is the capital which has been definitely — and often irrevocably — committed to the process of production. Here is the capital entrusted to the stream of activity; it is in jeopardy until recovered in the form of revenue, and there is no assurance of full recovery. I realize, of course, that there is some overlapping, as in all taxonomy. Cash on hand may be in effect committed, and cost factors attaching to marketable inventory may be all but recouped. I also realize that there is some recovery of costs (in the case of land, for example) even in the event of forced liquidation.

The point is that a very large section of the so-called assets of business enterprises, especially in the public utility and industrial fields, consists of costs in process rather than available funds or currently recoverable values. This means that the continual bickering regarding the relation of deferred charges to "real assets" is meaningless. Excluding money resources all of the assets are deferred charges, costs incurred. In this area the test for assets is not that of separate physical existence, or of immediate realizability. The question is: Is there a reasonable basis for applying the particular cost factor to prospective revenues? If an affirmative answer is justified, the charge under consideration is at the moment an element in the asset total. With the situation clarified along this line there is no longer any excuse for regarding organization and development charges, properly incurred, with suspicion, even if no basis for assigning such charges to specific tangible properties is available. In the last analysis virtually all costs are the prices of services assumed to be needed in business operation. Some services are acquired by the enterprise in service form; other services are acquired congealed in the form of technical facilities. But this distinction has no fundamental meaning for accounting purposes.

"Costs" rather than "assets" is the significant term in present-day accounting. Costs are incurred and are charged to cost accounts. From time to time the pool of costs is analyzed for the sake of determining the charges to be applied to current revenues on the one hand and prospective revenues on the other. After absorption of the expired costs the amount to be deferred emerges as an "asset" balance.

I think it might help our understanding if the practice were revived of dividing the balance sheet horizontally into two distinct sections, the current account balance sheet and the capital account statement.

In the accounting for costs three interrelated stages may be distinguished. First, there is the task of recording costs as incurred, properly classified. This is the simplest part of the work of handling costs and under modern accounting methods is accomplished in an effective manner at most points. Second, costs must be traced in terms of the flow of operations, with adequate reclassification by departments and other significant divisions. Third, costs must be matched with periodic revenues. The last two phases are closely related and bristle with difficulties. Here is the crux of cost accounting.

In the original recording of costs there is one weak spot which is very widespread and has at least theoretic significance. Where the factors of production are acquired on an immediate cash basis, the amount of cost incurred is definitely available and there is no excuse for inaccurate recording. Where payment is deferred, on the other hand, the amount of cost may not be apparent and there is more than a possibility of misstatement. In practice, as a matter of fact, costs incurred on a credit basis are almost universally overstated to some extent.

As a means of emphasizing the point I have in mind a rather extreme case may be referred to. In recent years the United States Government has issued over three billions, in maturity amount, of "Savings Bonds" on a discount basis. For example, a bond with a maturity value of $1,000 payable in ten years is issued for $750, cash. The difference between these two figures is actually interest, interest which accrues during the life of the contract at a rate of 2.9%, compounded semiannually. With these conditions it seems quite clear that the total amount of the asset acquired by the borrower is restricted to amount of cash received, $750, and that the effective liability at the outset is likewise $750. That is, no one would have the hardihood in this case to insist that the government's immediate assets and liabilities are expanded in the amount of $1,000 as a result of the transaction. It is also clear that in buying goods or services with the amount received from the issue of one of these bonds, the government is in a position to incur a cost of only $750.

In the field of business enterprise long-term obligations of this character are seldom if ever used (although bonds are frequently issued under terms by which part of the total interest is represented by discount). Nevertheless, interest in the form of discount is present in many business transactions, sometimes in substantial amount. The question is: Are we justified in failing to segregate interest charges of this character? Let us consider an actual case that came to my attention recently. A company buys a specialized machine at a contract price of $28,000. The contract requires an initial payment of $4,000 upon delivery, and a payment of $6,000 every six months for four successive periods. No interest as such is charged. In this situation most accountants without hesitation would debit

Equipment with the full amount of the contract price, $28,000, ignoring the question of discount. But is this sound? Is it not more reasonable to take the position that a part of the total amount paid is actually interest and should be so recorded? Assuming a rate of 6%, compounded semiannually, the amount of discount is $1,697.41. This means that the cost of the equipment is only $26,302.59. Accepting this interpretation the charge to Equipment, and the amount subject to depreciation, is $26,302.59, and the discount of $1,697.41 is accrued as an interest charge over the life of the contract. The difference between the conventional treatment and the revised procedure, it may be insisted, is substantial. With the conventional treatment the amount of cost incurred is overstated by nearly $1,700, and the amount of this overstatement is charged to operations over the life of the machine. With the revised procedure the discount is excluded from plant cost and is accrued as interest over a two-year period.

In purchases of goods and services on current account, likewise, the element of discount may be assumed to be present. Here, however, the period covered is usually so short and the amount of implied discount so small that no very strong case can be made for a modification of the usual procedure. The most that is needed is an occasional statistical analysis of the conditions under which goods and services are acquired on account.

Please do not understand from these remarks that I am endorsing the introduction into the accounts of estimated interest on investment. Nothing of the kind is involved. I am simply suggesting the possibility (and the desirability in some cases) of a more careful classification — as to accounts and periods of time — of expenditures actually made in the acquiring of cost factors on a credit basis.

With respect to the second and third phases of cost accounting — departmentalizing and matching with revenue — I have one major suggestion and several minor comments to offer. In particular, I wish to emphasize a proposition which is very generally neglected or denied but which has a great deal of force, I believe, throughout the range of human experience and activity. Stated in general terms, the proposition is that where two or more factors are necessary to a given result it is unreasonable to impute the effect to the essential ingredients or causes seriatim. Or, turned about, the proposition is that where two or more results flow from a single agent it is unreasonable to impute the significance of the agent to the several effects seriatim. Applying this thesis to the problem in hand, we have the statement that *all costs legitimately incurred are homogeneous in their relation to revenue* or that *all revenues should be proportionately attributed to each of the necessary costs.*

This view of essential relationships in measuring business performances amounts to a denial of the propriety of the ranking of costs which is so characteristic of business thinking and is so often reflected in accounting procedure. It denies the propriety of playing favorites with costs. Cost favoritism is of three kinds — class favoritism, department favoritism, and period favoritism. The first is illustrated by the persistent tendency to subordinate depreciation in the income statement, to treat the depreciation as a doubtful, optional, take-it or leave-it kind of cost. On every hand we see such statements as "net profit before depreciation is $13,642,915.25" or "we earned our preferred dividend and had a balance left for depreciation of $322,604.12." One might as well say "net profit before cost of materials," or "net profit before labor cost," or "net profit assuming there were no costs." There is nothing imaginary or questionable about depreciation cost. Depreciation is an actual cost, an out-of-pocket cost. In the case of depreciation, indeed, the expenditure must be made in a lump sum, in advance, for a period of years. The amount paid for the unit of equipment is simply the prepaid wages of the robot, the mechanical agent. Like its human prototype, the machine has a limited service life. As in the case of the human factor, too, the possible services of the machine are likely to prove to be very perishable if not used in accordance with a normal schedule of activity. As the services of the machine are requisitioned and placed in operation, or lost through failure to utilize, appropriate slices of the prepaid amount are charged to operating cost accounts or written off as losses. That is depreciation accounting in a nutshell. The procedure is very matter-of-fact, entirely devoid of mystery. It must be granted, of course, that the length of service life is not definitely known in advance and that partly as a result of this fact the determination of the periodic expiration is largely a matter of judgment, in the light of all pertinent data. But if, in a given period, plant facilities necessary to production are actually used, it is hard to see how the conclusion can be avoided that plant cost must be included in operating charges to the extent, at least, of a reasonable minimum amount. To hold otherwise denies both the objective physical conditions and the obvious economic implications. Moreover, although depreciation charged to revenues in a given period may not be fully recovered, it is fair to conclude that depreciation is not peculiar in this respect (assuming that the plant facilities in question are of modern type and that the cost thereof is in line with current costs of similar facilities). If revenue, for example, amounts to only 90% of the total of the applicable costs, including depreciation, this means that 90% of each cost factor is recovered, not that some are recouped in full and others are lost in full. There is little or no evidence of a selective arraying of cost components in the complex process of market price determination.

Another important example of class cost favoritism, which I cannot forbear mentioning, is that represented by the tendency in income statement presentation to strike an intermediate "gross profit" balance. Here again there is a preferential ranking of cost which has no substantial justification and tends to lead to misunderstanding on the part of both management and customer. There is no objection to the classifying of applicable costs in as much detail as may be helpful, but there can be no profit, "gross" or otherwise, until the total of costs has been matched with the total of revenue. The "gross profit" tradition is a relic of the early history of accounting for mercantile concerns, and it is high time that it be relegated to the limbo of outworn procedures in favor of a presentation of operating data which is consonant with the conceptions of cost accounting that have been developed in the industrial field. Please do not misunderstand me. I am talking here about the general income statement of the enterprise for the accounting period. I am offering no objection whatever to reckonings of departmental margins, or to ratios computed by applying this or that cost or group of costs to total revenues. Such calculations may be misleading, if taken too seriously, but they are often genuinely helpful. In this connection I might add that I like the suggestion of Mr. C. B. Clark, of The J. L. Hudson Company, to the effect that departmental assignments of cost be confined to the strictly inescapable costs and that the departmental balance be conceived as the contribution of the department to the common costs and to profit, if any.

This brings us to the question of departmental favoritism in cost accounting. I must not take time to dwell on this point although I consider it important. Business is full of biased cost accounting, particularly with respect to joint or common costs. We have all seen many examples of it, and in view of the difficulties involved in cost assignment it is not easy to find a remedy. One of the common types of unfair allocation results from the failure to charge a particular activity with incidental benefits furnished by another department without apparently increasing the cost of operating the latter. (The action taken by the superintendent of the water and electric departments of a particular municipality affords an illustration. The superintendent, interested in making a favorable showing for the electric department in comparison with a private electric utility, refused to permit any part of the cost of operating pumps used in pumping water into the filter tanks to be charged to the electric department, notwithstanding the fact that the flow of water on the way to the tanks was used to cool electric department apparatus.) In all such cases the only sound approach —

assuming departmental reckonings are required — is that which insists on an assignment of a reasonable portion of the cost of the department rendering service to the department receiving the benefit. This conclusion conforms to the essential fact that under the prevailing conditions the cost factors embodied in a particular department are actually rendering service in two directions.

Unfair departmental allocation which is not intentional is, of course, common, particularly where there are indirect influences, not readily traced. As an example of indirect relationship may be mentioned the case where the employees of one department are permitted to buy goods of another department at a substantial discount.

The third type of cost partiality listed above, period favoritism, is the most far-reaching and dangerous of all. It is crudely represented by the postponing or the advancing of maintenance expenditures by a management with a weather eye on the effect on the reported profit for the current period. It may be more subtly represented in depreciation policy, in the handling of deferred charges, and in inventory methods. I shall give some further attention to this point under another head.

A special type of questionable cost ranking which deserves some attention is reflected in the familiar tendency to stress differential cost computations, particularly in connection with price estimates. This is a big subject and nothing more can be done here than raise the issue once more and indicate my own opinion. I submit that in business accounting average periodic cost, including all necessary factors of production, is a more significant concept than differential cost. I am inclined to argue, too, that the prevailing emphasis on differentials and short-run policy actually has an unfortunate influence on long-term business operation. In making decisions with respect to particular sections of prospective output, no doubt, there is some justification for giving close attention to probable cost increments. On the other hand, once the output of a particular period has been determined and is water under the bridge, I fail to see much excuse for favoring particular segments of revenue in the matter of cost accounting. If 10,000 units were produced at a total cost of $100,000, the cost of each and every unit is $10. Moreover, even in the delicate matter of taking on additional orders in a period of depression it is easy to exaggerate the importance of differentials. For the sake of holding a skeleton organization together and maintaining a market position it may be necessary on occasion to price products below the level of cost computed on any basis. In other words, neither differential nor average cost is a decisive fact in extraordinary conditions.

I can perhaps best emphasize my slant on this problem by saying that I have always been suspicious of the old story that the last straw broke the camel's back. I have always suspected that the other straws had some influence on the result.

So much for the general problem of cost ranking. A number of other aspects of the process of tracing costs and assigning costs to periodic revenue should be mentioned. First, the accountant should not be unduly influenced by apparent physical connections — "what the eye can see and the hand follow." Stop watches, scales, calipers, gauges, etc., are none too helpful in cost accounting. The problem is one of reasonable economic association rather than physical incidence. I recall that Henry Carter Adams made this point years ago by pointing out that coal burned in a freight locomotive while standing on a siding under a full head of steam to let a passenger train through might be construed, at least in part, as a cost of passenger traffic. Similarly, the entire cost of a sheet of leather may be charged to product even if 10% of the sheet by weight goes to the scrap pile. When this aspect of the situation is more generally and clearly understood, we shall have little difficulty in seeing the reasonableness, under some circumstances, of postponing the application of a portion of advertising and other selling charges, and of office and administration costs, to the revenues of a period subsequent to that in which such costs are incurred.

At the same time the accountant must recognize that the

problem of matching costs and revenue will continue to have baffling areas no matter how rational the point of view adopted and no matter how carefully the work of allocation and assignment be carried out. The success of specific, detailed assignment will always be limited, and it will always be necessary to place considerable reliance upon mass, periodic application. In other words, the very nature of the problem is such that we can hardly expect to find completely convincing methods of distributing the more general classes of charges in relation to realized revenues per period.

With respect to common costs the accountant is beginning to realize that such costs are to be found in virtually all enterprises. Indeed, it is hardly going too far to say that common costs are the rule and specific costs flowing in water-tight compartments to specific destinations the exception. The effect of this development may already be seen in the tendency in many enterprises in the direction of the abandonment of fine-spun schemes of allocation which at bottom have little to commend them other than their arithmetical precision.

Finally, a word should be offered with regard to standard costs and the related subject of losses. As you all know, real progress has been made in the last ten years in the development of standard cost procedures, and such procedures have come to have a settled place in the framework of cost accounting. The principal danger in the use of standard costs lies in the possibility of taking such estimates too seriously from the standpoint of the general income statement for the period. Costs actually incurred in excess of standard should not be deferred merely because they are in excess; nor should costs recognized in the income statement be increased to standard if the actual costs fall below this level. Neither the total stream of cost incurred nor the amount broadly applicable to the year's revenues is affected by the existence of cost budgets and standard cost accumulations, except in the sense that plans alter expenditures and use of existing facilities. Moreover, although standards may be useful in drawing the line between expenses and losses, particularly in departmental computations, we should not be too quick to assume that any variance in excess of standard should be reported as a loss in the income statement or treated as a charge to surplus. No doubt there is a valid though shadowy distinction between expenses — costs of revenue — and outright losses. For example, it does not seem unreasonable, at least at first sight, to treat the depreciation of completely idle plant, in excess of normal stand-by facilities, as a loss.

IV. THE PERIOD OF RECKONING

THE FOREGOING discussion has neglected a group of questions bearing upon the process of income determination which are particularly associated with the nature and significance of the accounting period employed.

Modern accounting essays the difficult task of breaking the continuing stream of business operation into time sections. The result, at the best, is no more than a series of careful estimates. To prepare an income statement for a particular month, quarter, or year requires the severing of many living threads; each report is tentative in that its final validation depends in part at least upon future events. It is no wonder that former Justice Brandeis and others have suggested that there can be no wholly dependable computation of net income until the particular enterprise has run its course. And if modern business activity were carried on in the form of specific terminable ventures, like the trading voyages of an earlier day, it is very likely that the venture or project rather than the period would be emphasized as a basis of income reckoning. As matters stand, however, we are committed to a program of periodic measurement, and it falls to the accountant to make this program as sound and effective as the intrinsically limiting conditions permit.

In the past ten to fifteen years there has been a considerable drive in the direction of short-term statements. Many concerns have adopted the practice of preparing semiannual or quarterly income reports, and occasionally an organization has gone as far as the issuing of monthly reckonings. I should like to sound a warning note in this connection. In view of the difficulties in the way of making satisfactory annual statements, there is a question as to the propriety of interim matchings of revenues and costs. If the highly artificial and tentative character of short-term reports were fully understood, there would be less reason for anxiety, but as a matter of fact such reports seem to be taken very seriously by many readers. With respect to the stock market, there seems to be a decided tendency to capitalize in perpetuity the prospects of a company as revealed by the last quarter's showing in determining the price of the shares. An unfavorable report appears and the price of the stock falls 50%; the company reports a profit and the price of the stock jumps 100%. Examples of these extreme fluctuations are numerous. It may well be argued that we are becoming too sensitive to every wind that blows and that such hypersensitiveness is a disturbing rather than a stabilizing factor. I do not mean to imply that too frequent reporting is the dominant element in this situation, but I suggest that it may be one influence.

Certain types of short-term reports, of course, are almost indispensable to the operating management. In some cases even daily reports of the volume of business and other evidences of activity may be desirable. I am raising a question only with respect to matchings of revenue and cost, with a disclosure of profit or loss, which cover such a short period of time, and are based on such arbitrary assignments as to be valueless or even misleading.

Short-term income reckonings are likewise dangerous in that they tend to develop questionable conceptions of operating expenses. When business activity is viewed from the standpoint of a particular month or quarter, a rather technical and narrow interpretation of revenue charges tends to emerge. Thus, if a portion of plant is idle during the month, or is utilized at less than "normal" capacity, an emphasis on the short-run view may lead to the conclusion that part of the depreciation is an outright loss rather than a cost of revenue. I suggest again that what is needed is more stress on a broad, long-run view of operating activity. A business enterprise has its being not in any ideal or standard milieu but rather in a world in which accident and bad judgment are commonplaces. From a short-run, departmental point of view costs which appear to make no specific contribution to production have the appearance of losses, but from a long-run enterprise standpoint virtually all charges take on the character of costs of revenues.

Aside from the technical difficulties and imperfections associated with business operation is the effect of impinging external changes. All enterprises, in varying degree, are subject to economic fluctuations. But it does not follow that the effect of such fluctuations is nonoperating loss or gain, as the case may be. In undertaking production in the face of special risks, it is to be assumed that the circumstances are realistically contemplated and that it is expected that revenues in the long run will be sufficient to cover all charges incurred. And technical operation and economic speculation are generally inextricably bound together.

One of the most controversial developments in accounting is the effort to deal with the limitations of periodic income determinations by the adoption of some accounting policy designed to exert a stabilizing influence. This development dates back some distance in accounting thinking and practice but has been especially important in the last decade. It has a number of manifestations. One is the "fat-year, lean-year" depreciation doctrine. Under this doctrine, in its extreme form, depreciation is conceived as an elastic cost which varies with operating net, and hence may properly be adjusted for the purpose of minimizing the fluctuations in such net. It obtains some support from the familiar conception (referred to earlier) of plant assets as a limited stock of services to be rendered. If this conception is sound, it follows — it may be argued — that when plant is temporarily idle there is no depreciation, as no services are being requisitioned, and that when plant is being operated either at subnormal or supernormal capacity the depreciation charge should be correspondingly contracted or expanded to match the changing flow of productive service. This line of argument is plausible and may be given a limited endorsement. It should be pointed out, however, that there is a marked difference between a thoroughgoing output or activity method of spreading depreciation cost and a manipulation of depreciation designed to bring about a desired effect upon net income. With a production method of apportionment, depreciation is being objectively determined without regard to final effect upon the showing of profits; under the fat-year, lean-year policy, as commonly applied, an important cost is being gauged by reference to a conclusion which itself is supposed to result from the process of matching revenue and cost. And there would seem to be little propriety in any practice in which effect is employed to determine cause. It should also be noted that there is a great difference between the spreading of the depreciation of relatively short-lived plant assets in terms of seasonal and other short fluctuations (as, for example, the writing off of an airplane motor in terms of flying hours) and a policy which seeks to smooth the recorded path of the enterprise through the uncertain ups and downs of the business cycle. When depression has reduced plant activity to 50% of so-called average or normal output, for example, it is not at all reasonable to conclude that the expiration of the potential store of plant services is similarly reduced. In many cases physical decay is not proportionately arrested with declining activity. More important is the fact that limited life is often largely the result of obsolescence and related factors, and there is little evidence that the effect of such factors is modified by falling or rising output.

Another means of stabilizing reported net income is found in the various schemes of spreading irregularly recurring losses. Perhaps the principal example is the practice of accruing reserves for insurance through estimated charges to operation. This practice has considerable appeal. If the enterprise enters into agreements with insurance companies and pays regular premiums for protection from the effects of possible casualties, it seems clear that a regular cost, actually incurred, takes the place of irregular, uncertain losses. If, then, the enterprise becomes a "self-insurer," so called, is it not proper for a regular expense to be accrued based either on the premiums which would otherwise be paid or an annual average of estimated losses over a considerable period? The answer is that the conditions are by no means the same in the two cases. An enterprise which has taken out insurance policies covering certain risks has thereby changed the setting in which it operates; no longer is the business subject — to the extent of the coverage — to the risks in question; they have been shifted to another party, and a regular service cost has thereby been substituted for uncertain, irregular losses. In one case, therefore, it is sound to charge operations with the cost of insurance, a cost actually incurred; in the other case, the introduction into actual expenses of an insurance cost which might have been incurred but was not, or an estimated average loss which may never be validated, is objectionable. Such accounting is purely artificial; it gives an appearance of stability and regularity where there is no actual stability or regularity.

I am not saying that it is improper for an enterprise to carry its own losses where careful examination of the situation shows this to be expedient. Large companies, with many separate properties, and varying working conditions, may find it desirable to carry certain risks which it would be possible to remove or minimize through insurance contracts. Also I am not saying that fire losses and other casualty losses occurring irregularly are not business expense — costs of revenue — from the long-run point of view. It is purely a question of incidence. No amount of technical accounting will change the objective circumstances. If labor costs are high in one year as compared with another, it is not usually suggested that average labor costs — or labor costs as they would be under altogether different conditions — should be substituted for the charges actually incurred. Similarly, there is no adequate justification for the substitution of insurance costs which might have been incurred for losses actually suffered. If the decision to forego insurance protection was deliberately and reasonably made, this means that the management has accepted operating conditions under which periodic net income will actually be more irregular than might otherwise be the case. Then it is not up to the accountant to issue reports which place the operations on the alternative basis which the management has rejected.

"But," the objector says, "there will be a lack of comparability between the statements of the insured company and those of the self-insurer if there is no accrual of an average loss as an estimated operating charge in the accounts of the latter." This objection is an old friend, always popping out at one. Some concerns borrow money and pay interest; therefore, other concerns should in their accounts assume that their capital is borrowed and accrue interest thereon. Some concerns rent buildings; therefore, other concerns should assume that they do likewise. Some proprietors hire all managerial services; therefore, other proprietors should imagine that they are paying themselves salaries. So the story goes. I suggest that the way to promote rational comparisons of business entities of various kinds is not to be found in obliterating genuine dissimilarities through arbitrary accounting procedures. The way to begin a careful study of a field of California poppies, for example, would not be to paint out all variations in coloring. I can see that the economist-statistician who is analyzing and combining the figures of many enterprises is going to wish that there were more uniformity in the conditions of business operation. But even in this area, it seems to me, the investigator is helped most if the accounts of each enterprise are kept with scrupulous attention to the circumstances under which the enterprise carries on its activity.

It may still be argued, perhaps, that losses like those due to fire actually accrue in much the same way that depreciation cost accrues. But this position is hardly tenable. Plant represents a cost actually incurred and depreciation accounting consists of the process of assigning this cost to periodic revenues. This situation has no counterpart in the accruing of possible fire loss. If at the end of a particular period no loss has occurred, it is quite fantastic to say that a loss has accrued during the period. It is not even fair to hold that the assets are placed in greater jeopardy as a result of the good fortune of the past year. There may, indeed, never be a fire casualty during the entire life of the plant. This means that the credit balance in the reserve for insurance at any particular time is not a contra to recorded costs of property but is genuine earned surplus which has been appropriated without passage through the door of income recognition.

The accruing of estimated casualty losses is likewise objectionable in that persistent understatement of net income may be involved, aside from the questionable periodic distribution of profits. With no definite objective control on the estimates and with the management desirous of accumulating a substantial reserve balance, there is a tendency to accrue in excess of a fair estimate of either average loss or alternative insurance cost. This would not be improper if a process of appropriating earned surplus were substituted for charges to operation, but the procedure cannot be approved if a continuing concealment of earnings is involved.

Incidentally it may be pointed out that the phrase "self-insurer" is misleading. Strictly speaking, there is no such thing as "self-insurance." A concern may decide to forego insurance and accept the risk, but this is not an alternative insurance plan. In the nature of the case a program of insurance is characterized by a shifting of risk to an outside agency which is in the business of carrying risk. Even if an insurance reserve were accumulated in an amount equal to the total possible loss which might reasonably have been covered by insurance contracts, and were funded in cash or securities, this would not be an insured condition. Such a state of affairs would simply mean that a concern had accumulated profits or converted capital in the form of a large fund which was not needed for the normal purposes of the business and which would be likely to remain unutilized, in large measure, indefinitely.

The most interesting and important effort to minimize the fluctuations in reported earnings is the "last-in, first-out" approach to the measurement of periodic cost of sales and inventory. This policy, as most of you know, has been very actively sponsored by many businessmen and accountants in recent years and has finally received some official endorsement in income-tax administration. Under this policy the inventory each period is built up from the costs first incurred, including the preceding inventory, and cost of sales is assumed to be represented by all costs incurred which are not absorbed by the inventory computation. Or, turned about, the policy provides for the application to current revenue of the most recent costs in appropriate amount and the inclusion in inventory of the costs not so absorbed. In a period characterized by advancing or falling prices the procedure exerts a stabilizing influence on the reported course of net income, a feature which is usually emphasized as its greatest virtue. That is, in a period of rising prices the procedure tends to apply the highest of the available costs to sales, thus cutting down the showing of net, and in a period of falling prices, similarly, the effect is to bolster the reported profits. Last-in, first-out is especially favored for extractive industries and other lines handling large amounts of materials subject to sharp fluctuations in price. It is argued that more significant periodic operating data are derived by matching revenues with the latest costs, and that a more equitable series of taxable incomes flows from such procedure. It is also argued that the use of last-in, first-out, like actual hedging, tends to exclude from reported income the effect of fluctuations in inventory prices, and thus restrict the showing of profit to the amount realized by the business through the exercise of its intrinsic operating function.

This is far too big a subject to be discussed fully here. I would like to outline briefly, however, the reasons for my misgivings with respect to this new effort to reduce the fluctuations of business earnings through accounting procedure. In the first place, there can be no doubt that in few, if any, cases does the actual flow of the goods and services which are the tangible representatives of costs incurred conform to the assumed pattern. Indeed, it would be very unfortunate in most lines if this were the case, as the resulting loss through the retention of old stock in the inventory would be enormous. As a rule, the efforts of management should be directed to seeing to it that as far as the physical flow is concerned the cost factors move through the business in an orderly procession — that is, in "first-in, first-out" fashion. And without much doubt the actual flow in most enterprises follows the first-in, first-out course more nearly than either the weighted average or last-in, first-out patterns — the two main systematic alternatives.

It does not follow, of course, that the dollar flow must jibe with the physical movement, but the burden of proof is definitely on those who wish to hold otherwise. We are not merely keeping accounts with economic capital in dollars; it is our task to follow capital as it takes shape in particular structures, goods, services, and conditions. Take plant, for example. In the industrial field, at any rate, few would have the hardihood to suggest that last-in, first-out should be rigidly applied to plant; that the investment in plant should always be considered to be represented by the cost of the first batch of facilities. Instead, it is the *sine qua non* of good property accounting that the accounts show the cost of the existing layout of facilities. Now if this is sound in the case of plant, why shift to an entirely different position in the case of another group of cost factors, those represented by the inventory? It is of interest to note in this connection that the proponents of last-in, first-out commonly defend the notion that the basic or normal amount of the inventory is essentially a fixed asset like plant, apparently without seeing that the procedure they are supporting is not at all that which is considered proper for plant.

In the second place, there is reason for questioning the general force of the proposition that more significant operating data are produced through last-in, first-out procedure. It is probably true that current costs have more bearing on current selling price than do earlier costs. However, it should be remembered that the use of last-in, first-out does not result in charging revenues with end-of-year prices. Where there is no increase in the inventory, and the amount of inventory is relatively small in relation to total costs incurred, the cost of sales by last-in, first-out will include the total costs incurred for the year, and this figure may not be greatly different from that which would be computed under the first-in, first-out approach. What is more important, it may be urged that for managerial purposes it is more useful to apply the relatively recent costs to goods on hand than to goods sold. Completed sales and the related costs are "water under the bridge," closed transactions. Utilization of the inventory, on the other hand, lies in the future, and in planning such utilization the current level of costs should be considered.

With respect to the question of profit realization, I feel that no one has succeeded in making a strong case for the doctrine that reported income should exclude the effect of all changes in the cost of inventory. If sales exceed costs incurred applicable to such sales, a recognizable profit has been realized, and this profit is not obliterated or altered by the fact that a portion is utilized to acquire new cost factors at a higher price. Business income, at least in the eyes of the law, is not measured by change in purchasing power or increase in physical resources, but by the excess of dollar funds acquired from customers over associated dollar costs incurred. The conventional conception of income, it is true, is subject to serious limitations, and accountants should not neglect to explore possibilities of further analysis. We are in no position, however, to throw overboard the conventional conception. Further, it is by no means true that the use of last-in, first-out procedure will result in complete elimination of the effect of inventory price movements from acknowledged profits and thus restrict the showing of net to the effect of technical production. As I suggested earlier, business activity is an amalgam of technical effort and adaptation to changes in impinging business conditions, and there is no scheme of accounting which can change this essential fact.

A technical objection to last-in, first-out procedure lies in the fact that different results are obtained through the use of this procedure if it is applied continuously throughout the year in pricing issues or shipments from those which are secured when the computation is made in terms of the data for the year as a whole. Under the former technique, indeed, the difference between the effect of last-in, first-out and first-in, first-out may not be very marked.

As far as income-tax considerations are concerned, the case for last-in, first-out is strong. Under an income-tax administration which glorifies the annual reckoning, and which has only to a limited degree permitted the forwarding of losses, it is clearly to the taxpayer's advantage — in fields where net income tends to fluctuate sharply — to cut off the peaks and fill the valleys by every allowable device.

From a balance sheet standpoint the thoroughgoing application of last-in, first-out leaves much to be desired. Under this policy the inventory may be either greatly overstated or understated by comparison with current costs. If, for example, a sugar refining company happened to acquire its first inventory at 25 cents per pound, and maintained the same physical inventory in subsequent periods, the use of last-in, first-out would result in a constant inventory at a 25-cent level, even in the face of a relatively permanent decline to a price of, say, 5 cents per pound.

Whatever else may be said it remains true that last-in, first-out procedure does tend in some degree to minimize the fluctuations in reported net income. This leaves us facing the essential question: Is such stabilization desirable? As I have already tried to indicate, I feel that an answer in the negative is justified. A clear distinction must, of course, be drawn between actual stabilization of business and apparent stabilization through accounts. I am offering no objection here to programs which attempt to reduce business fluctuations, but I am questioning efforts to alter the appearance of business affairs without modification of the objective conditions. Certain fields of business, it is generally agreed, are subject to sharp fluctuations in prices and volume of sales from year to year. Where this is the real situation, it is surely not desirable to introduce accounting methods which bring about an artificial averaging or smoothing. That is, if there are good years and bad years, this condition should be sharply disclosed, not obscured by the accounts and reports.

The problem is one of adequately qualifying annual statements without creating misconceptions. The proper solution, I submit, lies in supplementing annual reports, not in doctoring them. As some of us have been recommending for a long time, accountants should make more use of comparative, cumulative, and average income statements, as a means of throwing the single-period statement into proper perspective. Further use of well-arranged statements of funds may also be helpful. But I object strongly to the presentation of an averaged statement as if it were the candid report of the course of operation in the particular year. Entire elimination of short-run reckoning is preferable to artificial modification of such reckoning.

V. COSTS AND VALUES

As SUGGESTED earlier, recorded costs may be generally assumed to indicate true economic significance, actual value, at the moment of incurring. With the passing of time, however, the book figures become less dependable measures of effective, current cost, and in periods of sharp and prolonged price movements the shortcomings of the data shown by the accounts may be serious.

With respect to the more current elements — those cost factors which pass through the business in a few days, weeks, or months — the final absorption of charges usually occurs before the divergence between recorded prices and immediate market prices is substantial. With respect to plant costs, on the other hand, the period of residence in the enterprise is a matter of years, and in that time it is more than likely that the change in costs of construction and other prices will be sufficient to create a marked disparity between the recorded charges and the corresponding costs prevailing in any particular period. In other words, while the costs of labor's services and materials are usually charged to revenues roughly in terms of the level of prices in effect at date of absorption, the depreciation charge, drawn from costs incurred at a much earlier date, may be quite out of line with current plant cost. In view of this situation it is not surprising that the interest in the valuation problems of accounting persists, notwithstanding the shift in emphasis from the balance sheet to the income statement. There is a continuing feeling of dissatisfaction, especially among cost accountants, with the operating statements based upon unadjusted book costs incurred in prior years. Such costs, many seem to feel, are not adequate as a basis for considering changes in selling prices or for making comparisons between periods and between different plants and departments.

Among the maze of suggestions and recommendations as to

how plant costs might be revised, two main propositions stand out. First, there is the proposal that recorded costs be regularly converted into the common denominator of current dollars as a basis for depreciation charges. This possibility has been discussed most clearly and completely by H. W. Sweeney in his interesting and valuable book, *Stabilized Accounting*.[1] The idea here is to accept cost as the measure of charges to operation, with cost defined, however, in terms of purchasing power rather than original dollars. Secondly, there is the familiar recommendation of the appraiser that current replacement cost be substituted for recorded cost in the determination of periodic charges. The two proposals, although distinct in conception, tend to yield somewhat similar results when applied in practice. The costs of complex plant resources include a wide range of material and service prices, and the movement of such prices conforms in some degree to the movement of the general price index — the measure of the change in the value of money. The swings in the costs of construction, it is true, tend to be somewhat wider than the fluctuations in the fabric of prices as a whole, but the degree of overlapping is such that the changes in the two indices are regularly in the same direction. It is this fact which affords some justification for the paradoxical statement that "the proponents of replacement cost valuations are in effect defending adherence to the original cost basis." Interpreting cost incurred in the sense of economic power committed to the enterprise, there is a measure of truth in this observation.

From the standpoint of managers and owners interested in applying truly significant costs to revenues in the measurement of operating performance, it seems fair to conclude that the replacement cost approach is somewhat more useful than the purchasing power approach to plant valuation. Business management is concerned in some degree with the maintenance of the integrity of investment measured in purchasing power but is perhaps even more devoted to the protection of productive

[1] New York, Harper & Brothers, 1936.

capacity and scope of activity. Moreover, it is presumably the specific costs of replacing the plant facilities in use, rather than the recorded costs converted into current dollars, which have a bearing on the prices of the product of such facilities.

With this by way of general background the question may now be asked: What should be the attitude of the accountant toward plant valuations as a means of promoting more effective determinations of income? A reasonable answer seems to be that although the accountant is not justified in wholesale condemnations of appraisals for the purpose indicated, he is likewise not compelled to accept valuation as a part of the regular framework of income accounting. The reasons for this somewhat unfavorable conclusion can be readily indicated. First, replacement cost of plant is of marked significance only in the case of standard, up-to-date facilities, which will presumably be replaced substantially in kind. Neither the original cost nor the replacement cost of facilities of an obsolescent character are potent factors in the economic process. For such resources the only sound approach to valuation is via the route of the remaining services which the resources may be expected to render in the light of all the attendant conditions. This is a point of which professional appraisers are notoriously neglectful. Now, for standard facilities recently acquired the recorded costs are presumably reasonably in line with significant current costs (barring periods of extraordinarily sharp price movements), which means that the practical case for revision of book costs is none too strong, as a rule, even in the very area in which the appraiser's approach is most fully justified. Secondly, the effect upon operating charges of the substitution of replacement costs or other values for recorded costs is seldom decisive, even where the movement in construction cost has been marked. In most enterprises the depreciation charge is a relatively small slice of total operating cost, and hence moderate changes in this cost usually do not exert a marked influence on the total. Assume, for example, that in a given case the amount of depreciation is 10% of the grand total of costs. In this situation a revision of plant value by which the periodic depreciation charge is increased by, say, 25% results in a change in total charges assignable to revenue of only 2.5% — hardly a major adjustment. Similarly, the recognition of a write-down of plant by which a depreciation charge amounting to 10% of total expense is reduced 25% would mean a decrease in total costs of only 2.5%. In view of all the uncertainties involved in the process of income measurement at the best, modifications of the extent indicated are not likely to prove to have any material effect on general operating or financial policy. At the same time it should be admitted that even changes of this character may be significant in departmental computations. In the third place, enthusiasts for the revision of plant cost should remember that the price of the product of the particular enterprise seldom reflects the change in the prices of component cost factors, of either the current or fixed type, immediately and precisely. No doubt costs and product prices are related in the long run, but there is considerable friction and lag in the typical case. Fourth, there is no assurance that the replacement cost at the particular date will persist for any considerable period; indeed, it is almost certain that there will be continuing change throughout service life. This point bears particularly on the claim that depreciation charges should be based on replacement costs in order to insure the retention of funds in the business (assuming that they are collected from customers) sufficient to cover replacement cost at date of retirement. As an indication of what it will finally cost to replace the plant (if it ever is replaced), the estimated replacement cost in a particular period is scarcely more reliable than recorded dollar cost.

More important perhaps than any of the foregoing is the fact that the accounting for income cannot be shifted completely to a replacement cost basis without coming into conflict with the legal point of view. In the eyes of the law, in general, income is determined by charging recorded costs to realized revenue. This is a consideration of consequence in income-tax reporting and in the determination of the legal rights of the various parties. This point of view, of course, is not the whole story. Nevertheless, the accountant is inevitably coerced in considerable measure by the legal framework, and in his search for ways of improving the reporting of operating data for managerial purposes he should not lose sight of the legal criteria of the general income statement.

Assuming that valuation data are to be introduced into the accounts for the purpose of modifying cost reckonings, how shall this be done? This is not the place to discuss technical details, but the nature of the two main possibilities may be indicated. In the first place, the enterprise may be considered to make a fresh start in life from the point of the appraisal. The appraisal, that is, may be viewed as a phase of quasi-reorganization. With this approach the valuation data are treated as taking the place of recorded costs, and are dealt with thereafter as if they represented actual costs. The amount of the increase or decrease in the proprietary equity resulting is treated as a permanent adjustment of economic capital, and there may be a corresponding adjustment of legal capital through the issue of a stock dividend (in the case of the write-up) or a reduction in par or stated value (in the case of a write-down). Net income thereafter is reported solely on the revised basis — a lower level in the case of the write-up and a higher level in the case of the write-down. This entire procedure, it may be added, emphasizes the appraisal as a very special event, undertaken under exceptional conditions. It does not lend encouragement to schemes which contemplate continuous revaluation and periodic adjustments of costs and earnings to take into account the movement of either general prices or costs of plant.

The main alternative is to treat the results of valuation as useful supplementary data and at the same time preserve the framework of income accounting on the recorded cost basis. At a minimum, this means the issue of separate estimates of costs and income on the appraisal basis and reference to the appraisal data through the use of balance sheet footnotes and comments. At a maximum, it means the incorporation of the results of valuation into the regular accounts, in such a manner as to permit a showing of costs on the revised basis coupled with an adjustment which in effect restores the influence of original recorded cost in the general income statement. To carry through such a compromise procedure, the effect of the valuation upon the plant accounts should be segregated in the ledger (in both gross and net terms). The influence of the valuation upon the stock equity is carried in a contra or adjunct account modifying the equity as a whole, without division between capital and surplus. Charges to operations are based on adjusted costs, for the sake of placing departmental operating data on the revised basis, for what that may be worth to the management. Finally, in the preparation of the periodic income statement the amount by which the charge to operation is overstated or understated — from the standpoint of original cost — is transferred from the suspense equity account as an adjustment of operating data prepared on the valuation basis. By this means the final figure of net income and of change in earned surplus is placed on a cost basis. This general procedure commends itself to those who wish to give internal cost accounting the benefit of plant charges revised in terms of current prices and at the same time pass all realized profit and loss, throughout the history of the company, through the door of recognized income and earned surplus.

In the foregoing comments I have avoided consideration of valuations from the standpoint of the balance sheet, the statement of financial position. No doubt in the past the balance sheet point of view has been of marked influence in encouraging valuations of plant and the use of such well-known expedients as "cost or market, whichever is lower" in pricing inventory. However, I think that at the present time most accountants are inclined to agree that the real issue between cost and value lies in the area of income determination.

A careful examination of the whole picture, including sympathetic consideration of the possibilities of appraisals and conversion through the use of index numbers, tends to the conclusion that the accountant has been on the right track in giving his allegiance to the cost basis. At times, no doubt, this allegiance has been little more than a blind adherence to tradition, but it may very well be a deliberate and enlightened point of view. With such a point of view the accountant will be in a position to exert a substantial influence, in a constructive direction, on proposals calling for basic amendment or reform of accounting concepts and procedure.

AUDITING DEVELOPMENTS DURING THE PRESENT CENTURY

INTRODUCTION

It was with especial pleasure that I accepted the invitation to serve as the lecturer on the Dickinson Foundation in 1941 because of the very high regard which I have for the memory of the late Sir Arthur Lowes Dickinson, in whose honor the Arthur Lowes Dickinson Foundation in the Graduate School of Business Administration of Harvard University was established.

It was my privilege to become acquainted with him while I was still very young in the public practice of accounting. I last saw him in 1933 at the International Congress on Accounting in London when, in bringing the greetings and good wishes of the New York State Society of Certified Public Accountants to the Congress, I had the opportunity to express the indebtedness of our profession in America for the guidance given it by Sir Arthur in the early nineteen hundreds. He was a worthy exemplar of those ideals and objectives which he so wisely and persuasively urged upon the young profession in that vital and growing period of forty years ago.

My appearance before you today coincides approximately with the completion of forty years of my activity as a public accountant, first as a member of the staff of my firm and for thirty years as a partner with those who founded it. I shall seek to present some of the developments of that period in complying with the request that I devote these lectures to a consideration of some phases of the subject of auditing.

Since a considerable portion of the independent public accountant's audit work consists of so-called balance sheet audits or examinations, I shall discuss with you some of the developments relating to work of the accountant in performing engagements of that character. Also, I shall seek to identify some of the major influences responsible for these developments.

Auditing has been sometimes described as the analytical phase of the accountant's work and accounting *per se* as the synthetic phase. In practice the line between the two often becomes very dim; in fact, that line is frequently not apparent at all because of the overlapping of the two phases. The form of auditor's report or certificate recommended by the American Institute of Accountants for use in normal circumstances refers to the accountant's examination and tests of the records underlying the financial statements, but also it includes an opinion that the statements set forth the position of the company and the results of its operations "in conformity with generally accepted accounting principles applied on a basis consistent with that of the preceding year."

Robert H. Montgomery, in the sixth edition of his work on *Auditing Theory and Practice*, describes a balance sheet audit or examination as comprising "the minimum examination of the financial statements, system of internal control, accounting procedures, accounting records, and other supporting evidence, which the auditor believes is appropriate in the particular case and in accordance with generally accepted auditing procedure to enable him to express an opinion as to the position of the company, the results of its operations for a period, and the conformity of the balance sheet and statements of income and surplus with generally accepted principles of accounting consistently applied." [1]

Further, he lays down the principles or rules of a balance sheet audit or examination, which indicate but do not limit the audit phase of the accountant's work, as follows:

Balance sheet audits are not all alike in the nature and extent of the work because of the variations in the kinds of business encountered and

[1] New York, The Ronald Press Company, 1940, p. 8.

in the systems of internal check and control in use, but the procedures followed by the auditor should be designed to give him reasonable grounds for belief:

1. That, except as otherwise noted, all the assets shown in the balance sheet were actually owned by the client at the balance sheet date and were carried at amounts arrived at by application of generally accepted accounting principles;
2. That there were no other assets of a material amount which were not, but which should have been, shown;
3. That the liabilities shown in the balance sheet were actual or contingent liabilities;
4. That all liabilities of materiality are expressed in the balance sheet;
5. That the nature of surplus is adequately disclosed, that the statement of income is reasonably classified and informative, and that there is no substantial misstatement of the net income for the period;
6. That the capital stock is properly classified and stated, and that no stock of any class has been issued in excess of amounts duly authorized.[1]

One of the best comments I have seen on what might be called the accounting phase of auditing, and which is all the more interesting because of its coming from outside the accounting profession, is the following portion of the report made in 1939 by the New York Stock Exchange's Stock List Subcommittee on Independent Audits and Audit Procedure:

. . . there seem to be those who, when faced with certain inevitable limitations and qualifications in the audit phase, entertain doubts as to the value of the entire independent audit. They seem for the moment to overlook the importance of the accounting phase. This is partly, of course, the result of the recent McKesson & Robbins case, in which the fraud rested on the falsity of the factual matter which is the basis of all accounts. It may be worth noting, however, that a distortion of emphasis may result also from a circumstance of terminology; the same word "audit" is used for the entire procedure, and also for one of its two phases . . . .

. . . financial statements of industrial companies are not statistical

[1] *Ibid.*, pp. 8–9.

presentations of fact fixed in the form which the stockholder reads. While properly based on facts, these statements represent the judgments of the Company's management in the application of conventional methods of stating assets and liabilities and in appropriate allocations of income and outgo items to specific periods of time. For example, plant and property are usually stated on the basis of cost, or on some other conventional basis — and not at a figure supposed to reflect present day value. Other items are usually stated at going concern values, and profits are calculated on this basis.

The importance of a periodic review by outside experts to see that these numerous judgments have been made in accordance with accepted accounting principles consistently followed by the Company must be apparent to every one — entirely apart from any methods the business world may employ to assure itself of the authenticity of the data underlying the accounts. The independent public accountant is thoroughly qualified to make such a review. For this he has been specially trained. The public is entitled to rely upon his opinion regarding the soundness and consistency of the accounting judgments made by the Company in the preparation of its reports to stockholders. If the independent public accountant does not concur in the results of these judgments, he will take exception to the Company's method by a statement in his auditor's opinion accompanying the financial statements. If his exception is of sufficient importance, he will express no opinion, and explain in his report why it is withheld. The independent public accountant's opinion on the soundness of judgments and consistency of methods is of real importance — for even with correct factual data at the base, the possibilities of accounting errors and misrepresentations are very great.

In an address by John Haskell, Vice President of the New York Stock Exchange, in 1939, on "What Is Expected of the Independent Auditor from the Viewpoint of the Investor," he made the following statement — again interesting because expressed by a layman:

The New York Stock Exchange believes that the investor expects many things of the independent auditor, but first I shall mention some which we believe should not be expected. We do not expect the auditor to make a detailed verification of all transactions of listed companies. We do not expect him to be a superman or detective endowed with the second sight of catching — from his examination of the books and such tests and checks as he may make of the records to the underlying data

— every minor defalcation that may have been committed. We do not expect him to qualify as a general appraiser or valuation expert of all the countless materials which go to make up the stream of commerce and industry.

On the other hand, the Exchange and the investor do expect that the independent auditor will not permit the use of his name in connection with a report on which the public may rely if any restrictions are imposed upon his freedom of access to any of the records or information which he considers necessary in order to express his professional opinion that the financial statements present fairly the position of the Company and the results of its operations.

We expect the independent public accountant to make an audit study to satisfy himself of the adequacy and effectiveness of the Company's system of internal control.

We expect that, by test checks and methods of sampling and observation, the auditor will go beyond the books of record to satisfy himself of their conformity with the underlying facts.

We expect the auditor to apply sound judgment so that, over a period of time, and irrespective of the emphasis of the day on certain items, all phases of the Company's business will be covered. The investor relies upon the impression created by the financial statements as a whole and it is obvious that a well-rounded audit offers greater safeguards than one in which excessive emphasis is placed on certain phases to the neglect of others.

The Exchange and the investor expect the independent public accountant to be independent in fact as well as in name.

We count upon his having wide experience, professional competency and a detached, unbiased viewpoint. We expect and demand of all professional honesty and the highest personal integrity.

Aside from the auditing of the records themselves, the Exchange and the investor expect that the independent auditor will continue to assume great responsibility as to the accounting judgments which govern the final results set forth in financial statements, so that these judgments may be in accordance with generally accepted sound accounting principles.

We expect the independent auditor to be particularly alert to maintain basic distinction between capital and income in the preparation of reports to stockholders. From the viewpoint of the investor, even more than from the viewpoint of short-term creditors and others, the cardinal importance of the earnings statement must be emphasized. Safeguards must be provided against misstatements of earnings by the absorption of losses which should be made against income through charges to capital or capital surplus, earned surplus or by other methods that violate this basic distinction.

Although we do not expect the auditor's report to guarantee financial statements, we expect it to set forth an opinion upon which the auditor is willing to stake his professional reputation that he has satisfied himself that his examination has been as extensive as the general standards of his profession have established and that, beyond this, he has satisfied himself, by methods and to the extent deemed appropriate, that the financial statements fairly present the position of the Company and the results of its operations in accordance with sound accounting principles.

We believe that the investor expects the auditor's certificate or report accompanying the completed financial statements to be as clear, concise, unequivocal and illuminating as your professional ability can make it. It should make clear, in language the investor understands, the distinction between statements and phrases included by way of explanation for the added information of the investor and any exceptions to the data in the financial statements or in the methods used in their preparation with which the accountant is not in full accord.

Finally, we expect the independent auditor and his profession to lead in the development of effective methods and progressive steps in the constant evolution of sound and more understandable reports. Federal statutes and rules and the variegated, conflicting, over-lapping crazy-quilt of local regulations establish minimum standards with which all must comply, but the investor expects that corporations whose securities are listed on the New York Stock Exchange will observe much higher standards. He counts on your profession to see to it that, in the field of audits and reports, added safeguards and constant development of sound practices will surpass the minimum standards which must apply to all.

I. HISTORICAL DEVELOPMENTS

I recall that in the early days of my work in the office of my firm the usual audit which we were called upon to make was focused largely on an examination of the cash records, the comparison of paid checks with the recorded expenditures (either directly with the cash book, if the accounts were so organized that this could be readily done, or first with the check stubs for one or more bank accounts and then the check stubs with the cash book), examination of petty cash vouchers, checking of postings from customers' ledger accounts to the receipt side of the cash book, comparison of deposits per the check book with the cash book, and, naturally, reconciling of bank balances between bank pass book and cash book, a count of the petty cash on hand, and such other examinations as in the circumstances of the particular client seemed to afford a basis for the most thorough verification of the integrity of the cash accounts. Those features of the accounts which, in the modern audit, require so much time and attention, such as the testing and review of receivables, not only to ascertain their existence but, even more, their probable collectibility, the examination of the inventories, and the review of depreciation and depletion allowances, received proportionately a lesser part of the accountant's time than today.

There were various reasons for this: (1) many of the concerns under audit were of moderate size, the ownership was closely held and frequently in the hands of the management, and the primary purpose of the examination was to give a sort of clearance to the treasurer or cashier, or whoever was acting in a position of trust in respect to the funds of the concern, so that the owners might be assured on that point; (2) in comparatively few instances were financial statements certified for the purpose of filing them with banks to obtain credit or for publication to stockholders; (3) the periodic determination of profit or loss on a consistent basis was not yet emphasized as it is today; (4) among a great many businessmen there was, as yet, no recognition of the need for care in following sound accounting principles in the preparation of their financial statements. Those who were conservatively minded naturally had their accounts kept on that basis and in some cases kept their accounts on an ultraconservative basis. Those who were unduly optimistic and of that class who, like Micawber, were always looking forward to something turning up to make it possible for them to dispose of stock which had been on hand a long time without finding a customer, did not like to have their style cramped by being reminded of the need for dealing realistically with the inventory and writing down such items from cost to a figure more nearly approaching realizability. Not infrequently the bankruptcy court took care of their situation before they had become converted to the desirability of following sound principles in the keeping of their accounts.

Changes in Trends of Auditing

With the rapid growth of American business following the Spanish-American War, the increase in the size of many enterprises (sometimes through consolidation with others, as during the trust forming period of the late eighteen nineties and the early twentieth century), and the auditing of larger concerns, there developed the necessity for making the audit one of selected tests of the accounts rather than an endeavor to examine all of the transactions of the period even in the cash account.

The newer approach was primarily that which has come to be known as the balance sheet examination, viz., substantiation, so far as practicable, of all items, both assets and liabilities, entering into the balance sheet, and a general review of the operating accounts for the period intervening since the last previous annual audit, together with a comparison of the various revenue and expense groups with the corresponding operating accounts of the previous period or periods, inquiry into the causes for marked fluctuations, and such tests of the items entering into the operating accounts as seem appropriate in the circumstances of the particular engagement. Especially in those cases where the examination was for the purpose of submitting a certified balance sheet to a bank for credit purposes, the audit of the items entering into the operating accounts as distinguished from balance sheet items was frequently quite limited, though even there the experienced accountant recognized the light that would be thrown on the balance sheet position from a test examination of the operating accounts.

One result of this development was more and more emphasis on the importance of the accountant's review of the manner in which the management had dealt with the recording and classification of transactions of the company from the standpoint of the application of sound accounting principles and the consequent dependability of the determination of income and presentation of financial position.

During the decade preceding the First World War, the banking credit of commercial concerns was increasingly being based not alone on good character but also on a more definite knowledge by the lending bank of the financial affairs of the borrower. In the large cities the commercial banks were establishing credit departments which studied with care the financial statements [1] filed with them by borrowers and supplemented the statements with such information concerning the nature of the borrower's business organization and other features of the concern as they could learn. Credit

[1] The development was, first, the filing of unaudited statements prepared by borrowers and, later, the filing of certified statements in compliance with the requirements of the lending banks and of the Federal Reserve Banks.

men in the banks were perhaps the earliest group outside the accountancy profession which recognized and supported the now generally accepted accounting principle of valuing inventories at cost or market, whichever is lower. They recognized that it is a principle born, not out of pure logic, but rather out of long business experience and observation. They grasped the principle that it is wise to provide for potential losses, and not to count your chickens before they are hatched. The banker's experience has taught him that by some strange perversity of fate potential losses much oftener become actual than is true of possible profits. Hence they became firm believers in writing down inventories when the price level fell below cost but not in writing them up when market prices rose. This principle is so widely recognized today that it is difficult to realize that only a few decades ago many businessmen clung firmly to the idea that if it was sound practice to write down inventories in a falling market, it was just as sound to write them up in a rising market.

The increasing use during the present century of certified financial statements in bankers' prospectuses for security offerings emphasized still more the need for the auditor majoring on such questions as inventory valuations and their reflex action on the determination of annual operating profits, the allowance to be made for possible loss on receivables, the allowances for depreciation of plant and exhaustion of wasting assets, the ascertainment, so far as possible, of all direct and contingent liabilities, the disclosure of write-ups of property and credits to surplus arising therefrom, and so forth.

An influence which contributed much to the improvement of accounting practices and strengthened the hand of the public accountant who had long been urging such improvement arose out of the taxes imposed during the First World War. It was a very practical influence because in so many cases it appealed to the business pocketbook. So long as income taxes were at a low rate they had little effect on the accounting practices of business concerns. When, however, in 1917 income taxes were materially increased and a heavily graduated excess profits tax was enacted and for the following year a still heavier war profits tax was imposed, with a further increase in the rates of income tax, business concerns became receptive to such suggestions as stating inventories on a conservative basis and making adequate allowances for depreciation of the plant.

Prior to this time the depreciation policies of many industrial concerns had been on the hit or miss order, where indeed there was not an utter absence of depreciation allowances. There were still quite a few businessmen who were contending that, as long as they were maintaining their plants in good operating condition, renewals and replacements were a sufficient offset to the depreciation allowance which accountants had been urging upon them. In some cases, where ultra-conservative management had been absorbing in operating expenses costs of expansion of the plant, this might have been the case, but there were many others where the argument was fallacious; the auditor, however, could do little except bring out the facts in his report and qualify it accordingly.

The incidence of high taxes completely changed the picture. Businessmen were now ready to recognize the applicability of the inventory principle of cost or market, whichever is lower, and many a concern about that time established a reasonably consistent depreciation policy which has been followed since. The United States Treasury does not have the same broad powers to prescribe accounting methods as does a regulatory body like the Interstate Commerce Commission. Its indirect influence, however, has been very considerable because the business concern that pursues a less conservative policy in its accounts in respect of matters like inventory and plant depreciation than it claims in its tax returns is at a decided disadvantage from a tax standpoint, and this is generally recognized.

The accounting necessary under government contracts during the First World War, particularly those on the cost-plus basis, gave a stimulus born of necessity to better accounting methods. It paralleled and reinforced the influence of high taxes in leading to adoption of sounder inventory methods, better costing systems, departmentalized accounting, recognition of plant depreciation as an element of manufacturing cost, and the like. It was but natural that this practice led to calling on the public accountant for advice and guidance. In many cases, too, this led to the periodical auditing of the accounts.

One of the most helpful influences in furthering the practice of having published financial statements accompanied by certificates of independent public accountants was that exerted by the New York Stock Exchange. As the culmination of informal activity in this direction for some years, the president of the Exchange on January 6, 1933, made an announcement that since April of 1932 all corporations applying for listing of their securities had been asked to include in their listing agreements an undertaking that future annual financial statements, published more than three months after the agreement, would be audited by independent public accountants and accompanied by a certificate of such accountants, setting forth the scope of the audit and qualifications, if any, made by them in respect thereto, and that the Committee on Stock List had considered many reasons advanced why this procedure should not apply in particular cases but had made exceptions only in the case of certain railroad companies. The announcement further stated that after July 1, 1933, all listing applications, excepting for the time being railroad companies reporting to the Interstate Commerce Commission, would have to contain a certificate of independent accountants as to the balance sheet, income statement, and surplus statement for the most recent fiscal year, and an agreement that annual reports to stockholders would thereafter be audited and accompanied by a similar certificate.

Especially from the time that Mr. J. M. B. Hoxsey became executive assistant to the Stock List Committee of the Exchange during the 1920's, the Exchange had been doing its utmost to encourage the preparation of financial statements published by listed corporations on the basis of sound accounting principles. The support of the Exchange in this way, which antedated the enactment of the securities acts, was most helpful to accountants in their efforts for improvement in corporate accounting practice. The services of Mr. Hoxsey, representing the Exchange, in accounting conferences with the officers of listed corporations, with the independent accountants examining the statements of such corporations, and with the Committee of the American Institute of Accountants on Cooperation with Stock Exchanges, were of the greatest value in furthering the recognition and adoption by corporations of sound accounting principles and the improvement in form and content of published statements.

Influence of Regulatory Bodies

The increasing demand for accountants' services, and the changes in trend of the type of auditing service rendered, which I have just mentioned, lead us to consider the influence on accounting practice which governmental bodies have had in recent decades and which have naturally had a bearing on the work of the independent accountant as an auditor. The Interstate Commerce Act of 1906 gave the Commission authority to prescribe, not only uniform annual reports to the Commission, which it had had the power to do for some twenty years previously, but also the accounts to be kept, any deviation from which was forbidden. This had a decided influence on railroad accounting and has caused a higher degree of standardization of accounting in that field than in any other branch of industry or commerce. Also, the Commission recognized that some of its earlier instructions for the preparation of reports to it had not been based on sound accounting principles; for instance, the Commission had formerly permitted bond discount to be charged to property account but in its new classification of construction expenditures recognized the force of the accountant's contention that discount is nothing else than interest paid in advance and consequently should not be permanently capitalized. On another question, i.e., that of allowances for depreciation of property, the Commission has never gone to the full length to which industrial concerns as a whole have come during the last quarter century. It has made depreciation allowances compulsory for equipment but not for track or structures.

Incidentally, I happened to note in the first edition of Montgomery's *Auditing Theory and Practice* the following extract from an article in a financial paper, which is of interest because of the points mentioned which have significance in the auditing of railroad accounts:

> No one doubts that the Baltimore and Ohio of today is a magnificent property. But that is all the more reason why it should seem very strange that some of those who are still in the board should apparently have forgotten the experience of sixteen years ago. Early in September of 1896, despite the profit and loss surplus of $23,737,000 then existing, Stephen Little was employed to go over the old Baltimore and Ohio's books. Before the end of that month the announcement that a receiver had been appointed for the company came like a bolt out of the blue. In his report Mr. Little gave the following causes for the Baltimore and Ohio's trouble:
>
> 1. The inflation or overstatement of net income,
> 2. The mischarge of worn-out equipment to profit and loss,
> 3. The capitalization of charges to income,
> 4. The capitalization of so-called improvements and betterments of leased lines,
> 5. The payment of unearned dividends,
> 6. The understatement of liabilities, etc.[1]

[1] New York, The Ronald Press Company, 1912, p. 430.

It is of interest to note that not one of the six "causes for the Baltimore & Ohio's trouble," which are stated above and in respect of which the company's books were not, in Mr. Little's opinion, on a sound basis, implied any monetary dishonesty but represented a failure to apply sound accounting principles.

The Interstate Commerce Commission has apparently had little influence on the development of accounting principles or practice outside the railroad field. So far as the public accountant is concerned, the effect of the authoritative powers of the Interstate Commerce Commission in respect of railroad accounting has apparently been to discourage the use of the public accountant's services by the railroads. This has probably been due in part at least to the erroneous impression which has gotten abroad that the Commission periodically audits the accounts of the railroads.

The Securities Act of 1933 specifically exempts from its provisions "any security issued by a common carrier which is subject to the . . . Interstate Commerce Act. . . ." Hence, the financial statements included in prospectuses of railroad security offerings are not required to be certified by independent public accountants.

A drastic criticism of the status of railroad accounting after three decades of governmental regulation was expressed by Jules I. Bogen, editor of the New York *Journal of Commerce*, in a paper read before the American Management Association in 1939. The paper, which was entitled, "An Objective Appraisal of the Independent Audit," contained the following paragraph dealing with one of the numerous hasty suggestions made as the result of the shock of the McKesson & Robbins case:

Thirdly, it has been proposed that a federal statute be passed setting up auditing and internal management check standards for all corporations engaged in interstate commerce. Now there is one industry where accounting has been subject to such federal regulation since 1906 — the railroad industry. And if there is any type of accounting which requires really fundamental reform, it is railroad accounting. If that is what rigid government regulation of accounting does, I think it is the last thing we want.

It is of interest to note in passing some marked divergences between the developments in railroad accounting and those occurring in the industrial and mercantile field during the past quarter-century. Illustrative instances are (a) the treatment of surplus charges and credits, and (b) allowances for depreciation of property.

In the financial statements of industrial concerns it has become more and more the practice to absorb in the current income account items which under the practice of an earlier day would have been shown as direct charges or credits to the surplus account because of having had their origin in transactions of a prior period, because of being considered nonrecurring, or for some other reason. Where the items are of large amount, the current net income may be first stated and the special or extraordinary items, if of large amount, deducted from or added thereto. In the published statements of railroads, however, the profit and loss account (equivalent in effect to the account more generally termed surplus in industrial accounting) is still the account to which such items are directly charged or credited, despite the fact that over a period of years they have an important effect on the net income of the period.

In a recent railroad prospectus the net income of a guarantor railroad corporation was shown for each year of the past decade. Following was a statement of the net debits charged directly to Profit and Loss for each year of the decade. The annual net income amounts for the ten years aggregated approximately $53,000,000, and the net debits to Profit and Loss some $20,000,000. A part of the latter amount was of a special character, such as retirement losses arising out of a rearrangement of certain facilities for joint operation thereafter with another railroad, but a substantial portion represented write-offs of advances apparently made to finance current losses of such joint operation and net debits for retired road and equipment.

The net debits for retired road and equipment appear to have arisen out of the absence of any obligatory requirement for setting up allowances for depreciation of roadway and structures, though the Commission has required such allowances to be set up currently for depreciation of rolling stock since the promulgation by it of the classification of accounts which became effective in 1907.

The annual net income shown as such would apparently have been materially less had some of the items charged or credited directly to Profit and Loss been treated in the same manner as has become general practice among industrial companies.

Another illustrative instance which might be mentioned is the 1940 annual report of a railroad company which showed a net profit of approximately $200,000 in its Income Account, net debits of almost $900,000 to Profit and Loss Account for Retired Road items, and miscellaneous credits and debits amounting, net, to a credit of somewhat less than $500,000. There is no explanation in the Profit and Loss Account as to whether the Retired Road amount includes any extraordinary items such as abandonments. This is one of the railroads the financial statements of which are accompanied by a certificate of independent accountants. The certificate stated the opinion that, subject to certain considerations not here material, the ". . . balance sheet and related statements of income and profit and loss fairly present, *in accordance with the requirements of the Interstate Commerce Commission*, the financial condition of the Company . . . and the results of its operations . . ." (italics supplied).

About the time of the enactment of the Interstate Commerce Act of 1906 there was an acceleration of the movement for regulation of public utilities other than the railroads, including street railways, electric light and power companies, and gas companies. This regulation came from the various states, and came earlier in some than in others. Also, the reaction on accounting methods of the utilities varied in different states. The regulatory acts in some states gave power to commissions to prescribe the form of accounts to be kept, whereas this was not so in other states. The question may well be raised whether direct regulation of accounts does not tend to make the prescribed methods the maximum of performance which is likely to result rather than the minimum from which the regulated companies should progress. Indeed, experience would indicate that this is the tendency which develops in practice.

Most, if not all, of the state public service commissions permitted, through the uniform system of accounts prescribed by them, the use of the so-called retirement reserve method [1] instead of service life depreciation allowances in respect of the operating properties of the utility companies. Years before, utility companies (particularly in the street railway days) had contended that there was no necessity for their setting up allowances for depreciation of property, as the renewals and replacements currently made were claimed to be a sufficient offset to wear and tear. Accruing obsolescence was blithely ignored. Public accountants urged on the utilities the need for recognizing accruing depreciation but with little success, and I well recall that back in the early 1900's our firm usually found it necessary to qualify its reports on the accounts of public utilities because we found no allowances made for depreciation and an unwillingness to recognize the need for them.

Unfortunately, the permission given by the public service

[1] Based on making allowances to provide for absorbing the cost of property retirements estimated to occur within a relatively short period of years. The effect was primarily to equalize the charges against annual operations

commissions, under their legal powers, to allow public utilities to use the so-called retirement reserve method brought about an accounting impasse. The accounting profession as a whole was, I believe, convinced that service life depreciation was a sound principle for the public utilities just as much as for industrial concerns. In the circumstances, however, there was nothing that accountants could do but assure themselves that full disclosure was made of the actual procedure and make their certificates subject to a reservation as to the adequacy of the retirement reserve.

The telephone companies were a notable exception to the utilities generally, and followed the service-life depreciation plan. I have heard some electrical utility operators say they wish now it had been the practice in their industry at a much earlier date to use the service-life depreciation plan rather than the retirement reserve method. It is unfortunate that the commissions did not use their influence and powers to secure the introduction years ago of the service-life plan. At that time it might have been done with less hardship than to make the change now.

Today the commissions are urging, or even requiring, the service-life depreciation method, but it seems to me they must also be practical about it and recognize that there must be a period of transition to permit of the change-over from one method to the other. There are too many problems of financial policy involved to permit of an overnight change. So far as annual depreciation allowances are concerned, many utilities are gradually bringing their former retirement allowances up to the amounts required for service-life depreciation purposes. To bring the accumulated allowances or reserves up to the full amount required, however, will take a considerable time for many of them. Equity requires that the

---

for the cost of property retirements, rather than to accumulate a reserve equal to that which would normally accrue under service life depreciation practice.

commissions recognize their concurrence in the use of the retirement reserve method over many years and that they should accordingly seek to work out the transition problem in a way that will impose the least hardship on the utilities and their security holders.

In 1936 the Federal Power Commission prescribed a new uniform system of accounts for the electrical utilities coming within its jurisdiction, and the National Association of Railways and Utilities Commissioners recommended a similar system which was adopted by many of the state utilities commissions. The most significant features of the new system of accounts are the stated requirement for service life depreciation practice in place of the former retirement reserve method, and the so-called "aboriginal cost" requirement that "all amounts included in the accounts for . . . plant acquired as an operating unit or system shall be stated at the original cost incurred by the person who first devoted the property to utility service," with supplemental accounts to record the differences between such original cost and the cost of the property to the present corporate owner.

The "aboriginal cost" requirement has led accountants to the conclusion that, if the studies necessary to determine "original cost" as defined by the Commission indicate it to be substantially less than corporate cost, which latter is the cost of the property to the present owner, disclosure of the difference is essential in the balance sheets of utilities which independent accountants may be called upon to certify.

Time does not permit of going into all the questions which arise out of this revolutionary concept of cost of property in a public utility enterprise. Some of them are (a) the disposition eventually to be made of the difference arising from the use of the two cost bases, (b) the segregation of the difference between tangible and intangible assets, and (c) the effect on the determination of depreciation allowances. This is in addition to the difficulty in many instances of getting at a dependable "original cost" of property which may have changed hands a number of times over a period of years, with varying methods of accounting for property costs in force during such period, particularly in the matter of such elements of cost as capitalizable interest and overhead, and with possibly incomplete or inadequate records available from predecessor owners in which case resort must be had to estimates of cost at time of the original acquisition.

Despite the fact that public utilities (other than railroads) are for the most part under just about as effective a control as the railroads through the various state commissions, the Federal Power Commission, and the Federal Communications Commission, which have jurisdiction in the case of the utilities, the development in respect of the examination of their financial statements and the certification thereof by independent public accountants has been different from that of the railroads. Today published statements of most utilities bear the certificate of independent public accountants. This development was already under way prior to the enactment of the Securities Act of 1933, but it received a further stimulus therefrom in that, whereas railroads are exempt from the provisions of that Act, other public utility companies are not, and are required by the Act to have their financial statements certified by independent public accountants when offering securities to the investing public.

A series of Federal laws were enacted from 1933 to 1940, all of which have important accounting and auditing implications. The first was the well-known Securities Act of 1933, which required registration (first with the Federal Trade Commission, and from 1934 on with the Securities and Exchange Commission) of securities to be offered to the public. Among its provisions which are both of interest and importance to the accountant are that a balance sheet and profit and loss statement of the issuer, which are to be included in the documents filed with the Commission, shall be "certified by an independent public or certified accountant"; that the balance sheet shall show "all of the assets of the issuer, the nature and cost thereof, whenever determinable, in such detail and in such form as the Commission shall prescribe (with intangible items segregated), including any loan in excess of $20,000 to any officer, director, stockholder, or person directly or indirectly controlling or controlled by the issuer, or person under direct or indirect common control with the issuer, and all the liabilities of the issuer in such detail and such form as the Commission shall prescribe, including surplus of the issuer showing how and from what sources such surplus was created . . ."; that a profit and loss statement for the three latest years, similarly certified, shall be filed which shall show "earnings and income, the nature and source thereof, and the expenses and fixed charges in such detail and such form as the Commission shall prescribe . . . ," and that "such statement shall show what the practice of the issuer has been . . . as to the character of the charges, dividends or other distributions made against its various surplus accounts, and as to depreciation, depletion, and maintenance charges, in such detail and form as the Commission shall prescribe, and if stock dividends or avails from the sale of rights have been credited to income, they shall be shown separately with the statement of the basis upon which the credit is computed, and such statement shall also differentiate between any recurring and nonrecurring income and between any investment and operating income."

Broad powers are given the Commission for the administration of the Act, some of which, as just indicated, touch on accounting questions. The liability of the auditor and of others participating in the registration for any untrue statements of material facts or omissions to state material facts required to be stated or necessary to make the statements in the registration statement not misleading has been the subject of much public attention and needs no detailed comment at this time.

The Securities Exchange Act, enacted in 1934, provided for the regulation of securities exchanges, for the registration of corporate securities listed thereon, and for the filing of annual reports with the Commission by corporations having such listed securities outstanding. The Securities and Exchange Commission, which was created by that act, was given broad administrative powers including some referring to accounting matters. Although the certification of financial statements included in such annual reports is not obligatory under the Act, the Commission was authorized to require it by regulation and it has promulgated such requirement.

Accountants have taken seriously the provisions of the two securities acts and have sought to impress the importance thereof on their clients as well, particularly in respect of those accounting matters which are particularly within the scope of the auditor's duties. The requirements of the acts and the activities of the Securities and Exchange Commission have given valuable support to accountants in their continuous efforts for improvements in accounting practice and for the adequacy of disclosures essential to presenting a complete picture of financial position and results of operations.

The Public Utility Act of 1935 with its rigorous control of public utility holding companies by the Securities and Exchange Commission contains further important accounting provisions. Among them is one "to prevent the payment of dividends out of capital or unearned surplus" excepting with the approval of the Commission. This distinction between earned and unearned surplus is of interest to the accountant because, although it has become a recognized distinction in accounting practice, corporate laws of but few states specifically provide for, or mention, such a distinction. Because of the absence of a statutory requirement for such a distinction, some lawyers have at times objected to its being made in the balance sheets of their clients.

Accountants generally, I believe, feel that, as expressed on occasion by both the Securities and Exchange Commission and the New York Stock Exchange, the omission from the corporate law of a state of a requirement for what would otherwise be regarded as good accounting practice does not justify a failure to apply such accounting practice or principle by a corporation incorporated in such state. In other words, accepted accounting principles have a validity which does not necessarily arise out of specific enunciation or sanction of law.

By amendments to the Federal Power Act made in 1935, the Federal Power Commission is now empowered to "ascertain and determine, and by order fix the proper and adequate rates of depreciation of the several classes of property of each . . . public utility." It is further provided that ". . . public utilities subject to the jurisdiction of the Commission shall not charge to operating expenses any depreciation charges on classes of property other than those prescribed by the Commission, or charge with respect to any class of property a percentage of depreciation other than that prescribed therefor by the Commission." Still further, "no . . . public utility shall in any case include in any form under its operating or other expenses any depreciation or other charge or expenditure included elsewhere as a depreciation charge or otherwise under its operating or other expenses."

In theory at least, the auditor might find himself in an embarrassing situation if it appeared that the Commission had decreed an unduly low or unduly high rate of depreciation on public utility property, and the company is not permitted under the Act to set up its depreciation allowance at any different amount from that prescribed by the Commission, regardless of how completely the opinion of managers or officers might agree with the view of the auditor. In such a case, apparently, the only recourse of the auditor would be to qualify his report and to indicate whether, in his opinion, the prescribed allowance is inadequate or excessive. Since at best the computation of depreciation allowances is to a considerable extent a matter of estimate, however, and since it is to be presumed that the Commission will wish to have the depreciation allowances as nearly as may be in accord with what all concerned believe to be the proper allowance, it seems unlikely that many, if any, situations of this kind are likely to arise in practice. There is always the danger, however, that expediency may influence a regulatory body when it is making a decision in a particular case. Mr. George O. May effectively pointed out in the February, 1941, *Journal of Accountancy* the need for avoiding any departure from sound accounting principles on the ground of expediency.[1]

The Trust Indenture Act of 1939 (enacted as an amendment of the Securities Act of 1933) imposes various obligations on the issuer of securities coming within the scope of the Act, including the requirement that in the case of conditions precedent, compliance with which is subject to verification by accountants (such as preservation of specified ratios, amount of net quick assets, negative-pledge clauses, and other similar specific conditions), a certificate or opinion of an independent public accountant is to be furnished. The Act prescribes the following recitals as the basis of any certificate or opinion so issued:

> Each certificate or opinion with respect to compliance with a condition or covenant provided for in the indenture shall include (1) a statement that the person making such certificate or opinion has read such covenant or condition; (2) a brief statement as to the nature and scope of the examination or investigation upon which the statements or opinions contained in such certificate or opinion are based; (3) a statement

[1] Vol. LXXI, No. 2, "Accounting Principles and Regulatory Expediency," pp. 116–118.

that, in the opinion of such person, he has made such examination or investigation as is necessary to enable him to express an informed opinion as to whether or not such covenant or condition has been complied with; and (4) a statement as to whether or not, in the opinion of such person, such condition or covenant has been complied with.

The Investment Company Act of 1940 grew out of the study which the Securities and Exchange Commission had been directed by the Public Utility Act of 1935 to make of "the functions and activities of investment trusts and investment companies, the corporate structures, and investment policies of such trusts and companies, and the influence exerted by such trusts . . . upon . . . investment policies."

So-called investment trusts had been a relatively small factor in the American financial picture until the late 1920's when they had a mushroom growth with a widespread participation by the public. The prices at which the securities of such trusts were issued, or to which they quickly rose, went even beyond the inflated prices of securities generally, and approached the dimensions of the "South Sea Bubble" in England some two hundred years before.

After the crash in the stock market in 1929 the prices of investment trust stocks generally nose-dived as rapidly and drastically as they had previously risen. The Commission as a result of its study was of the opinion that there had been various abuses by those who dominated the companies and that protective measures were desirable. In contradistinction to much of the other New Deal legislation, the Commission and representatives of the investment companies were able to agree on the legislation to be enacted.

Representatives of the American Institute of Accountants appeared before the Senate Committee having the bill in charge and also conferred with the Commission so that when the bill came out of committee it contained provisions in respect of the reports to be filed with the Commission by the investment companies and of the examinations of the financial statements to be made by independent public accountants which met in a large measure the views of the accounting profession.

Under the Investment Company Act, not only financial statements in reports filed with the Commission, but also those in reports required to be transmitted to stockholders, must if required by the Commission be certified by independent public accountants. The Act deals in some detail with the accountant's certificate, as indicated by the following provision:

> The certificate of such independent public accountants shall be based upon an audit not less in scope or procedures followed than that which independent public accountants would ordinarily make for the purpose of presenting comprehensive and dependable financial statements, and shall contain such information as the Commission may prescribe, by rules and regulations in the public interest or for the protection of investors, as to the nature and scope of the audit and the findings and opinion of the accountants. Each such report shall state that such independent public accountants have verified securities owned, either by actual examination, or by receipt of a certificate from the custodian, as the Commission may prescribe by rules and regulations.

The concluding sentence, embodying a statutory requirement for an explicit statement regarding the verification of securities owned by the investment trust or company, is to be noted.

An earlier development than any of those regulatory enactments already referred to, which has had some influence on accounting but which, because of its timing, has had the effect of rather limiting the contact of the public accountant with its particular field, is that of statutory bank examinations.

At the time that the Federal Government first instituted, through the Comptroller of the Currency, a system of national bank examinations, and the banking departments of the different states instituted periodical examinations of state banks and trust companies, the profession of public accountancy in the United States was hardly born. Indeed, if there were any men then practicing as public accountants, they were only a scattered few and none of them would have had a staff capable of examining even a moderate-sized bank. The consequence was that the periodical examination of banks was undertaken by the governmental authorities abovementioned instead of public accountants being retained, as has been the general practice in England and Canada.

The much earlier development of the profession in England caused it to be called upon to undertake bank examinations when the need for them became evident in England. Consequently, the professional accountant has continued through the years to include the examination of the accounts and assets of banks among his activities in both England and Canada, with a supervisory relationship by the governmental authorities which does not include periodical examinations unless there seems to be special reason therefor.

Some banks retain accountants to assist the examining committees of their boards of directors. At the present time, however, the auditing of banks by professional accountants is not widespread, many banks considering the statutory examinations as sufficient.

Similarly, in the case of insurance companies, when state supervision of the companies, including an examination of their accounts and assets from time to time, came into being, it was undertaken by the commissioners or departments in various states because there was no public accounting profession [1] of either scope or standing which could undertake the periodical examination and the certification of the published reports, and thus permit the supervision by the governmental bodies to be devoted to phases of regulation other

[1] The State of New Hampshire in 1851 created a commission of three to make annual examinations of insurance companies, and the Commonwealth of Massachusetts in 1858 provided that "it shall be the duty of said commission to visit and examine whenever they shall deem necessary any insurance company."

than the examination of the accounts of the insurance companies. It is of interest, however, that a number of large life insurance companies have published statements certified by independent public accountants ever since the Hughes investigation in 1905, and that a considerable increase in the number of companies issuing certified statements in their annual reports has occurred in recent years.

It may be noted in passing that accounting for both banks and insurance companies lagged behind the development of accounting for industrial and mercantile enterprises. Published bank statements for many years were rather crude and could hardly be said to have measured up to the requirements of disclosure of all material information such as they expected to find in the statements required of their borrowers. It has been only in recent years, for instance, that notations have appeared on bank statements of the investments which are pledged to secure certain types of deposits or in respect of fiduciary powers, and only comparatively recently that any substantial number of banking institutions have published an income statement.

The accounting of insurance companies, particularly of life companies, has continued largely unchanged for many years, and their accounting methods and the statutory form of statements submitted to their policyholders are still rather primitive in some respects. The April, 1941, *Journal of Accountancy* contained an article by Mr. Charles E. Mather on "The Income Statement of Life Insurance Company" [1] which is stated to be based on the auditor's conviction that life insurance companies should provide their policyholders with reports at least as informative as those issued by the average commercial corporation to its stockholders. He suggests that the usual balance sheet should be supplemented by a new form of income statement (presented in the article) in place of the "rather cryptic" statement now customary.

[1] Vol. LXXI, No. 4, pp. 322–333.

Social Uses of Accounting

In an *Encyclopaedia Britannica* article on Money it was pointed out that money has come to include anything that performs the work of money; that the most important function of money is that of facilitating exchange; that the earliest economic writers saw plainly that division of employments was only possible through the agency of a medium of exchange, and that a second function of money is that of affording a ready means for estimating the comparative values of different commodities.

Not only does money talk but money symbols are one means of expressing various phases of our modern civilization, including its social conditions and development. With the widespread ownership not only of our large corporations but of many of medium size as well, and with the public today having investments in every phase of business, industrial, mercantile, public utility, and so on, published financial statements have assumed ever-increasing importance. Such statements are indicative of the success or failure of individual enterprises and a reflection, in a broad way, of the business of the country as a whole.

With the recognition that in our modern society capital, labor, and the consumer all have an interest in the national economy, and consequently in the success of business and in the distribution of its produce, the financial statements of business concerns obviously have a social interest. The dependability of the representations contained in such statements by reason of the opinion of the accountant expressed thereon — in the terminology of the man in the street, "certified" — makes the accountant, in a sense, a party to such uses as financial statements may properly have in the consideration of social questions and their attempted solution.

I cannot help feeling that, with the pendulum having apparently swung to an extreme in the present state of labor relations (as evidenced by numerous strikes which appear to be seriously slowing down the defense program), the time must come when disputes between capital and labor, in so far as they relate to wage rates and the division of the avails of production effort between those who contribute capital and those who contribute labor, respectively, to what in effect is a joint enterprise, must rest for their solution in no small measure on what financial statements disclose concerning the operations of the business. The balance sheet and income account, which may normally suffice for the purpose of stockholders who should be informed from time to time of the financial status and operating progress of an enterprise, will need to be supplemented in negotiations or arbitrations between capital and labor with more detailed data pertinent to the questions at issue. Nevertheless, these basic financial statements with the support of examination and certification by independent accountants are a starting point for the analyses required to afford the data necessary to permit the negotiating parties or arbitrators to come to conclusions equitable to both sides.

As between capital and consumer, what is indicated in the paragraph immediately preceding has been in use for years past in rate proceedings relating to railroads and other utility corporations. There is there involved, of course, the special factor of monopoly, partial or complete, with the necessity of determining fair charges for service on the basis of not merely "what the traffic will bear" but also of what should be regarded as the limit of a fair return on the capital employed in such an enterprise. To be sure, proceedings of this kind under the past decisions of the United States Supreme Court have, in respect of the capital employed, had to take into account factors other than those shown directly in the financial statements. For instance, the amount allowed for property employed in the operations of a utility is not usually confined to its cost (either new or depreciated), but such cost is considered as one of the elements in arriving at the fair value of the property at the time reasonable rates are being set.

It has been stated that when, some forty odd years ago, in *Smyth* v. *Ames*, the United States Supreme Court held that present fair value, rather than original cost, was to be the substance of the rate base, those who were seeking to have railroad rates reduced apparently felt they had obtained a victory in the public interest. During the years leading up to that decision the price level had been, broadly speaking, tending downward. Today, after a period during which the price level had risen greatly, the prudent investment theory has been strongly advocated by those seeking to have rates for electric light and power and other forms of public service reduced. The prudent investment theory, as expressed by the Massachusetts Public Service Commission in the *Middlesex and Boston Rate Case* (1914), is that "capital honestly and prudently invested must, under normal conditions, be taken as the controlling factor in fixing the basis for computing fair and reasonable rates; that if there is mismanagement causing loss, such loss must be charged against the stockholders legally responsible for the mismanagement; . . ."[1]

In a brief filed by the Attorney General of the United States as *amicus curiae* in a case then pending before the Supreme Court, he defined "prudent investment" as "the amount reasonably and honestly invested in public utility properties used and useful in the public service." Also, in arguing for abandonment of the fair value rule for rate-making purposes, he said, "the rule of prudent investment, combining as it does exactness, ease of application and a proper principle for the determination of just compensation, is the standard for rate making best adapted to modern busi-

[1] 2 Ann. Rep. Mass. P. S. C. 99.

ness conditions and practice in this country."[1] Apparently, the Attorney General would make it possible to use the books of account more directly and with less adjustment of the figures shown therein than has been the case in rate determinations based on the fair value theory. The question may well be raised whether he is not oversimplifying the problem of rate making when in expressing his preference for the prudent investment theory he includes among its advantages "exactness" and "ease of application." Rate making, if it is to be fair to all the interests concerned, will always present a complex situation, and exactness and ease of application are not likely to be found inherent in the use of the prudent investment theory. At best it is a question of relativity of ease of determination under the respective theories of fair value and of prudent investment. If the prudent investment theory is to be adopted in place of the fair value theory — and for purposes of the present discussion I express no opinion in favor of one or the other — it should be based on more fundamental considerations than fancied "exactness" and "ease of application."

A further development since the enunciation of the prudent investment theory in the Massachusetts case above cited is the present requirement of the Federal Power Commission, the Federal Communications Commission, and the utility commissions of various states that utility property accounts shall be so segregated that they will show the original cost thereof to the person who first devoted such property to public use, and separately any amount by which the cost to the present owner exceeds such original cost.

To the extent that fixed assets may now appear on the books of operating utilities at more than their cost to the present owners merely by reason of their having been written up because of assumed appreciation in value, I think little,

[1] *Denis J. Driscoll, Thomas C. Buchanan and Richard J. Beamish, et al.* v. *Edison Light & Power Company*, 307 U.S. 104 (1939).

if any, argument would be offered by accountants for recognizing such written-up values. Where, however, the properties appear on the books of the owning corporations at actual cost to them as contrasted with a lesser cost to the predecessor owner, the question of whether such predecessor cost is proper for rate-making purposes is still to be passed upon by the Supreme Court.

In the Supreme Court's opinion in the case of *American Telephone & Telegraph Co. et al.* v. *U. S. A. et al.* (1936), which sustained the right of the Federal Communications Commission to require property accounts to be set up on the original cost basis, the Court, while expressing no opinion on the manner in which such accounts should enter into any rate determinations, made it clear that both for purposes of reflecting the accounting company's assets and for computing depreciation allowances any excess of legitimate corporate investment over cost to the original owner would continue to be recognized as a part of the property investment. For such use, however, as the public interest may warrant, the information afforded by property accounts kept on the original cost basis will be available.

Another direction in which accounts may serve a social use is indicated by the recommendation in the 1940 annual report of the Comptroller of the Currency that he "be authorized, in his discretion, to forbid a national bank to declare or pay dividends on its capital stock until there has been satisfactory compliance with his requirements." He points out that "responsibility for the legality and propriety of each dividend should continue to rest upon the board of directors of the particular bank as at present, except where it affirmatively appears to the Comptroller that the declaration of a dividend should not be permitted because of the existence of violations of law or unsafe or unsound banking practices which, if continued, would endanger the safety of the bank and its depositors."

Senator Glass has introduced a bill in the Senate which, among other provisions, would make it unlawful for any insured bank to declare or pay any dividend on any of its capital stock when the Comptroller of the Currency (as to national banks) or the Board of Directors of the Federal Deposit Insurance Corporation (as to insured state banks) object thereto as being in the opinion of the Comptroller or Board, respectively, not "compatible with the best interests of such bank, its depositors or other creditors, or with the public interest."

Obviously, the accounts of the bank and the examination thereof would be a primary source of the data needed by the Comptroller or the Board in determining whether a proposed dividend would be undesirable in the circumstances of a given bank.

The foregoing examples of areas in which public authorities have assumed accounting or auditing responsibilities, or have exercised controls in those areas, will serve to indicate that the functions and responsibilities of the public accountant as auditor have been both increased and more sharply defined as the years have gone on.

II. PRESENT–DAY AUDITING PRACTICE

WHERE THE purpose of an audit is to enable the auditor to express an opinion upon the balance sheet and the related income and surplus statements, he will seek to establish by such internal and external evidence as may prove available the propriety of the amounts at which the various assets appearing on the balance sheet are stated, the amounts of the liabilities which should appear on the balance sheet (either direct liabilities which should be definitely included or contingent liabilities which should be noted thereon), the amount and description of the capital stock (or other form of capital as in the case of partnerships), and the amount of surplus (with proper classification, if required, between capital surplus and earned surplus and indication of any restriction on the distribution of the surplus, whether contractual or through such action as the reacquisition of the company's own stock and the holding of it uncanceled in its treasury).

The internal evidence in support of the financial statements may be said to include the records themselves from which the statements have been prepared, their coherence, various records tying in with one another, the subsidiary books being in balance with their respective controlling accounts, and the existence of a system of internal control and check which appears to be reasonably adapted to the circumstances under which the client concern operates and which appears to be satisfactorily functioning.

The external evidence may be briefly described as documents which originate outside the client's office, and particularly statements and confirmations which come directly to the auditor from outside sources. It may also be said to consist of the assets themselves which can be the subject of objective inspection, as distinguished from the record of ownership thereof, as, for example, stocks and bonds or notes receivable.

The existence of a system of internal check and control and the effectiveness or otherwise with which it appears to be functioning have been emphasized more and more in recent years as an important consideration in determining the scope and extent of sampling and testing in making an audit. Consequently it follows that the system of internal check and control must be the subject of observation and testing, both in an initial audit and by way of review as to changes for better or worse during succeeding audits.

Alertness by the auditor to every indication which he may gain from the nature and treatment of transactions which come under his review is indispensable in an effective audit. The most painstaking inquiry into the existing system is no substitute for alertness and imagination.

It may be observed, too, that an "over-all" impression of the organization and personnel of the business and its functioning is helpful, and may sometimes be even more significant than the apparent plan or system of internal check and control and its intended functioning. Such an over-all impression is something like the doctor's impression of his patient's appearance and progress, or loss of ground, as distinguished from the technical details or symptoms recorded on chart or questionnaire.

Accounting Evidence

In speaking of accounting evidence the auditor may be visualized as acting somewhat in the capacity of a judge or jury who considers the evidence submitted in support of the representations made in the financial statements or, going one step farther, in supporting or corroborating the entries made in the books of account from which the statements have been prepared. Just as in the case of a judge or jury, the purpose of the consideration of the evidence is that a conclusion may be reached as to the dependability or otherwise of the representations contained in the statements and an opinion be expressed accordingly.

Two important distinctions come to mind, however, between the position of the judge or jury and that of the auditor. One distinction is that a judge or jury has the evidence brought to it by parties in interest who are presenting their case for consideration. This is true only in part in the case of the auditor. For the most part he must search for the evidence, and to a considerable extent he must determine what evidence shall be presented to him.

Another distinction is that, of the evidence brought to judge or jury, some of it is not infrequently excluded on the ground that it is irrelevant, incompetent, or otherwise not acceptable under applicable legal rules of evidence. The auditor, however, is not so limited. Whatever evidence is before him may and should be considered for its informative and probative value. Some of it may have very little value, but even in such cases the possibility of helpful suggestion is not to be overlooked.

It follows that the type of evidence which comes before the auditor is frequently less conclusive than would be required in a court of law. However, he must consider it for what it may be worth and exercise his best judgment regarding its acceptability. The auditor is not bound by any rules of evidence in conducting his examination and, on the contrary, any effort to withhold any evidence from his consideration should ordinarily lead him to insist upon its submission.

The books from which the statements have been prepared are themselves part of the accounting evidence. They are presumed to be a record made approximately at the time the transactions occurred, and therefore are *prima facie* to be accepted as evidence to the extent that they are not contradicted by other more conclusive evidence of the actual nature of the transactions which they purport to reflect. Entries therein may on occasion, however, because of the absence of supporting evidence which should be available, be questioned until substantiated to the auditor's satisfaction.

Other accounting evidence includes any relevant documents which may throw light upon, or corroborate the truthfulness and correctness of, the entries in the books, or may yield information concerning contingent liabilities or other matters which have not yet become the subject of closed transactions and which may, therefore, merely be noted on the balance sheet or income statement or in the explanatory notes appended thereto instead of being recorded in the principal books of account. Among such documents may be mentioned bank statements, paid checks and notes, copies of deposit tickets, petty cash vouchers, invoices for materials or other merchandise purchased or for expenses incurred, pay rolls, cost records, copies of bills rendered to customers, approved debit and credit memoranda relating to adjustments of customers' or suppliers' accounts, construction authorizations, engineers' reports, leases and other contracts, minute books, correspondence relating to unusual transactions, inventories, computations of depletion and depreciation allowances, and so on.

Sometimes the evidence relating to certain transactions is largely or wholly oral, that is, explanations from officers or others who know the facts regarding transactions for which entries have been made but for which little or no documentary evidence is available. Obviously, oral evidence, in the form of explanations, is not to be disregarded by the auditor, though naturally the acceptability of the evidence so received may involve the exercise of even more judgment than when the evidence is in documentary form.

A considerable part of the practical work of the auditor is to test the dependability of the books of account by comparison of the accounting evidence with the entries to which it relates. The extent to which such evidence shall be accepted as conclusive is one of the elements in the work of the auditor that make it professional in character since it involves the exercise of judgment and educated opinion.

Since it is not practicable in the case of any but small concerns to examine all the transactions of the period which has elapsed since the last preceding examination, a second exercise of judgment relating to the evidence is the extent to which it shall be reviewed and compared with the book entries. This is no easy matter and, indeed, thinking and the exercising of judgment are usually not easy. Thomas A. Edison is reputed to have said that there is no extreme to which a man will not go in the effort to escape the labor of thinking.

The need for making such a judgment, however, cannot be evaded. It goes without saying that the greater the experience of the auditor the better the basis for his judgment, and the greater the assurance with which he comes to a conclusion about the extent to which, in a given case, his testing and sampling or, as it might also be described, the use to be made of the accounting evidence shall be carried.

Clients' Written Representations Regarding Inventories, Liabilities, and Other Matters

A development of more recent years, which may be regarded as in the nature of supplementary accounting evidence, is that of having responsible officers or other representatives of the client in positions of authority give to the auditor an "inventory certificate" and a "liability certificate." The purpose of the former is to have someone make a definite statement to the auditor, on behalf of the client, that the inventory of a stated amount (perhaps divided into a few broad classes) has been taken under the direction of the signer of the certificate; that to the best of his knowledge and belief quantities are correct and were determined by actual count, weight, or measurement; that the entire inventory is the unencumbered property of the client, has not been pledged as collateral, and includes no items billed by the company prior to the balance sheet date or held on consignment; that the inventory is priced at cost or market, whichever is lower, and is not in excess of net realizable value; that the basis of pricing and method of computation is the same as was used at the end of the previous fiscal period and that the general basis on which cost is determined is as described (as first-in, first-out; average; last-in, first-out, etc.); that no obsolete, damaged, or unusable materials or merchandise are included in the inventory in excess of net realizable value; and that the amount stated is a fair and proper valuation of the inventory.

The liability certificate is a statement or representation that, to the best of the knowledge and belief of the signer, all liabilities have been taken up on the books of account as at the balance sheet date, including liability for all merchandise shipped and billed to the client prior to that date; that none of the assets of the company was, or is now, pledged or hypothecated as security for any liabilities except as disclosed in the certificate; and that, excepting for those indicated in the liability certificate, there were no contingent liabilities, no purchase commitments for the purchase of materials or supplies at prices in excess of the prevailing market prices, or repurchase agreements for merchandise previously sold, no other commitments, contracts, or leases which might adversely affect the company, and no unused balance of letters of credit outstanding at the balance sheet date. Further, the liability certificate should contain a statement of the approximate amount of any contractual obligations for plant construction, purchase of real property, equipment, and rights; a statement that there were no subordinations of liabilities at the balance sheet date, and that between that date and the signing of the certificate there has been no material change in respect of contingent liabilities, commitments, etc., except as indicated in the certificate.

The securing of such certificates has become widely recognized in the profession as an essential part of auditing procedure so that there may be no question of the client's having made a definite representation, on the one hand, of the propriety of the inventory taking and valuation and, on the other, of the liabilities, including those of a contingent character, which the client either knows or should know about. Naturally, such certificates must not be relied upon as substitutes for but as supplementary to inquiry by the auditor into the various items mentioned. The very request for these certificates, however, has the effect of facing the client squarely with the basis on which the inventory has been, or should have been, taken, and of perhaps having the client bring to the attention of the auditor information concerning those types of liabilities which are not necessarily recorded on the books of account, such as various classes of contingent liabilities, merchandise and construction commitments, and other contractual obligations, hypothecation of assets, etc. Also, it may lead to a disclosure of direct liabilities which have not been reflected on the books before their closing.

Some auditors go so far as to require comprehensive written representations by executives of the client in respect of various phases of property accounting, reserves for depreciation and depletion, and the validity of the accounts and notes receivable, as well as some other special features. This is not a general practice, though some extension of the request for clients' written representations regarding the property accounting may at times be helpful. Retirements of fixed assets are not always reported to the accounting department, and a request for the signature of a superintendent or plant manager to a certificate that all sales, dismantlements, and abandonments of plant and equipment during the period of audit have been reported might cause him to recall retirements which had not been reported. Engineers have not infrequently found that when an inventory is taken of fixed assets a portion of those carried on the books is found to be missing, apparently because of failure on the part of those responsible for reporting retirements to the accounting departments. Where there seems reason for requesting such a certificate from an operating official, the logical corollary certificate would be by the controller or other accounting officer that all reported sales, dismantlements, and abandonments of plant items reported to his department had been properly recorded.

Developments in Auditing Procedure

Some illustrations of present-day auditing procedures which reflect the application of what has been learned from the auditor's experience through the years are as follows:

(a) Review of the composition of the surplus balance and of the consideration for which capital stock and other securities were issued is now considered an essential part of the auditor's duties. The procedures in this respect would now also include a review of minutes of stockholders' and directors' meetings at organization and for significant matters in subsequent years, the certificate of incorporation, and any changes in capital stock issues since organization. More attention is now being paid on the occasion of an initial audit to establishing the basis of fixed assets, unless other public accountants have satisfactorily covered the ground in prior examinations. This may involve a general review of the fixed asset accounts from the date of organization of the company. In earlier years when the property account frequently had its inception merely as an offset to the face value of securities issued, that account was more or less accepted "as is," and the auditor was frequently content to accept the balance of property accounts at the opening of the year for which he made his initial audit, without attempting to establish the basis of the amount at which the fixed assets were carried.

(b) Many accountants now feel that a second or cut-off bank reconciliation is a desirable part of auditing procedures in respect of cash. This procedure is a development during the past decade. It was adopted as a means of ascertaining whether any checks were outstanding when the first reconciliation was made but improperly excluded therefrom, and of detecting other possible irregularities which might more readily be brought to light by a second cut-off without notice than at a regular reconciliation date. There may be cases in which for special reasons it is impracticable or unreasonable to resort to the second reconciliation plan. If such be the case, the principal objectives of the second reconciliation may be attained by obtaining bank statements and paid checks at a date following the first reconciliation, and (1) seeing whether any checks included therein were apparently issued in the preceding period but were not listed as outstanding in the first reconciliation, (2) comparing such outstanding items with the returned paid checks so far as they may have been paid by the bank, (3) noting that deposits in transit over the first reconciliation date were promptly credited in the subsequent bank statement, and (4) learning of any charge-backs of deposited items.

(c) Another procedure now generally followed is to obtain duplicate bank deposit slips from the bank (or to have the bank authenticate for the auditor copies prepared from the client's records), usually for a short period, and to compare the detail of the items shown thereon with the source of postings to customers' and other accounts. Perhaps the warning should be given that since, in those banks where the block system is used, the tellers do not compare the items making up the deposit in detail with the deposit slips at the time originally received, the value of this check is in such cases not so conclusive as might be wished. Even in such circumstances, however, it has some value. An effective method which may be used when it is practicable for the auditor to be present at the client's office during a period is for the auditor to make such comparisons immediately after the cashier has made up his deposit, and to see that such deposit is transmitted to the bank without further access thereto by the cashier.

(d) Auditors now endeavor, in all cases where practicable, to obtain outside direct confirmation of balance sheet items. In addition to asking banks to confirm independently the balances on deposit at the balance sheet date, the banks are asked to confirm direct or contingent liabilities of the client which may be known to them, endorsements, collateral held, items held for collection, etc. Collection agencies are also asked to confirm notes or acceptances held by them. Legal counsel is asked for information regarding suits or other liabilities known to them. Life insurance companies are asked for computations of cash surrender value of life insurance policies which may be held. Consignees or consignors of merchandise are requested to confirm balances shown by the client's records. Trustees of bond issues, registrars and transfer agents of capital stock issues, and sometimes the secretary or other pertinent official of the state of incorporation are asked for information which they can supply for the confirmation of security amounts shown by the client's records. Deposits held by such organizations as transportation lines, custom brokers, and public utilities are also confirmed directly with the holders.

(e) Improvement in plant accounting records which accountants have been urging for many years has been effected by many corporations. When this has been done, such records permit the auditor to review more intelligently the changes in fixed asset accounts. This is particularly true when a work order or work authorization plan for the accounting pertaining to plant changes is in use.

(f) Auditors pay more attention today than in earlier years to a review of the client's files of contracts or agreements as a source of information concerning possible liabilities, such as service or operating agreements, officers' and employees' bonus agreements, pension plans, purchase agreements, etc.

(g) While not a generally accepted procedure, circularization of creditors is not infrequently resorted to, especially if a review of the internal procedures for recording creditors' invoices indicates them to be unsatisfactory.

Extensions of Auditing Procedure

Over the years during which I have been observing the development of auditing procedure I have seen it continuously extended. For instance, I recall that forty years ago when we were verifying bank balances we usually relied upon the bank passbook, which was balanced by the bank upon request of the depositor, for the amount of the balance standing to the credit of the depositor. Confirmation of deposit balances by banks directly to the accountant was in its infancy and not yet generally resorted to. Monthly bank statements, which had their origin in the Middle West, were just beginning to be heard of in the East. As a result of the development in respect of this item on the balance sheet, every effort is made today to obtain the assurance which comes from confirmation of bank balances directly to the auditor, by verification on the part of the bank of duplicate deposit tickets when details of cash receipts are being traced, by confirmation of notes payable or any other obligations of the client held by the bank, and of drafts, notes, or similar items held for collection.

In respect of two other important assets, usually classed as current on the balance sheet, there has been a marked development of auditing procedure through the years and a definite extension thereof as normal procedure where it is practicable and reasonable in the circumstances of the particular engagement. These two items are inventories and receivables.

Broadly speaking, there were for years in this country two schools of thought in respect of contact of the auditor with inventories of goods on hand. One school held to the thought of the much older profession in Britain where the auditor had not sought to establish physical contact with inventories except, presumably, in abnormal cases. It felt that the work of the auditor, since he is not to be considered an expert in materials or a valuer, should be confined to such evidence as the inventories (vouched for by those who were responsible for the stocktaking), financial books, stock records, and related documents, together with inquiry into the method of stock-taking and making accounting tests and checks of the inventories and supporting records.

Another school of thought, however, held that we should not be content with the practice and experience of the past but should seek to establish by physical contact with the inventory, through observation of the methods by which it is taken and by test inspection of quantities where this be practicable, the probable correctness of the inventory quantities. Some accountants had reached the point where they had been able to persuade many of their clients to assent to the inclusion of such physical contact with inventories in the scope of the auditor's examination. It was recognized, however, that this had not yet become a general practice in the profession, and could not therefore be regarded as normal procedure which could be expected to be followed in the absence of unusual circumstances indicating express need for such procedure.

The special committee appointed by the American Institute of Accountants in 1939 to consider possible extensions of auditing procedure adopted the view of the second school of thought and made the following recommendations regarding auditing procedures in respect of inventories:

(A) That hereafter, where the independent certified public accountant intends to report over his signature on the financial statements of a concern in which inventories are a material factor, it should be generally accepted auditing procedure that, in addition to making auditing tests and checks of the inventory accounts and records, he shall, wherever practicable and reasonable, be present, either in person or by his representatives, at the inventory taking and by suitable observation and inquiry satisfy himself as to the effectiveness of the methods of inventory taking and as to the measure of reliance which may be placed upon the client's representations as to inventories and upon the records thereof. In this connection the independent certified public accountant may require physical tests of inventories to be made under his observation.

In cases where the inventory is determined solely by means of a physical inventory at the end of the accounting period (or at a date prior or subsequent thereto but within a reasonable time thereof, with adequate records supporting the interim changes), it will ordinarily be necessary for the foregoing procedures to be followed at that time.

In cases where the concern maintains well kept and controlled perpetual inventory records supported by (1) a complete physical inventory at a date not coincident with the balance-sheet date, or (2) physical inventories of individual items taken from time to time so that the quantity of each item on hand is compared with the inventory record for that item at least once in each year, it will be satisfactory to undertake the procedure outlined at any interim date or dates selected by the auditor, his purpose being to satisfy himself as to the credibility of the perpetual inventory records and whether they may be relied upon to support the inventory totals as shown on the balance-sheet.

(B) That hereafter, in the case of inventories which in the ordinary course of business are in the hands of public warehouses or other outside custodians, direct confirmation in writing from such custodians is acceptable procedure; except that, where the amount involved represents a significant proportion of the current assets or of the total assets of a concern, the independent certified public accountant shall make supplementary inquiries.

The committee, however, took the precaution of accompanying its recommendations with the following warning:

It should be clearly understood that in undertaking these auditing procedures regarding inventories, the independent certified public accountant does so for the purpose of satisfying himself as to the credibility of the representations of the management regarding quantity and condition and does not hold himself out as a general appraiser, valuer, or expert in materials.

The recommendation of the committee in respect of physical tests of inventory was "viewed with alarm" by the profession in Great Britain and Canada. If an editorial in *The Accountant* [London] of June 24, 1939, written soon after the approval of the report submitted by the Committee to the Council of the American Institute at its May, 1939, meeting, may be regarded as indicative of the reaction of the profession generally in Britain, the extended auditing procedure in respect of inventories now to be regarded as normal procedure in this country is not likely to be adopted by our professional brethren across the sea, at least for some time to come.

An editorial in *The Canadian Chartered Accountant* of August, 1939, indicated a feeling probably akin to that expressed in *The Accountant* on the part of the profession in Canada.

The situation in respect of the circularization of receivables was somewhat different from that relating to physical contact with inventories. The same questions raised in respect of inventories, namely, that the auditor lacked the training for distinguishing between different qualities of even such relatively common materials as, for instance, steel, or of even recognizing commodities or products of various kinds in such fields as the chemical industry, did not for the most part obtain in respect of establishing the authenticity of the notes and accounts receivable by communication with the debtors.

In at least one line of business, that is, stock and commodity brokers, the confirmation practice had been an accepted procedure for many years past, and an audit would not have been considered complete or satisfactory if the auditor had not, through such communication with customers, had the opportunity to ascertain whether, upon being independently informed through statements of account from the client mailed under the control of the auditor, they took exception to the correctness of the balances standing to their debit or credit, or of the securities shown in such accounts as long or short, or of the commodity commitments indicated thereon.

In the industrial and mercantile fields the practice had been used to some extent, particularly where the system of internal check and control did not appear to be effective, or where the receivables consisted of a relatively few accounts of exceptionally large amount. Although the confirmation practice was gradually coming into greater use, it certainly could not be said up to 1939 that it was an essential auditing procedure in the absence of which the auditor would not give an unqualified certificate.

Practical problems were seen in making even a small test of the receivables of certain types of concerns, such as department stores and furniture instalment houses, automobile finance companies and small loan companies, milk companies and others in the field of house-to-house distribution, and the larger public utilities, where there may be in the case of one company anywhere from tens of thousands up to even a million or more accounts or notes receivable. In many of these cases the average receivable would be small, and both the type of many of the customers and the relativity of small individual accounts to the aggregate of the receivables would call for an undue amount of time from the auditor for the confirmation procedure with a consequent expense to the client which might well be disproportionate to any conceivable value of the results to be obtained.

In the case of at least one class of concerns, namely, the public utilities, it was seen that there is a factor of control of receivables which is additional to that of accounting check and control, namely, the cutting off of service in the event the consumer does not live up to the prescribed terms of payment, and his inability to get service elsewhere in the event of such termination of service. This gives a still greater assurance to the dependability of utility receivables for the purpose of the auditor's review of them. This service control factor, combined with the small balance for the average consumer, leads me to the conclusion that in the case of a utility with a large number of consumers and with a well-organized system of consumer accounting and internal check and control, confirmation of any but the smallest percentage of consumers' receivables is, if not quite impracticable, certainly unreasonable.

The recommendation of the committee was as follows:

That hereafter, wherever practicable and reasonable, and where the aggregate amount of notes and accounts receivable represents a significant proportion of the current assets or of the total assets of a concern, confirmation of notes and accounts receivable by direct communication with the debtors shall be regarded as generally accepted auditing procedure in the examination of the accounts of a concern whose financial statements are accompanied by an independent certified public accountant's report; and that the method, extent, and time of confirming receivables in each engagement, and whether of all receivables or a part thereof, be determined by the independent certified public accountant as in other phases of procedure requiring the exercise of his judgment.

The Institute's Committee on Auditing Procedure has since issued a statement that,

in the case of the receivables of department stores, instalment houses, chain stores, and other retailers, there might be question as to the reasonableness of applying the positive form of confirmation, but it is believed that there is no question as to the practicability and reasonableness of applying the negative form of confirmation which requires no reply unless the recipient challenges the balance shown. When dealing with housewives, as is the case in department stores particularly, the negative form is more practicable than the positive, as it places the recipient definitely on notice that the creditor's books show a stated balance, and that the auditor assumes the correctness of that balance unless the debtor objects within reasonable time.

In audits generally the so-called negative form is, in my opinion, usually the preferable form, because of its greater economy of time and expense. It serves the primary purpose just as well as the positive form, which calls for a reply from the customer, for the objective is for the auditor to assure himself that the customer is informed of the amount standing to his debit. If the customer does not admit liability therefor, it is to be assumed he would register an objection just as certainly when the negative form is used as if the positive form were employed. If the customer concurs in the correctness of the amount as stated, no reply is necessary, with consequent economy of postage and of the time otherwise necessary for the handling and checking of the replies.

It is important that in the use of either form of confirmation the procedure be such that undelivered communications to the debtors be returned by the postal authorities directly to the auditor.

Internal Check and Control

The term "internal check and control" has relation to the manner in which the departmentalization and flow of transactions having a financial aspect is arranged in a business concern, and with the apportionment of duties of various members of the concern's staff so that so far as possible the work of recording by one person or department is a check or control on that of others; further, that complete control of the recording of a series of transactions as, for instance, starting from the recording of shipments through to collection of payments made by customers, shall not be in the hands of any one person; and that so far as feasible the handling and recording of funds from customers shall not be by the same person or persons who originate or record the debits to customers or the credits for adjustments in their accounts. Per contra, the incurring and recording of liabilities for materials, merchandise, wages, or expenses shall not be under the control or subject to the unrestricted approval of the person or persons making or recording disbursements. For instance, the recording of the data for and the preparation of the pay roll should not be under the control of those who pay off the men.

The formulation of an opinion, not only of whether a proper system of internal check and control exists, but even more whether it is functioning properly, is difficult at best. The scope of the examination to be made involves two unknown quantities which react upon each other: on the one hand, the nature and extent of the sampling and testing to be made of the recorded transactions must be determined, in part at least, in the light of the system of internal check and control, and, on the other hand, the effectiveness of such a system must be judged to a considerable extent by the results of the auditing tests.

There are differences of opinion among experienced accountants as to the value or otherwise of questionnaires, whether they relate directly to the performance of the work called for by the auditing program or to the features of the system of internal check and control. Some accountants have felt that the use of them has a tendency to emphasize mere routine and to deaden initiative. It may be observed that among doctors the best diagnostician is not necessarily the one who does the best or most complete paper work on a case. Similarly, in the army, the best and most resourceful officer is not necessarily the one most adept in the voluminous paper work which army regulations and practice call for. Nevertheless, in my opinion, it is on the whole desirable that the auditor record the more important features of the system of internal check and control as he makes his inquiry into it for the first time, and that in succeeding audits he note any significant changes that he observes.

It should be understood that when an auditor gives a certificate on the financial statements of a company he is not necessarily endorsing, or completely satisfied with, the system of internal check and control he finds in effect. He has to take it as he finds it for the current examination, and determine how far it shall influence the scope and extent thereof. The number of instances in which the auditor will find an ideal system of internal check and control in existence and functioning 100 per cent to his satisfaction will be relatively few. Human perfection is practically nonexistent. In the final analysis he must determine whether, in all the circumstances and after considering the system as it is in plan, and as it is apparently functioning, he is satisfied that the financial statements do, in his opinion, present fairly the position of the client and the results of its operations for the period under review. Naturally, the effectiveness of the system of internal check will be one of continuing interest to the auditor so that suggestions to the client for the improvement of the system are a logical result of evident defects — or failure to function — which come to the auditor's attention.

Corporate Accounting Control

The McKesson & Robbins case, with its deep-laid conspiracy in high places, gave a tremendous shock to the business and financial world. For some time it was the current topic of conversation in business circles. However, the matter did not remain simply a topic of discussion. The boards of directors of a number of corporations conferred with their independent auditors to acquaint themselves more fully with the scope of the examinations being currently made for their corporations and sought to assure themselves that in its broader aspects "it couldn't happen here."

In the 1938 annual report of one of our largest corporations, which was published soon after the McKesson & Robbins disclosures, the president made a statement concerning the accounting practices and policies of the company, the organization of the accounting functions, the activity of the internal auditing staff, and the examination by the corporation's independent auditors. The purpose of the statement was to describe "how the various items in the financial statements were established in relation to the policies laid down for their determination." In the description of the corporation's accounting organization and methods and the internal check and control the controller played an important part.

A subcommittee of the Stock List Committee of the New York Stock Exchange, in its report of August 11, 1939, made the following recommendation regarding the position and responsibility of the controller:

> More emphasis should be placed on the responsibility of the controller and the assurance to him of adequate authority and facilities. The scope of his responsibilities should be fixed by the board of directors, and he should report periodically to them, in addition to making his customary reports to the operating management.
>
> The controller or chief financial officer should sign the published financial statements of his company, even in those cases where the statements are accompanied by the report of the independent public accountant.
>
> Independent and efficient accounting and internal auditing departments are a vital factor in assuring the accuracy of the books and published reports. The importance of the controller or internal auditor in these connections is paramount and the board of directors should take an active interest in his selection.

Function of the Controller: The Controllers Institute of America has developed the following brief definition of the duties of the controller of a corporation:

> The duties of the controller shall be to maintain adequate records of all assets, liabilities, and transactions of this corporation; to see that adequate audits thereof are currently and regularly made; and, in conjunction with other officers and department heads, to initiate and enforce measures and procedures whereby the business of this corporation shall be conducted with the maximum safety, efficiency, and economy. He shall attend all meetings of the board of directors and of the execu-

tive committee, and he shall report to the president and/or the board of directors as said board of directors may prescribe. His duties and powers shall extend to all subsidiary corporations, and so far as the president may deem practicable, to all affiliated companies.

This definition has been formulated with an eye to the ideal. For instance, the provision that he shall attend all meetings of the board of directors and of the executive committee is at present probably the exception rather than the rule if the controller is not himself a member of the board of directors.

The Controllers Institute has further elaborated on the duties of the controller by enumerating them as follows:

1. The installation and supervision of all accounting records of the corporation.

2. The preparation and interpretation of the financial statements and reports of the corporation.

3. The continuous audit of all accounts and records of the corporation, wherever located.

4. The compilation of production costs.

5. The compilation of costs of distribution.

6. The taking and costing of all physical inventories.

7. The preparation and filing of tax returns and the supervision of all matters relating to taxes.

8. The preparation and interpretation of all statistical records and reports of the corporation.

9. The preparation, as budget director, in conjunction with other officers and department heads, of an annual budget covering all activities of the corporation, for submission to the board of directors prior to the beginning of the fiscal year. The authority of the controller, with respect to the veto of commitments or expenditures not authorized by the budget, shall, from time to time, be fixed by the board of directors.

10. The ascertainment currently that the properties of the corporation are properly and adequately insured.

11. The initiation, preparation, and issuance of standard practices relating to all accounting matters and procedures and the coordination of systems throughout the corporation, including clerical and office methods, records, reports and procedures.

12. The maintenance of adequate records of authorized appropria-

tions and the determination that all sums expended pursuant thereto are properly accounted for.

13. The ascertainment currently that financial transactions covered by minutes of the board of directors and/or the Executive Committee are properly executed and recorded.

14. The maintenance of adequate records of all contracts and leases.

15. The approval for payment (and/or countersigning) of all checks, promissory notes, and other negotiable instruments of the corporation which have been signed by the treasurer or such other officers as shall have been authorized by the by-laws of the corporation or from time to time designated by the board of directors.

16. The examination of all warrants for the withdrawal of securities from the vaults of the corporation and the determination that such withdrawals are made in conformity with the by-laws and/or regulations established from time to time by the board of directors.

17. The preparation or approval of the regulations or standard practices required to assure compliance with orders or regulations issued by duly constituted governmental agencies.

Internal Auditing: An important contribution toward an effective system of internal check and control, especially for large companies, is the use of an internal auditing staff. Its work is to conduct a continuous audit which will be more extensive as to detailed examination or verification of the various classes of transactions recorded in the corporation's accounts than is practicable for the independent auditor. In the present day the extent and complexity of the business of a large, and often far-flung, corporation requires the independent auditor to devote a large part of his time to the study of the accounting principles applied by the corporation and the consistency with which they have been followed from period to period.

The more that internal auditing is utilized as a safeguard against peculations and in order to insure proper accounting for the avails of the business done, the more the independent auditor can devote his attention to the consideration of the proper application of sound accounting principles and the formulation of his opinion regarding the dependability of the financial statements which the management submits to stockholders and creditors.

Among the salient features of the organization and work of an internal auditing staff or department and of its relation to the work of the independent auditor may be mentioned the following:

Distinction between work of the internal auditor and that of the independent auditor: One consideration in establishing an internal auditing organization is that the cost of auditing may be lessened by reason of the independent auditor's being justified in relying on the detailed examination and verification by the internal auditor. Especially in this day of the widespread use of mechanical bookkeeping appliances, it would involve unwarranted expense to have the independent auditor devote himself to the detailed checking of the bookkeeping records. By confining the auditing work of the independent auditor to test checks of the accounts and to reviewing the reports of the internal auditors, he can devote his efforts primarily to those matters which are of major importance in reviewing the financial statements of position and operations and the manner in which the various items appearing therein have been built up.

In distinguishing between the work of the internal auditor and that of the independent auditor, it may be noted that the former is likely to be engaged in verifying transactions in the light of accounting policies laid down by the management, whereas it is the function of the latter to determine whether or not those accounting policies are sound.

Coordination of work of the internal auditor with that of the independent auditor: Programs of coordination must be individually developed according to the particular needs and form of organization of different companies. A few general points may be mentioned for consideration when such a program of coordination is being formulated:

(a) From the very nature of his work, the internal auditor will have a familiarity with the everyday routine and details of the business of which the independent auditor should avail himself, both by reviewing such formal reports as the internal auditor may make to his superiors and by conference on those matters arising in the course of the independent examination concerning which the internal auditor should be able to give information;

(b) In determining the scope and extent of the independent auditor's examination, the field covered by the internal auditor and the apparent effectiveness — or otherwise — of his work should be considered by the former;

(c) When a corporation has many branches and a number of factories spread over a wide geographical area, the independent auditor will not necessarily visit all of them every year. In such cases the work of the internal auditor will supplement that of the independent auditor in respect of the points not visited in a particular year;

(d) In some instances the internal auditor may, under the direction of the independent auditor, prepare analyses, schedules, and accounting exhibits which the latter may require. This procedure may be considered as supplementary to the normal practice of having the accounting department prepare various schedules for use in the audit.

Significant types of auditing work by the internal auditor: The work of the internal auditor is closely related in many respects to the work of the independent auditor, but in most cases he will go further in making detailed verifications. There is not always the necessity to verify completely all the transactions, however, for in many cases a "spot test" would be quite sufficient. The exercise of judgment on the part of the internal auditor, therefore, is without question a basic factor in the efficient conduct of his activities.

(a) Participation by the internal auditor in inventory taking has in many corporations become one of his important duties. The internal auditor is regarded as being in a favorable position to accept this responsibility because of his familiarity with the company's product and the absence of the limitations of time which are necessarily placed on the independent auditor. The internal auditor can actively participate in the taking of the inventory and is aided by his continuing familiarity with the unit quantities and values of his company's materials and products.

(b) In large companies, the purchasing process is usually classified into various steps, and most of the normal purchasing progresses along such routine steps. It is not difficult for the internal auditor to verify the generality of the purchases and the classification of them; however, he may have a few special problems with which to contend. Certain commodities may be of a perishable nature and must be purchased as needed; also some departments or personnel find it necessary to make special purchases, as, for example, repair parts. It is instances such as these that sometimes require the internal auditor to go into considerable detail to see that these items are properly handled for accounting purposes. Purchases are sometimes made for direct shipment to customers, and the internal auditor should follow these transactions through to see that the customers were properly charged. Purchase returns are another class of item to be looked into carefully and in detail by the internal auditor.

(c) The accounting aspects of the sales procedures which are the concern of the internal auditor center about the satisfactory establishment of accountability, entailing adequate inventory control, shipping or delivery procedures, and, in the case of cash sales and scrap sales, suitable control over such transactions. He is also concerned about the provision of adequate managerial information for control, which requires adequate analysis of sales transactions and current reports covering these data for management use. The duties assigned to the internal auditor may also include inquiry into the service aspects of the sales transactions, the promptness of delivery, accuracy of filling the orders, systematically and accurately prepared billing papers, and general courteous treatment in all matters in respect to customer relations.

Work of the internal auditor not strictly limited to the realm of accounting: The close relationship of the internal auditor to the management provides the latter with a means for gaining special information needed for dealing effectively with particular problems. For instance, it may be necessary to establish further the accuracy of certain company information and to analyze its bearing upon a proposed contract. In such a case the internal auditor may be required to go into facts surrounding the proposed transaction beyond their strict accounting significance and report upon practices or policies which are involved. Again, he may have the task of examining and appraising the reasonableness of the bases on which intercompany or interdepartmental relations rest and the general accuracy with which charges and credits between them are made. The extreme importance of budgetary activities as a means of effective management control may make it necessary to use the internal auditor for review and appraisal of such activities, either completely or in respect of particular aspects thereof.

These are only a few illustrations of special duties of the internal auditor. The internal auditing staff may be considered to be a flexible group which, in addition to regular duties, is ready to function in whatever manner will most effectively serve the management of a corporation.

Organization of internal auditing staff or department: In order that such a department serve effectively, it should have a status in the organization independent of other departments which must come under its review and appraisal. It is desirable that the head of the department be responsible directly to the controller or to another officer who is above the direct functional activities, the accounting of which is being audited. The size of the internal auditing staff will necessarily vary with the needs of the corporation. Although the staff members may be classified, either by rank (such as executive, senior, semisenior, or junior) or by operating divisions (such as factory, retail, warehouse, or traveling), it is desirable not to continue staff members in the same routine or geographical area over too extended a period of time. Rotation of assignment with a fresh mind coming to a particular field or section of the accounts, though under the continued direction of the head of the department, has its values.

The headquarters of the internal auditing department will normally be at the head office of the corporation. In addition to the chief auditor, those staff members concerned chiefly with the auditing activity at the central office will be stationed there. The size and character of personnel, the nature and scope of the internal auditing program, and the management policies in respect thereof will naturally have to be worked out in the light of any limitations imposed by the funds made available for the department.

The auditing program should include provision for reports to be made by staff members, not only at completion of a particular assignment, but also during the progress thereof if special circumstances develop during an assignment. Concurrent study of the corporation's accounting practices should be part of the work of the internal auditor with recommendations for any simplification and improved control as the natural result.

Conservatism in Financial Statements

As the auditor proceeds with his work he is likely to get an impression whether the accounting policy of the management is conservative or otherwise. The provision made for uncollectible receivables; the manner in which the inventory is priced, and especially the treatment of goods which have been on hand for a considerable length of time and in which styles may have changed or which are shopworn; the provisions for depreciation and depletion; the resolving of the doubt in favor of charging borderline items to operations rather than capitalizing them or, conversely, the attempt to nurse earnings by capitalizing everything that can possibly be claimed as an addition to or improvement of plant; the liberality of and promptness of provision for possible losses, or for claims of one kind or another against the concern or an evident policy of deferring write-offs as long as possible, all contribute to the feeling which the experienced auditor gains either that the accounting policy of his client is conservative or the reverse. Sometimes the auditor will find that ultraconservatism has reigned and that it has led to understatement of earnings or possibly to equalization thereof between years by taking advantage in less favorable years of the ultraconservatism of other years. Inventories, perhaps, have been priced at below either cost or market and, if no disclosure of the practice has been made, a secret reserve has thus been created.

It seems likely that, taken by and large, any substantial secret reserves which had been built up in the accounts of corporate enterprise generally in the United States would probably have been exhausted by the losses of the depression period. In fact, it seems likely that this was generally true as early in the depression period as 1933. To the Americans present at the International Congress of Accounting held in London in July of that year, however, it was interesting to note the animated discussion by the British accountants which followed extended reference to secret reserves in the paper presented by Mr. Henry Morgan, F.S.A.A., past president of the Society of Incorporated Accountants and Auditors, on "The Auditor's Responsibility in Relation to Balance Sheets and Profit and Loss Accounts" from the British point of view.

I had the privilege of hearing the discussion and judged

from the interest in the subject that secret reserves are (or at least were) more often present in the case of British corporations than is the case on this side of the ocean. One of the British accountants told me it was supposed that the large London banks had heavy secret reserves because when some heavy loss was incurred — as, for instance, due to the notorious Hatry failure — the banks were able to absorb it without any apparent effect on their surplus and undivided profits.

It is not always easy to keep on an absolutely even keel in making accounting decisions or distinctions in classifying expenditures as falling into either the capital or the expense class. In deciding what should be the amount of provision for possible losses or matters in litigation, in determining the allowances to be made for depreciation and depletion, the ultimate outcome of which cannot be known for years to come, etc., judgment is bound to lean to one side or the other, and I am frank to say that I am in favor of an accounting policy that leans toward the conservative side. Conservatism, however, must not go so far as to distort the presentation of the financial position and the operating results.

This is particularly a case in which disclosure is of the essence. I do not believe that present-day accounting practice in the United States justifies an ultraconservative accounting policy which would give rise to secret reserves (directly or indirectly) without disclosure, though I recognize the difficulty of laying down any definition of, or determining when, a "reasonable" point has been passed. Obviously, each case must be determined on its own facts. However, I am here setting forth the substance of a tentative statement of general principles to be followed when dealing with secret reserves, which I formulated while I was listening to the above-mentioned discussion of the subject in London in 1933:

(1) If the reserves are not required to provide for any contingent liabilities or to provide for any uncertainties of value in respect of any assets, such reserves are in effect a portion of the company's surplus and, if of relatively material amount, there is no accounting principle which justifies the failure to disclose the amount and nature of such reserves in the balance sheet; further, any reserves of such character should at the time of creation be treated as an allocation of profits or surplus and not be merged or obscured in the profit and loss (or income) statement;

(2) If the so-called "reserves" represent a provision for the amount which it is believed may be required for the discharge of liabilities which are only momentarily contingent, or which represent a reasonable exercise of conservatism in valuing assets, disclosure of the specific amounts of such reserves in either balance sheet or profit and loss statement does not seem essential; also, in such a case the items come nearer to being provisions or allowances than reserves;

(3) When reserves of the character contemplated in (1) are discontinued, the amount thereof should be credited directly to surplus and not passed through the profit and loss statement of the year of such discontinuance;

(4) In the event of any charges being made to reserves of the character contemplated in (1), the nature and amount of such charge should be disclosed in the year in which made, in most cases preferably in the year's profit and loss statement;

(5) In the event of its being found that any material portion of reserves contemplated in (2) is no longer required, such amount should be credited to surplus account (to earned surplus, if the debit was to earned surplus) or, if included in the year's profit and loss statement, the amount should be described as an extraordinary item (not merely merged in the ordinary operations) and added to the net result from current operations for the year.

III. THE AUDITOR'S REPORT

THE EXAMINATION of the statements of a business or financial enterprise is, in the final analysis, but a stepping-stone to the preparation of a report by the independent auditor on the financial statements which are the subject of his review. In the case of large corporations with well-organized accounting departments the statements may be prepared by the client's staff and come to the auditor with the approval of the principal financial officer in practically the form in which it is expected they will be published to the stockholders or other interested parties, or be filed with the Securities and Exchange Commission or other regulatory bodies, or otherwise utilized. In the case of some concerns the statements may, in fact, be prepared by the auditor from the books after giving effect to the results of his examination, in which event he will naturally discuss with the client any adjustments which may have been made in the figures as shown on the face of the books, and the form of presentation to be used. As to any such adjustments, the auditor will naturally seek to obtain the concurrence of the client. In either event, the statements are regarded as the representations of the client. In the former event they are not only theoretically so but even physically so. In the latter event they are so because the client adopts them as his and decides whether they shall be promulgated.

In both instances the disclosure of all material facts essential to a proper understanding of the position of the enterprise and of the results of operations for the indicated period is most important. The standard of disclosure which should ever be before the auditor in considering his responsibilities when reporting on the statements is well stated in the requirement of the Securities Act of 1933 that as to "any part of the registration statement purporting to be made upon his authority as an expert or purporting to be a copy of or extract from a report . . . of himself as an expert, he had after reasonable investigation, reasonable ground to believe and did believe, at the time such part of the registration statement became effective, that the statements therein were true and that there was no omission to state a material fact required to be stated therein or necessary to make the statements therein not misleading. . . ."

There might seem to be cases where the question of disclosing data which is not obvious or implicit in the items of the financial statements themselves is rather academic because of the statements relating to the affairs of a close corporation or a partnership or proprietorship and all those who are likely to see the statements are already fully informed as to the affairs of the concern. Detailed disclosure might in such instances seem almost superfluous. Yet even in such instances the auditor must, if he makes no reservation or qualification in his report, require disclosure in the spirit of the requirement above quoted from the Securities Act because he can never know what use may be made of his report or into whose hands it may come.

Reliance on the apparent absence of privity of contract between the auditor and third parties into whose hands the report may come would be ill-advised. Especially where there are those who have an interest in the affairs of a closely held concern other than the direct management, as, for example, bank and merchandise creditors, it is of the utmost importance that all essential disclosures be made. Such disclosures may relate to many different circumstances as, for example, hypothecation of certain assets, commitments other than those in the ordinary course of business, contingent liabilities, restrictions on surplus arising out of bond indentures or holdings of treasury stock, most or all of which would not ordinarily appear on the face of the client's books of account.

Explanatory notes on, or appended to, financial statements are not in themselves a recent development. To some extent they have been used ever since the inclusion of certified financial statements in prospectuses or security offerings became at all general. However, the use, both in number and in scope, of notes appended to the balance sheet and the income statement received a stimulus from the passage of the Securities Act. The auditor, in taking seriously his responsibilities when certifying the financial statements to be included in registration statements, whether for new security issues or as annual reports required to be filed with the Securities and Exchange Commission, felt it essential that there be adequate disclosure of material information which would not normally or readily appear on the face of the formal financial statements but which is essential to an understanding of the position and operating results of the reporting company.

Directors and officers, also, and especially their counsel, have in most instances favored fullest disclosure of pertinent information in statements coming within the scope of the Securities Acts, so that there might be no question later as to anyone having been misled by lack of adequate disclosure of material facts and circumstances. Indeed, the question has been raised whether the precautions taken to make sure that no desirable disclosure has been omitted have not, in some instances at least, led to such a flood of explanatory notes that the financial statements proper are overshadowed by the volume of explanatory matter which must be studied at great length before the reader may draw dependable conclusions from the balance sheet and the income statement.

To some extent this is an illustration of the human tendency to go from one extreme to the other. Forty or fifty years ago reports to stockholders and bankers' prospectuses almost invariably contained extremely condensed financial statements, and the reader had to rely on his imagination to a considerable extent as to various phases of the company's financial position or its operations. A majority of the industrial corporations publishing reports at that time did not disclose the amount of their sales, and very often the income statement contained only a few items beginning with the operating profit after the manufacturing costs and selling and administrative expenses had been deducted from the sales.

The disclosure of essential information which can be made in the description of items on the face of the financial statements has undergone improvement, and in the ordinary case the nature or volume of it is not such as to raise any question as to the need for it. It is in respect of the notes appended to the balance sheet and income statement that the volume in some instances is such as to raise the question whether it may not defeat the purpose of the notes. In the words of the old adage, the woods cannot be seen for the trees.

Although the heavy responsibilities of the Securities Acts, and the tendency of the courts to bear down on the accountant and directors in respect of their legal liabilities to a degree which seems at times unreasonable, have naturally led to extreme caution to insure full disclosure of all material information, nevertheless a balanced viewpoint should prevail. In the first place, notes regarding nonessential or relatively immaterial matters should not be unduly elaborated; in fact, they should when feasible be excluded. Further, and this is still more important, explanatory notes should not be resorted to as an "out" in respect of items which ought to be adjusted. An item in either the balance sheet or income account which is in itself not properly stated cannot be satisfactorily dealt with by a note indicating that it has some other significance or should otherwise be interpreted than one would infer from a reading of the statements. In other words, as Mr. J. M. B. Hoxsey, who for so many years rendered such valuable service to the New York Stock Exchange, sometimes said, "A note reading that, assuming that two and two make five, such and such would be the result, is not a warranted substitute for correct treatment of an item in the financial statements."

As to reasonable disclosure of financial information to its stockholders, the annual reports of the United States Steel Corporation, practically from its organization some forty years ago, were regarded by accountants and other students of financial affairs as heralding the beginning of a better day. For a long time relatively few industrial corporations emulated its example. After the First World War, however, and particularly during the past decade, there was marked improvement, and it may be said that today there are a substantial number of corporations which put out reports containing financial statements that meet the requirements of: (a) sufficiently detailed presentation of both position and operations to give the stockholder an intelligent understanding of the results of the company's activities and of its present position, (b) satisfactory form of presentation, and (c) supplemental explanatory information required for the understanding of items in the financial statements which have special features, or for the presentation of matters which are still indeterminate or otherwise are not susceptible of definite inclusion in the formal statements.

I do not wish to imply that we have reached the ideal in respect of published corporate reports. Many companies have not yet attained the standard set by those who have led with a good example. I do wish to emphasize, however, that over the years there has been marked progress and that the improvement was already evident before the incidence of those influences which, during the past decade, have contributed substantially to improvement in both form and substance of published financial statements.

Evolution of the Auditor's "Certificate"

In the course of time auditors' reports have become broadly classified as being of either the long form or the short form of report, the latter being also colloquially referred to as a "certificate." The long form of report is not standardized and should not be, for it is to be used in those instances in which there are reasons for bringing to the client's attention varied information and details concerning the financial statements which have been under examination, such as particular features of the scope of the examination, significant developments calling for extended descriptive text, comments on the accounting methods in use, possible criticisms, suggestions respecting the treatment of various items or the improvement of the client's accounting methods, and so on. The report of this type should be anything but stereotyped. It relates to a particular engagement, with the circumstances peculiar to it, and should be framed accordingly. Obviously, it should be so organized and expressed that it will be informing and intelligible to the client and of real assistance to him.

A word or two of caution regarding the use of the long form of report may not be amiss. If the examination is limited in any way, or if the results are such that the auditor has any reservations or believes qualifications to be in order, the report should bring out the facts clearly. He should not rely on stating in his report merely the work done and leaving to inference the omission of other work which would be required for an unrestricted examination.

The short form of report or certificate grew out of the need for setting forth briefly the opinion of the auditor upon the financial statements submitted to stockholders, bond holders, banks, or others to whom the client wishes to submit primarily the financial statements. It was felt that the primary purpose of the auditor's report in such circumstances is to indicate that an examination had been made by an independent accountant, and that in his opinion the balance sheet and related statements of income and surplus set forth fairly the position of the corporation, partnership, or individual enterprise, and the results of its operations for a given period.

In the course of time a brief form developed which with minor modifications was widely used, and which read in substance as follows:

> We have examined the accounts of the Blank Company as at ...., 19......, and
>
> We certify that, in our opinion, the above balance sheet correctly sets forth the company's financial position on that date and the accompanying income account correctly summarizes the results of its operations for the year then ended.

When only a balance sheet was being published or otherwise utilized, the clause relating to the income account was omitted from the certificate.

In 1932 the Special Committee of the American Institute of Accountants on Cooperation with Stock Exchanges began a careful consideration of the general line of development of the activities of the New York Stock Exchange in relation to the annual reports of corporations. The work of the Institute Committee led to its recommendation of a form of auditor's report reading as follows:

> To the XYZ Company:
>
> We have made an examination of the balance sheet of the XYZ Company as at December 31, 1933, and of the statement of income and surplus for the year 1933. In connection therewith, we examined or tested accounting records of the Company and other supporting evidence and obtained information and explanations from officers and employees of the Company; we also made a general review of the accounting methods and of the operating and income accounts for the year, but we did not make a detailed audit of the transactions.
>
> In our opinion, based upon such examination, the accompanying balance-sheet and related statement of income and surplus fairly present, in accordance with accepted principles of accounting consistently maintained by the Company during the year under review, its position at December 31, 1933, and the results of its operations for the year.

The publication of this form of report or certificate by the Institute included the following notes regarding its use:

Notes

1. It is contemplated that before signing a report of the type suggested, the accountant should have at least made an examination of the character outlined in the bulletin, "Verification of Financial Statements," as interpreted in the communication of the Committee on Stock List to the Governing Committee dated October 24, 1933.

2. The report should be addressed to the directors of the company or to the stockholders, if the appointment is made by them.

3. The statement of what has been examined would, of course, conform to the titles of the accounts or statements reported upon.

4. In the second sentence, any special forms of confirmation could be mentioned: e.g., "including confirmation of cash and securities by inspection or certificates from depositaries."

5. This certificate is appropriate only if the accounting for the year is consistent in basis with that for the preceding year. If there has been any material change either in accounting principles or in the manner of their application, the nature of the change should be indicated.

6. It is contemplated that the form of report would be modified when and as necessary to embody any qualifications, reservations or supplementary explanations.

This report was so framed as to constitute answers to the following questions:

1. Whether, in the auditor's opinion, the form of the balance sheet and of the income, or profit and loss account, is such as fairly to present the financial position and the results of operation;

2. Whether the accounts, in the auditor's opinion, are fairly determined on the basis of consistent application of the system of accounting regularly employed by the company;

3. Whether, in the auditor's opinion, such system of accounting conforms to accepted accounting practices.

It was felt that the auditor's report or certificate should make it clear that a detailed audit had not been made, even though it might well be assumed that the business and investing public would so understand. Consequently, there was inserted in the suggested form of report, after the description in general terms of the scope of the examination, the clause "but we did not make a detailed audit of the transactions."

It is interesting to note that the Chairman of the Committee of the Controllers' Institute of America on Stock Exchange Relations, with which committee the Exchange also conferred, expressed himself warmly in favor of a standard form of certificate, one paragraph in the committee's communication to the Exchange reading as follows:

> We recognize the fact that agreement on terminology is always very difficult, because most people have certain preferences of language, and for this reason, we can see that agreement by public accountants on a particular form may not be easy to secure. We urge, however, that the Stock Exchange stress the necessity for such uniformity of language as to the major body of the certificate with the committee of the American Institute of Accountants, so that as far as possible all accounting firms will use the same language for the main part of their certificate. The wording of specific exceptions and qualifications, we appreciate, would naturally have to be left to the individual firms, since standardization to that extent we do not believe to be practicable.

The suggested standard short form of report (certificate) met with almost instant and widespread acceptance. Although the final communication containing the suggested form and the correspondence which preceded its adoption [1] were not published until January 21, 1934, the suggested form was used for the great majority of reports published by listed companies for the calendar year 1933.

This form of report continued in general use until 1939. At that time a special committee of the American Institute of Accountants, appointed after the McKesson & Robbins development, recommended the following "Short Form of Independent Certified Public Accountant's Report or Opinion":

[1] Published in pamphlet form by the American Institute of Accountants under the title of *Audits of Corporate Accounts*.

To the Board of Directors (or Stockholders) of the XYZ Company:

We have examined the balance-sheet of the XYZ Company as of April 30, 1939, and the statements of income and surplus for the fiscal year then ended, have reviewed the system of internal control and the accounting procedures of the company and, without making a detailed audit of the transactions, have examined or tested accounting records of the company and other supporting evidence by methods and to the extent we deemed appropriate.

In our opinion, the accompanying balance-sheet and related statements of income and surplus present fairly the position of the XYZ Company at April 30, 1939, and the results of its operations for the fiscal year, in conformity with generally accepted accounting principles applied on a basis consistent with that of the preceding year.

The Committee emphasized that "while the proposed form is submitted as a standard, it is not prescribed or recommended for invariable use but should be adapted to the needs of the particular case."

Aside from some minor improvements in phraseology, the revised form in my judgment does not represent any marked improvement of the form promulgated in 1934, or convey any greater understanding to the lay reader concerning the nature of the examination or of the opinion expressed by the accountant on the financial statements. The first paragraph of the 1939 form, in slightly different language, has the same content as the corresponding paragraph of the 1934 form: (a) it identifies the financial statements which have been the subject of the examination; (b) it describes the general character of the examination, viz., by audit tests and a review of the accounting methods; and (c) it emphasizes that a detailed audit was not made. In addition, the 1939 revision stressed the obvious, viz., that the examination was by methods and to the extent which accorded with the judgment of the accountant.

It was first proposed to eliminate from the revised form the explicit statement that the examination did not include a detailed audit of the transactions, the committee's thought being that a sufficient period had elapsed since the adoption of the 1934 form to make further use of this emphasis unnecessary. It is interesting that some expressions of opinion, not only from within but also from without the profession, indicated a feeling that a longer period of education of the business and investing public was desirable, and the substance of the phrase was therefore continued in the revised form.

The second paragraph of the 1939 revision embodied two changes from the 1934 form: One was the elimination of the phrase "based upon such examination" which was inserted in the original form to link explicitly the opinion with the examination described in the previous paragraph; the other was the explicit relation of consistency of the latest statements (as to the application of generally accepted accounting principles) to the corresponding statements of the preceding year. The latter was deemed desirable in the interest of precision; it seemed better than reliance upon the note which had been promulgated as one of six explanatory notes with the 1934 form of the report. That note reads as follows:

> This certificate is appropriate only if the accounting for the year is consistent in basis with that for the preceding year. If there has been any material change either in accounting principles or in the manner of their application, the nature of the change should be indicated.

When the Federal Trade Commission, which was originally charged with the administration of the Securities Act, promulgated its first rules and regulations relating to that act, it included therein the following article in respect of the auditor's certificate:

> Any certificate by an independent certified or public accountant with respect to any part of the registration statement, any papers or documents used in connection therewith, shall be dated and shall state that such accountant . . . has, after reasonable investigation, reasonable grounds to believe, and does believe, at the time of the date of such

certificate, that the statements therein are true and that there is no omission to state a material fact required to be stated therein or necessary to make the statements therein not misleading, except as specifically noted.

If in any case such accountant . . . is unable to satisfy himself concerning the correctness of any item in the said part of the registration statement, papers or documents, he shall refer to such items in his certificate and give appropriate explanation thereof.

If anything comes to the attention of such accountant . . . or he obtains knowledge of any facts before the effective date of registration which would make any of the material items therein untrue or indicate that there was an omission to state a material fact required to be stated or necessary to make the statements therein not misleading, he shall bring such immediately to the attention of the Commission.

In determining what constitutes reasonable investigation and reasonable grounds for belief, the standard of reasonableness shall be that required of a person occupying a fiduciary relationship.

Where a partnership of certified or public accountants certifies to a registration statement or any part thereof or any document used in connection therewith, the certificate shall be signed with the partnership name and by a member thereof.

Some months later the Commission amended the first paragraph of the article quoted above to read as follows:

Any certificate by an independent certified or public accountant with respect to a registration statement or any papers or documents used in connection therewith shall be dated and shall conclude with a statement substantially to the following effect:

> "Subject to the foregoing comments, we have, after reasonable investigation, reasonable grounds to believe, and do believe, at the date of this certificate, that the statements contained in the attached balance sheets and in the attached profit and loss statements truly and fairly reflect the application of accepted accounting practice to the facts disclosed by our investigation, and that there is no omission to state a material fact required to be stated therein or necessary to make the statements therein not misleading."

It will be noted that the Federal Trade Commission sought to have the auditor's certificate include language similar to that used in Article 11 of the Securities Act, to which I have already referred as establishing broadly the standard of disclosure to be followed in the preparation of financial statements.

Upon the passage of the Securities Exchange Act in 1934, the Securities and Exchange Commission succeeded the Federal Trade Commission as administrator of the Securities Act of 1933, as well as of the Securities Exchange Act.

The onerous nature of the liability provisions of the 1933 Act was charged by financiers and businessmen with being responsible for impeding public financing. The new Securities and Exchange Commission under the vigorous leadership of its chairman had a study made of the situation and revised the forms, instructions, and general rules and regulations for the administration of the Securities Act. In addition it prepared those applicable to the newly enacted Securities Exchange Act. In this study and in the formulation of recommendations to the Commission, which it adopted for the purpose of breaking the "log jam" affecting financing, a member of the faculty of the Harvard Graduate School of Business Administration, Dr. T. H. Sanders, rendered important service.

The Securities and Exchange Commission abandoned the rule of the Federal Trade Commission which, as already indicated, prescribed at least a portion of the language to be used in the auditor's certificate when appended to financial statements filed with the Commission, and promulgated the following rule:

> The certificate of the accountant or accountants shall be dated, shall be reasonably comprehensive as to the scope of the audit made, and shall state clearly the opinion of the accountant or accountants in respect of the financial statements of, and the accounting principles and procedures followed by, the person or persons whose statements are furnished. In certifying to the financial statements, independent public or independent certified public accountants may give due weight to an internal system of audit regularly maintained by means of auditors employed on the registrant's own staff. In such case the independent accountants shall review the accounting procedures followed by the

registrant and its subsidiaries and by appropriate measures shall satisfy themselves that such accounting procedures are in fact being followed. Nothing in this rule shall be construed to imply authority for the omission of any procedure which independent public accountants would ordinarily employ in the course of a regular annual audit. The certificate of the accountant or accountants shall be applicable to the matter in the registration statement proper to which a reference is required in the financial statements.

Following the adoption of this rule, the Commission accepted registration statements in which the financial statements bore the certificate of accountants in the customary Institute form, amplified by either explanations or qualifications, when called for by the circumstances of a particular case.

In the report of the Securities and Exchange Commission on its investigation in the matter of McKesson & Robbins, Inc., the Commission expressed its views concerning the principles on which it believed the form and content of the auditor's certificate should be based. Subsequently, it revised its rule (effective March 1, 1941) regarding the contents of accountants' certificates appended to financial statements filed with the Commission pursuant to the several securities acts and similar legislation, so as to read as follows:

(a) *Technical requirements*

The accountant's certificate shall be dated, shall be signed manually, and shall identify without detailed enumeration the financial statements covered by the certificate.

(b) *Representations as to the audit*

The accountant's certificate (i) shall contain a reasonably comprehensive statement as to the scope of the audit made including, if with respect to significant items in the financial statements any auditing procedures generally recognized as normal have been omitted, a specific designation of such procedures and of the reasons for their omission; (ii) shall state whether the audit was made in accordance with generally accepted auditing standards applicable in the circumstances; and (iii) shall state whether the audit made omitted any procedure deemed necessary by the accountant under the circumstances of the particular case.

In determining the scope of the audit necessary, appropriate consideration shall be given to the adequacy of the system of internal check and control. Due weight may be given to an internal system of audit regularly maintained by means of auditors employed on the registrant's own staff. The accountant shall review the accounting procedures followed by the person or persons whose statements are certified and by appropriate measures shall satisfy himself that such accounting procedures are in fact being followed.

Nothing in this rule shall be construed to imply authority for the omission of any procedure which independent accountants would ordinarily employ in the course of an audit made for the purpose of expressing the opinions required by paragraph (c) of this rule.

(c) *Opinions to be expressed*

The accountant's certificate shall state clearly:

(i) the opinion of the accountant in respect of the financial statements covered by the certificate and the accounting principles and practices reflected therein;

(ii) the opinion of the accountant as to any change in accounting principles or practices, or adjustments of the accounts, required to be set forth by rule 3-07; and

(iii) the nature of, and the opinion of the accountant as to, any significant differences between the accounting principles and practices reflected in the financial statements and those reflected in the accounts after the entry of adjustments for the period under review.

(d) *Exceptions*

Any matters to which the accountant takes exception shall be clearly identified, the exception thereto specifically and clearly stated, and, to the extent practicable, the effect of each such exception on the related financial statements given.

One material change in the rule, it will be noted, was the requirement that, "if with respect to significant items in the financial statements any auditing procedures generally recognized as normal have been omitted, a specific designation of such procedures and of the reasons for their omission" shall be included in the auditor's statement of the scope of his examination. A similar requirement had been recommended in the original report of the special committee of the American Institute of Accountants on auditing procedure which had been appointed immediately after the disclosure of the McKesson & Robbins conspiracy. Upon further consideration, however, the committee came to the conclusion that such a requirement would not be desirable and stated in its later report that it is the responsibility of the accountant — and one which he cannot escape — to determine the scope of the examination which he should make before giving his opinion on the statements under review. If in his judgment it is not practicable and reasonable in the circumstances of a given engagement to undertake the auditing procedures regarding inventories and/or receivables set forth in this report as generally accepted procedure, and he has satisfied himself by other methods regarding such inventories and/or receivables, no useful purpose will be served by requiring an explanation in his report. If physical tests of inventories and/or confirmation of receivables are practicable and reasonable and the auditor has omitted such generally accepted auditing procedure, he should make a clear-cut exception in his report.

Unfortunately the Commission did not seem to grasp the underlying philosophy of the Institute committee's mature conclusion, namely, that to state in the auditor's certificate that a given procedure had not been considered practicable and reasonable, even though satisfactory reasons for the omission be given, merely tends to confuse the reader of the certificate. The average reader would certainly not be able to determine from such a statement whether the omission was justified. Even another accountant would hesitate to say whether, despite the explanation given, the omission was justified without some examination on his part into the circumstances of the particular case. All of which leads up to the query of what useful purpose is served by seeking, in effect, to have the reader of the certificate attempt to form an opinion as to the adequacy or otherwise of the scope of the examination. No amount of regulation can supply lack of competency or integrity in performing professional service. Loss of professional standing — the severest form of loss to the practitioner — is the penalty for the former, and the liabilities of the law are the penalty for the latter.

Another material change in the Commission's rule was the addition of the requirement that in his certificate the auditor "shall state whether the audit was made in accordance with accepted auditing standards applicable in the circumstances." In the Commission's release accompanying its promulgation of the revised rule regarding accountants' certificates, it was explained that "in referring to generally accepted auditing standards the Commission has in mind, in addition to the employment of generally recognized normal auditing procedures, their application with professional competence by properly trained persons."

It seems strange that the Commission, the membership of which includes men with a professional background, such as lawyers, should have considered it necessary to require the accountant to emphasize his professional competence. It would seem rather odd if a lawyer in writing his opinion on a real estate title were to include therein a solemn statement to the effect that he was competent to examine real estate titles or that he had conducted his examination in a professionally competent manner. I cannot imagine an engineer who is making a report on his examination into the soundness of a bridge or other engineering project including therein a paragraph emphasizing his competence as an engineer and the performance of his engagement in accordance with accepted engineering standards. Surely, a doctor or surgeon called in as a consultant to express an opinion on the diagnosis of a difficult case of illness would not feel that in making a written report thereon he need include any statement of his professional competence or that he had made his examination of the patient in accordance with accepted medical or surgical standards applicable in the circumstances.

A physician was recently sued in New Jersey for damages by the parents of a child who contended that he had not handled the case properly. One of the experts for the defense, a man of eminent reputation in the particular field of medicine in which the case arose, testified, as stated in a newspaper report of the trial, that "Doctor ——— (the defendant) had in his (the witness's) opinion exercised the degree of knowledge, skill, and care usual in the general practice of medicine." The quoted sentence seems to me to state in a minimum of words the implied representation that any practitioner, not merely in medicine but in any profession, whether law, engineering, or accounting, makes when he undertakes to serve a client professionally, namely, professional competence and such performance as may be reasonably expected in the circumstances of the case. A specific statement thereof in the accountant's certificate seems superfluous and merely results in burdening the certificate with unnecessary phraseology.

In the endeavor, however, to cooperate as fully as possible with the Commission, the American Institute of Accountants waived the objections which it saw to the aforementioned requirements of the Commission's revised rule, and proposed the addition of the following sentence to the first paragraph of the 1939 form of Institute certificate:

> In our opinion, our examination was made in accordance with generally accepted auditing standards applicable in the circumstances and included all procedures which we considered necessary.

In further discussions between representatives of the Institute and of the Commission, the former emphasized the fact that the proposed addition to the Institute form of certificate must be based on opinion. The Commission, without questioning that fact, indicated that it regarded the new sentence as "a positive representation consistent with the implied representation he (the auditor) makes by holding himself out as a professional and expert accountant or auditor," and said that the proposed use of the words "in our opinion" appeared to be inconsistent with Section (b) (ii) of the revised rule.

In order to avoid an impasse with the Commission and upon being advised by counsel that, regardless of whether the statement was made categorically (without the use of the words, "in our opinion"), or specifically as a matter of opinion, it could be in fact only a statement of opinion, the Institute decided not to pursue the matter further. Consequently, accountants omit the words "in our opinion" from the aforementioned new sentence added to the 1939 Institute form of certificate, in respect of financial statements filed with the Commission since the effective date of the revised rule.

The question has naturally been considered by practicing accountants whether this addition to the Institute form of certificate should be confined to those cases in which the financial statements are filed with the Securities and Exchange Commission or whether it should be used generally whenever the short form of report (certificate) is appropriate. Unless the Commission feels led in the near future to reconsider its present position, it would seem likely that the amplified form of certificate will come into general use. Clients whose securities are listed on a stock exchange, and who must therefore file reports annually with the Commission, would probably wish to have the identical form of certificate used in such reports and in their published reports to stockholders. This in turn seems likely to lead to the use of the amplified form of certificate in reports to stockholders, or other interested parties, of companies whose securities are not listed. Such clients would presumably wish to have the auditor's certificate in their case read similarly to that appearing in the published reports of large companies of high standing in the business world. Here, too, as in respect of other matters of interest to the independent auditor, provisions of the securities acts and the regulatory requirements of the Securities and Exchange Commission will tend to influence the standards of accounting practice, not only in the case of companies coming within the Commission's jurisdiction but in the business and financial world generally.

Consistency of Application of Accounting Principles

In my opinion one of the most important statements ever included in an auditor's report or certificate was one which was made part of the form promulgated by the Institute in 1934. The accountant's opinion thereafter was to indicate whether the financial statements fairly presented the company's position and results of operations "in accordance with accepted principles of accounting consistently maintained by the company during the year under review." One of the explanatory notes for the use of the new form of certificate made it clear that the mention of consistency had particular reference to consistency in basis with that for the preceding year, and emphasized that if there has been any material change, either in accounting principles or in the manner of their application, the nature of the change should be indicated.

As one analyzes the nature of so-called accounting principles, it becomes evident that consistency in their application, coupled with disclosure of any change which appears warranted, is in a sense even more important than in the selection or application of a principle or one of its variations in a given case. Accounting "principles," as understood by the practicing accountant, mean as stated in one of Webster's definitions, "a general or settled rule or ground of action." Such principles are born out of reasoning from circumstances to a practical conclusion, and out of the experience of businessmen and accountants.

In considering accounting principles and their application, cognizance may well be taken of the following observations by President Emeritus Lowell of Harvard University in his book on *Conflicts of Principle*, written during the past decade:

> What appears as a universal principle is in fact often true only within the limits of the conditions in which it is properly applied, and becomes partially true, or altogether inapplicable, under new and unfamiliar circumstances. Yet we find a difficulty in emancipating ourselves from a conviction of its absoluteness and tend to rely upon it as an infallible guide where it is so no longer. . . .
>
> Considerations like these induce one to reflect upon the limited nature of principles commonly accepted as universal; upon the conflicts that arise when two inconsistent principles of that kind come into collision; and how far such conflicts may be avoided by recognizing that there are limits, with a debatable region in which neither can be rigorously applied.
>
> . . . Without attempting to assert that there are no propositions of absolutely universal application, it is enough for our purpose to say that many are commonly stated as universal when in fact they are not. . . .[1]

Although what I have quoted from President Lowell was written with quite a different purpose from that for which I have referred to it, I believe it has pertinency because of its caution against regarding a "principle" as being necessarily universal and capable of only one application. An accounting example of wide variation in application is the principle of "cost or market, whichever is lower" for determining the inventory amount to be used in stating both balance sheet and income statement. "Cost" in such case may be arrived at by a variety of methods, among them: specific costs, average cost, first-in — first-out, and last-in — first-out. Any one of these methods may be appropriate in a given situation, and in some situations the circumstances may be such that more than one may be suitably used.

[1] Cambridge, Harvard University Press, 1932, pp. 4, 5, 10.

It is at this point that consistency of application becomes vital. If the same cost method be followed from year to year the operating results, in so far as they are affected by the inventories at beginning and end of each fiscal period, are on a comparable basis. If, however, the inventory at the end of one period (and consequently for the beginning of the next period) has been stated on the basis of first-in — first-out, and at the end of the next period on the basis of last-in — first-out, the results of operations shown in the income statements of the two periods will certainly not be on a comparable basis and may be positively misleading. In such a case there must be disclosure of the change of basis and if the statements are to be truly informing, the income statement relating to the year of change should give, at least approximately, the effect of the change of basis. Also, in the auditor's certificate the change will have to be noted as an exception to the consistency of application of accepted principles of accounting, even though the change in inventory practice may be one of which he heartily approves.

The shift in emphasis from the balance sheet to the income statement, which has been so noticeable during the past two decades, has placed a premium on consistency in applying accounting principles to the stating of financial position and, especially, to the determination of operating results, and on the importance of adequate disclosure when a material departure from consistency has occurred, even though there may have been good reason therefor.

Audit Limitations

Forty years ago only a small percentage of business concerns had their accounts regularly audited. Today practically all companies with any public interest have periodical audits, either because it is required by statute or other applicable regulations, or because it has become recognized as good business practice. Today many companies in which there is little or no direct public interest follow the same practice. Even in the minds of those who are clients of the professional auditor, there has at times been a lack of understanding of just what should be the scope of the audit in normal circumstances and the purposes of having the statements "certified."

To many a layman "an audit is an audit," and many may have tacitly assumed that the work of the accountant involved verification or review of all the recorded transactions of the year. If some irregularity occurred in the petty cash, why didn't the auditor discover it? An irregularity of larger amount which, as a result of collusion or of other untoward circumstances, was not detected in the course of an audit of ordinary scope may have led to the query, why wasn't it discovered by the auditor?

It is well to bear in mind that no matter how ready the accountant may be to bear all the responsibilities that are properly his, there are practical limitations on both the scope and results of an audit conducted in normal circumstances and for the purpose of certifying the financial statements of a business corporation. In the first place, with the growth of business concerns during the last half century, it is obvious that for the great majority of them it is not a practical proposition to examine the records of all the transactions which have occurred during the year. Thus as a practical development has arisen the practice already discussed of making audits on the basis of testing and sampling the accounts, and with considerable reliance on the system of internal check and control.

With the widespread public interest in business enterprises today, the review of the accounting policies followed by a corporation and the determination whether its accounts represent the consistent application of sound accounting principles are recognized as of outstanding importance, and this part of the accountant's work may consume a considerable part of the time devoted to a given engagement. It is significant that in the course of the seven years during which the Securities and Exchange Commission has been reviewing the registration statements filed with it under the Securities Act (security issues) and the Securities Exchange Act (security listings and corporate annual reports) the questions which the Commission has raised regarding financial statements have in only a few instances been the result of financial irregularities as such but have dealt largely with the propriety or otherwise of the application of accounting principles to various circumstances and transactions of the registrants.

The necessity for recognizing both the value and the limitations of an audit was well stated in an address by Mr. George O. May fifteen years ago, when speaking to the Society of Certified Public Accountants of the State of New Jersey on the subject of "A Proper Courage in the Assumption of Responsibility by the Accountant." Mr. May, whose brilliant mind and wise counsel have served the profession so well, said *inter alia:*

> . . . An audit is a safeguard; the maintenance of this safeguard entails an expense; and this expense can be justified only if the value of the safeguard is found to be fully commensurate with its cost. The cost of an audit so extensive as to be a complete safeguard would be enormous and far beyond any value to be derived from it. A superficial audit is dangerous because of the sense of false security which it creates. Between the two extremes there lies a mean at which the audit abundantly justifies its cost.
>
> The problem is to determine this happy mean, to insure that the auditor does not fall short of a reasonable discharge of his duties, and the investor or lender does not attribute to the audit a greater significance than it can, as a practical matter, possess. And it must be recognized that skilled dishonesty, especially collusive dishonesty, may at times and for a time deceive even the auditor who conducts what is regarded as a reasonable audit, and that this should be so is not to be regarded as a defect in the system, since, as I have said, audit procedure represents a balancing of the consideration of risks on the one side and

cost on the other. As a matter of fact, investors and lenders need protection against deliberate dishonesty less than protection against unsound practices and undue optimism. . . .

It will be noted from the foregoing quotation that the final determination of what is a reasonable scope of an examination which will serve as a basis for an expression of the auditor's opinion in financial statements must rest on his judgment.

The practical limitations on an audit were well stated in a report by the Stock List Subcommittee on Independent Audits and Audit Procedure of the New York Stock Exchange in August, 1939. After emphasizing the importance of that part of the accountant's work which relates to the application of sound accounting principles to the factual data which form the base of the financial statements, the Subcommittee went on to discuss the audit phase of the accountant's work, as follows:

. . . In the case of large modern companies, the aggregate expense to industry of extremely detailed examinations of the voluminous material, by independent accountants, would be out of all proportion to the possible benefits to be gained in the occasional detection of irregularities in a few concerns. Most companies are honestly run, and the huge expense which would be incurred by all for detection of occasional misrepresentations in the few would in the aggregate be an economic waste to investors and to the public.

Even when this cost is not weighed in relation to American business as a whole, but only in relation to a single large modern concern, it is doubtful if even a most detailed examination would be a complete safeguard. The recent audit of McKesson & Robbins ordered by the Trustee following disclosure of the Coster-Musica frauds is probably one of the most detailed audits ever made of a large industrial concern by independent public accountants. Independent engineers were retained to examine and test check the quantity, quality and pricing of the inventory and many months were spent in an examination of hundreds of thousands of items and tens of thousands of pages of records. Even this audit could not cover all transactions, and the independent auditor's report included the customary phrase: "But we did not make a detailed audit of the transactions." We mention this only to indicate the burden which would be placed on corporations if all transactions were to be audited in detail.

The May, 1939, issue of the *Journal of Accountancy* contained an editorial in which consideration was given to the paper by Dr. Jules I. Bogen on "An Objective Appraisal of the Independent Audit," to which paper reference was made earlier in these lectures.[1] The editor summed up the matter succinctly when he said:

> Two courses are open to the (accounting) profession, and we believe that both are being followed: (1) continually to extend and improve auditing procedure so far as it may be reasonable and practicable to do so; (2) to educate the public to an understanding of auditing, and the essential, unavoidable limitations of the work of auditors.[2]

The latter course is in some ways the more difficult of the two. The American Institute of Accountants is diligently carrying on this effort for the education of the investing public. Its two pamphlet publications, *Financial Statements —What They Mean* and *Accounting and Your Pocketbook*, are useful contributions toward this end.

Accounting Research

One of the important, as well as significant, developments in the field of accounting in the last few years is the establishment of the Bureau of Research by the American Institute of Accountants. The Committee on Accounting Procedure of the Institute has the responsibility for directing the work of the accounting research bureau and for issuing the bulletins which set forth the opinions or conclusions of the Committee in respect of matters which have been the subject of study. A director of research is in immediate charge of this work. Dr. T. H. Sanders, a member of the faculty of the Harvard Graduate School of Business

[1] See p. 17.
[2] Vol. LXVII, No. 5, p. 259.

Administration, is serving in this capacity and has rendered valuable service in the planning and initiation of the research program.[1]

This research activity of the Institute arose from the conviction on the part of practitioners that it would be helpful to the profession, in considering principles or rules of practice where a diversity of procedure had developed, even when alternative practices were recognized as having justification in different circumstances, to narrow the diversity and, so far as possible, to find a basis for a principle or rule of universal application.

The matters which form the subject of research or consideration by the Institute's Committee on Accounting Procedure have a very direct relation to the work of the auditor because they bear on the basis for the opinion expressed in the standard form of short report that the statements present fairly the position of the concern and the results of operations "in conformity with generally accepted accounting principles." It is for the purpose of seeking clarification of, and as far as possible unity in the application of, principles that research activities are being carried on.

A number of important subjects which have been studied by the Bureau of Accounting Research and the Institute Committee have been covered by bulletins thus far issued by the Committee. As illustrations of the research activities of the Institute, reference may be made to three subjects, two of them where definite conclusions were expressed and another where the subject is still "in work." One of the two matters first referred to is that of foreign operations and foreign exchange on which a bulletin was issued in December, 1939. This bulletin was in response to a need arising out

[1] Since these lectures were delivered Dr. Sanders has resigned in order to enter upon war service at Washington. The present director of research is Professor James L. Dohr, a member of the faculty of the School of Business at Columbia University.

of a situation which had been cumulating for some years prior to the outbreak of the present war but which became still more acute after September, 1939, and which called for prompt consideration so that the Committee's views might come to the members of the Institute and the profession at large in time for use in examinations to be made of 1939 financial statements. It is encouraging to note that, although there has at times been criticism of the deliberation with which accountants reach a conclusion in matters where differences of opinion exist, it was possible in the particular instance to consider the situation with dispatch, to formulate various suggestions for dealing with the problem, and to reach conclusions which could be made the subject of a bulletin to the members of the Institute.

When, in the early part of the twentieth century, consolidated balance sheets and income accounts came rapidly into general use by corporations having subsidiaries, no distinction was observed between domestic and foreign subsidiaries. It was the general assumption, and quite justifiably so in the circumstances of the times, that the same basic consideration which made the inclusion of the accounts of one or more domestic subsidiaries in consolidated statements desirable similarly made the inclusion of foreign subsidiaries desirable. At that time there were no substantial restrictions on trade in any part of the world and between different nations, with the exception of tariffs, the effect of which was generally understood. Currency restrictions were practically unknown at that time, and currencies in general commercial use had a reasonably well-established value which did not fluctuate widely in their relation to each other. Relatively slight exchange fluctuations had the effect of starting the flow of gold in one direction or the other so that a corrective process was promptly set in motion. In these circumstances the business activities, the availability of profits for distribution, and the realizability of assets in the liquidation of a business were not fundamentally different in the case of foreign subsidiaries from subsidiaries operating in the home country.

During the decade immediately following the First World War there were radical fluctuations in currency values, and this introduced an added risk and difficulty in carrying on business in foreign countries. Even at that, however, the consolidating of accounts of foreign subsidiaries with those of the parent company in the published statements was in large part continued, though some questions began to be raised as to whether a distinction between the business of foreign and domestic subsidiaries had not developed which might make a different method of treatment desirable. In the 1930's the blocking of currencies and other restrictions on foreign business and foreign investments caused the question to become more acute. When war broke out in September, 1939, there were still further restrictions and still greater uncertainties as to the status of foreign investments and the availability of profits that might be apparently earned by foreign subsidiaries. The time had clearly arrived to reconsider the propriety of including the results of operations and the assets and liabilities of foreign subsidiaries or branches in the consolidated statements of American companies in the same manner as had been generally followed in the past. It was evident that, had the same conditions existed a generation ago (when consolidated statements were so rapidly coming into use) as today, it is most unlikely that foreign subsidiaries would have been consolidated in the same manner as domestic subsidiaries. The solution was not so simple, however, as merely untying the knot and putting the situation back in a position where a brand new solution could be generally applied.

The conclusion of the Committee was that disclosure of the essential facts was of the essence of any solution. Consequently, the following alternatives were suggested:

(a) To exclude foreign subsidiaries from consolidation and to furnish: (1) statements in which only domestic subsidiaries would be consolidated; and (2) as to foreign subsidiaries, a summary in suitable form of their assets and liabilities, their income and losses for the year, and the parent company's equity therein. The aggregate amount of investments in foreign subsidiaries should be shown separately, and the basis on which the amount was arrived at should be stated. If these investments include any amount of surplus of foreign subsidiaries and such surplus had previously been included in consolidated surplus, the amount should be separately shown or earmarked in stating the consolidated surplus in the statements here suggested. The exclusion of foreign subsidiaries from consolidation does not make it permissible to include inter-company profits which would be eliminated if such subsidiaries were consolidated.

(b) To consolidate domestic and foreign subsidiaries as hitherto, and to furnish in addition the summary described in (a) (2) above.

(c) To furnish: (1) complete consolidated statements, and also (2) consolidated statements for domestic companies only.

(d) To consolidate domestic and foreign subsidiaries as hitherto, and to furnish in addition parent company statements showing investment in and income from foreign subsidiaries separate from those of domestic subsidiaries.[1]

The second of the two matters above referred to is that of depreciation on appreciation of fixed assets. Considerable diversity in depreciation treatment had arisen during the decade of the 1920's when the practice of reflecting on the books apparent appreciation in property value reached its peak. Some concerns charged into the income statement of each period a depreciation allowance based on the appreciated or written-up value, but probably the greater number charged into the income statement only that part of the depreciation allowance which related to the cost of the property, and charged against the revaluation surplus (set up when the write-up for the appreciation was made) that part of the depreciation allowance which related to the appre-

[1] *Accounting Research Bulletins*, No. 4 (December, 1939), "Foreign Operations and Foreign Exchange," pp. 30–31.

ciation. Sometimes the full amount of the depreciation allowance on the written-up value was charged to current operations, but before stating the net income for the period a credit was brought into the income statement by transfer thereto of a portion of the revaluation surplus equivalent to the portion of the depreciation allowance for the current fiscal period relating to the appreciation reflected in the accounts.

In its bulletin on this subject the Committee took the definite position that ordinarily it is not desirable that property values be written up in the accounts but that, if for special reasons this nevertheless be done, it then follows that depreciation allowances on the full appreciated property amounts should be charged to operations. This pronouncement of the Committee appears to have been generally accepted in the profession.

Another subject which is being studied by the research bureau is the accounting treatment of inventories from both the balance sheet and the income statement points of view. Preliminary statements on the subject by the research bureau have appeared in the *Journal of Accountancy* for June and October, 1940, and the results of a questionnaire circulated among the members of the Institute's committee on accounting procedure were published in the April, 1941, issue of the *Journal*. The results of the questionnaire indicated that considerable further study would be necessary for the purpose of clarifying the numerous considerations entering into the accounting treatment of inventories and of stating more definitely the basic inventory principles and the procedures for their application in the accounting treatment of inventories.

IV. CONCLUSION

In bringing to a close this dissertation on auditing development during the first forty years of the twentieth century, and in considering the duty of the independent auditor in the years ahead, I cannot do better than to refer once more to the writings of Sir Arthur Lowes Dickinson. He closed his book on *Accounting Practice and Procedure* with the following paragraphs:

> In concluding this review of accounting practice and procedure, and the duties and responsibilities of the public accountant in relation thereto, it may not be out of place to call attention to the mental qualifications required by one who essays to attack and determine accounting problems.
>
> These are: ability, coupled with tact and honesty, to ascertain facts without friction and with impartiality; a mind unbiased by previous conceptions, and free to reach independent and reliable conclusions of fact; and a will strong enough to maintain such conclusions against the arguments, opinions, or desires of opponents interested in some opposite or inconsistent conclusion, and yet to adapt such parts of their arguments as may throw new light on the questions at issue. With such qualities, and with the added technical training and practical experience which are equally necessary, the individual is in fact an accountant qualified to deal with the many questions herein discussed, and to add new principles to those which it has been the endeavor to illustrate and explain in this volume.[1]

What I have just quoted from Sir Arthur is as vital and timely today as when it was first written over a quarter century ago.

[1] New York, The Ronald Press Company, 1920 (Sixth Printing), p. 249.

SURPLUS AND DIVIDENDS

I

SURPLUS

SOMEWHAT in the position am I of the youth who delivered an essay on the occasion of his graduation from high school. He began his paper as follows: "The subject announced for my essay was Shakespeare. However, on studying the subject this seemed too narrow a field, and I have changed the title of my essay to God, Man, and Shakespeare." Dean Donham, when he invited me to deliver these lectures, suggested as a subject "Dividends." But, like the high school graduate, I desired a wider field, and have combined the topic suggested by your Dean with another suggested by Professor Sanders, and will discuss Surplus and Dividends. Not insisting on three, I am content with two subjects for these talks.

One might indeed have used a threefold title, "Capital, Surplus, and Dividends," for one cannot well discuss "Surplus" without some idea of the nature of "Capital," to which Surplus is used in contradistinction.

Capital

It must be noted that capital, as used by economists, has a meaning distinct from that proper to accounting. In economics, capital refers to assets, wealth used to produce or acquire additional wealth. Accountants sometimes, and all too often, use capital with a content similar to the economic meaning, as in the phrases "capital assets" and "capital expenditure." This is confusing. In the technical accounting jargon, capital is a credit account, denoting proprietorship, while "capital assets" are debits — indicating something owned — and never the twain shall meet.

Much discussion has there been as to whether capital, as used in accounting as well as in jurisprudence, is *res* or *quantum*. One brilliant jurist has felicitously phrased the definition by saying capital is a "mathematical limitation," which, if I do not misinterpret the law Latin, is about the same (but expressed in terms which even an accountant may understand) as saying it is *quantum*, not *res*.

Capital was originally used in the accounts of an individual trader, but its significance is in connection with corporations. The individual does like to have a record of his proprietorship, both *ab initio* and as it is later modified by accumulated profits, losses, or withdrawals. A little more significance attaches to the capital of the several members of a partnership. But even in a partnership it is not always necessary to set aside capital from other categories representing proprietorship.

The significance of corporate capital is in connection with the generally found limited liability of the stockholders of a corporation, in contrast to the unlimited liability of the several partners. When the principle of limited liability was made a feature of modern corporations, it was thought some bait must be offered to enable them to borrow advantageously. And so there came the convention that in the corporation the creditor should be given assurance that to offset the disadvantage of being unable to hold the individual stockholders liable for debts the latter, unlike the individual trader or the partners, must be restricted as to the amount which they could legally withdraw from the enterprise.

This then is the "mathematical limitation" designed to give some assurance to creditors. It does not assure them that specific assets will be held to protect them as in the case of real estate covered by a mortgage. It does not protect the creditor against loss due to the vicissitudes of business. All that it says to the creditor is, "If you make a loan to this corporation there will be sufficient assets to repay you, *unless* the losses of the corporation — including not only the losses caused by unsuccessful operations, but as well those of a catastrophic nature, and those suffered in the process of liquidation — exceed the amount of the capital." It is this which causes many to speak of a corporation's capital as representing a buffer to protect creditors against loss. Like other buffers it may defend against a minor shock, but prove worthless against a head-on collision at sixty miles an hour.

There are many accountants who speak somewhat slightingly of what they call the "legal definition" of capital, or stated capital. But it cannot be too strongly insisted that it is in its legal character that the capital of a corporation is significant. It is a mildly interesting piece of information to learn how much the stockholders actually put into the business. But vastly more important is it to tell the creditors the size of this buffer which stands between them and possible loss. There is nothing sacrosanct about capital, *qua* capital. The law does not say the individual trader may not withdraw part of his invested capital either for his own personal use or, perhaps, to endow a chair in the university. If it does say that in regard to a corporation, it is essential to know just what is the amount of this mathematical limitation. And this is altogether a creature of the law.

Recognizing that the restrictions regarding the stated capital of a corporation are primarily for the protection of creditors, how far does the protection extend? If through mischance the buffer has been impaired, must the deficiency be made up? Two ways of regarding this may be illustrated by two common business transactions: demand loans on stock exchange securities, and the reserve of a national bank.

In the case of a demand loan, if the collateral declines in value, the creditor may call for additional security. The debtor, if at all possible, promptly furnishes this. He must make up the decline in the value of the security, or suffer perhaps unpleasant consequences.

The other conception of the significance of the capital of a corporation is illustrated by the legal reserve of a national bank, required to protect demand depositors. But if depositors draw on their balances to a sufficient extent the reserve must, like reserve regiments in a battle, be called out for protection, resulting in the reserve falling below the mathematical limitation. Unlike the case of collateral loans this does not result in an instant and insistent demand for additional legal tender to bring the reserve up to the normal amount. However, it does result in a restriction that the bank may not make new loans until the reserve is fully established. There results not a positive demand but a limitation on normal activities.

The question is, does the stated capital of a corporation resemble more the collateral security of a demand loan or the legal reserve of a national bank? Does its impairment require direct reimbursement, or merely a restriction on normal activities which may in time result in restoration of the amount?

The statement made by Donald Kehl [1] that "in strict balance-sheet surplus jurisdictions the stockholder not only stakes his capital but guarantees the maintenance of assets equal to capital" is incorrect as a general rule.

In very few cases an impairment of capital does call for additional contributions by the stockholders. If the stated capital of a national bank is impaired, the deficiency must be made up or the institution is liable to be taken over by the Comptroller of the Currency. This is analogous to selling out the collateral security when a demand to make up the depleted margin is not met. But this is not true of the common corporation.

In what respect does the stated capital resemble the legal reserve of a national bank? No general answer can be given

[1] *Corporate Dividends* (New York, The Ronald Press Company, 1941), p. 50.

to this question since it depends on local statutes. In some jurisdictions an impairment of the stated capital has no immediate legal effect on the activities of the corporation, assuming, as in the California statute, that the assets still exceed the liabilities. In other jurisdictions the impairment of the stated capital does result in limitation of the corporation's normal activities. Just as with the limitation of loans by a bank with impaired reserve, the corporation is restrained from paying dividends when its stated capital is impaired. This, if the business is at all successful, would in time reimburse the lost capital.

While capital ordinarily consists of funds contributed by stockholders, it is sometimes asserted that the capital of a corporation is increased by an increase in the value of capital assets. This is similar to, or perhaps based upon, a familiar doctrine in probate law by which two separate kinds of increase in wealth are recognized — one being income, the other an increase of principal. A somewhat similar separation of capital gains, although in a half-hearted and compromising way, is found in the provisions of the United States income tax regulations. But probate law and income tax regulations are specialized fields and, as the United States Supreme Court has said, do not apply to ordinary commercial accounting.[1]

The question of appreciation is of particular importance in connection with the determination of the amount available for dividends, and further discussion is deferred to the following lecture, which deals with dividends.

Surplus

Surplus is a term used in contradistinction to capital. Like capital, the term is somewhat ambiguous because of the variation in its content as used by economists and as used by

[1] *Merchants Loan and Trust Company* v. *Smetanka*, 255 U. S. 509, 521 (1920).

accountants. Just as capital in the economic sense refers to the assets themselves, so surplus is similarly used. To a certain degree this is reasonable, or at least it corresponds with the opinion of the man in the street. If one sows a bushel of wheat and harvests ten bushels (waiving the question of the cost of planting and harvesting) the nine bushels *is* the surplus. If one invests $1,000 cash in an enterprise and receives in return $1,500 net, the $500 cash *is* the surplus. But this use of the term is not openly countenanced by accountants, possibly the one exception being the distinguished British accountant, S. S. Dawson. Dawson has consistently argued that surplus is the assets, but I know of no other accounting author who comes out as openly as did he. Just as capital to the accountant is a mathematical limitation rather than a fund of assets, so surplus, to the accountant, is a mathematical measure, if not a limitation, rather than the excess assets.

What then is surplus? It always annoys me somewhat when a writer in accounting turns to the dictionary for definitions. The ordinary dictionary's use of words varies so often from that applicable to accounting terminology that such reference is of little value, and this statement is made with due apologies to the Committee on Accounting Procedure of the American Institute. Thus, e.g., in turning to the dictionary for a definition of assets one reads, "the property of an insolvent debtor applicable to the payment of his debts." In accounting one is not necessarily an insolvent debtor to have assets. And even the New Webster, which for some unaccountable reason many persons accept as authority, refers to "the practice of entering debit items in red ink," a feature which neither Littleton nor Peragallo seems to have discovered. So it gives little satisfaction to be informed by the dictionary that surplus in its accounting sense is "an excess of net income over fixed charges and dividends during a given period."

Every accountant will admit that surplus, as he uses it, represents an excess of net worth over some other quantity.

The difficulty is in determining with what other quantity the comparison is made. The main division of opinion is whether the excess is the amount above the stated capital or whether it is the excess above the amount originally contributed by the stockholders. On this point accountants seem unable to come to an agreement.

A more limited definition is made by those who say that surplus, when used without modifying adjective, should be limited to that portion of the total proprietorship which is a result of the major business activities.[1]

But the more frequently argued question is, as just stated, whether surplus is an excess over stated capital or over the amount contributed by the stockholders.

There are several sources of surplus: (1) Earnings obtained in the conduct of business. In so far as these are not immediately distributed as dividends they do constitute surplus whether called by that name or not. There is one possible exception which arises when the stock has been issued at a discount, whether this discount is revealed or not. If earnings have been made, there will result an excess over the amount of economic capital actually contributed by the stockholders. But if the stock was issued for less than par, it might not be the case that the earnings provided an excess over the stated capital. This matter was considered in the case of *Goodnow* v. *American Writing Paper Company*, and is discussed later. (2) Premium subscribed for the stock when issued. This is listed in the balance sheet ordinarily as surplus although in most cases with a modifying adjective. In many balance sheets a more specific name is given, such as Premium on Capital Stock which is sometimes subsumed with capital, sometimes shown as a part of the surplus. (3) The retirement of capital stock at less than the book value. Evidently this does not create an excess over the original stated capital. It does result in an excess over the

[1] C. R. Rorem, *Accounting Method* (Chicago, University of Chicago Press, 1928), p. 382.

capital stock outstanding. This may be illustrated by a corporation with $100,000 capital stock, issued at par. If the corporation buys $40,000 par value of this stock for $30,000, the situation is as follows: The original capital stock, $100,000, was represented by an equal amount of cash. Now cash, or other assets, on hand amounts to only $70,000, clearly not an excess over $100,000. The stock outstanding has been reduced to $60,000. The assets now amount to $70,000. This excess of $10,000 is to the existing stockholders a surplus which inures to their benefit. There is no question here as to whether this excess is available for ordinary dividends, but it would have to be distributed to the stockholders in case of liquidation. (4) Contributions and assessments, assuming that these are not paid to the corporation as additions to the stated capital.

This brings the discussion to the various subdivisions of surplus found in published accounts. The most vital distinction is ordinarily between capital surplus (or the more restricted term, paid-in surplus) and earned surplus. It is necessary, therefore, to discuss the significance of capital surplus, particularly as it relates to the premium on stock paid by subscribers.

There are those who stoutly maintain that capital surplus is part of capital, emphasizing the first word of the phrase. Others assert that the noun is the significant word and that capital in its adjectival use merely describes the kind of surplus presented. Those who assert that capital surplus is not really surplus because of the modifier are following the pattern of using the phrases "German Silver," "French Ivory," and "Welsh Rabbit" to indicate very clearly that the articles are in fact neither silver nor ivory nor rabbit. Those opposed follow the pattern of the phrases "Sterling Silver," "African Ivory," and "Jack Rabbit," holding that the modifying term does not at all detract from the character of the essential noun.

Is Premium on Capital Stock Capital or Surplus?

In the opinion of many accountants of high standing (expressed with great assurance) the premium, having been contributed by the stockholders, is just as much capital as the amount of their contribution which is specifically labeled "stated capital." Among those holding this view are S. J. Broad, who not only says that premium is to be considered as capital from an economic standpoint, but that it should be segregated from other surplus and added to legal capital so as to show in one total the aggregate shareholders' investment remaining in the business, and he says that the rule which permits a corporation to consider only part of a stockholder's contribution as capital and the balance as surplus is "a fictitious legal doctrine."[1] Marple draws a distinction: "in the eyes of the *law* [Capital Surplus] represents a surplus, while in *principle* it is part of invested capital."[2]

A distinguished and highly honored Certified Public Accountant states: ". . . it would be decidedly illogical for a group of stockholders to contribute the capital wherewith to form a corporation and to acquire certain property and then redistribute part of the same capital in the form of a dividend. It makes little difference if, when the capital is contributed, there is an agreement that a certain portion shall be segregated for the purpose of stabilizing dividends. Merely designating paid-in capital as surplus does not make it surplus earnings, and, in my opinion, any such designation is misleading."[3]

Whether it is illogical or not is not an accounting prob-

[1] *Journal of Accountancy*, Vol. 65, p. 281 (April, 1938). See also Kehl, op. cit., p. 133; W. A. Paton, *Accounting* (New York, The Macmillan Company, 1924), p. 747.

[2] R. P. Marple, *Capital Surplus and Corporate Net Worth* (New York, The Ronald Press Company, 1936), p. 10.

[3] F. H. Hurdman, in *International Congress on Accounting Proceedings, 1929* (New York, The Ronald Press Company, 1930), p. 585.

lem. Many financial transactions are illogical and foolish as, for instance, the financing of plant construction by the issuance of short-time notes or the paying of dividends which unduly reduce the cash on hand. The accountant is not concerned with the foolishness of a transaction but with whether the transaction took place.

Moreover, this very thing which is called illogical is often done. Transactions in which stockholders do contribute funds with the understanding that they may be returned are as follows: (1) The issue of preferred stock redeemable at the option of the corporation. (2) In the case of corporations dealing with mining or other wasting assets, stockholders do "contribute the capital wherewith to form a corporation" with the expectation that the corporation will redistribute part of the same capital in the form of a dividend. Such action is supported by legal decisions and by statute, and so far from being illogical it is a very sensible procedure. (3) Another instance of contributions being made with expectation that they will be returned to stockholders is found where a corporation already in successful operation issues additional stock at a premium sufficient to offset earned surplus already accruing to the corporation. This is again by no means illogical but quite the contrary. If such a contribution is not treated as surplus (assimilated to earned surplus), it is said there would be a distinct hardship to the original shareholders — this because a distribution of the surplus earned by the original stockholders would go in part to the newcomers who had in no way contributed to it. The crediting of the premium to paid-in surplus, regarded as akin to the previous earned surplus, helps to overcome this difficulty.[1] (4) Where it is found that the amount contrib-

[1] J. B. Taylor and H. C. Miller, *Intermediate Accounting* (2d ed., New York, McGraw-Hill Book Company, 1938), Vol. II, p. 215. See also the decisions in *Miller* v. *Payne*, 136 N. W. 811 (1912); *Equitable Life Assurance Society* v. *Union Pacific Railroad*, 106 N. E. 92 (1915); and *Smith* v. *Cotting*, 120 N. E. 177 (1918).

uted by the stockholders is in excess of that which can be advantageously used in the business is yet another instance. Thus, if a bank in a small city is organized with $100,000 capital, it may later prove that the business of that city does not justify so large a capital investment. W. W. Werntz favors "distributions from paid-in surplus when earnings do not exist but the company has funds not needed in the conduct of its business." [1] The essential thing to do is to return so much of the contributed capital as seems in excess of the economic needs. This could be done by a formal reduction of the capital stock. It is simpler when part of the stockholders' contributions were made in such a form as clearly to indicate that they are subject to return at the discretion of the directors.

Moreover, it is to be noted that in many balance sheets premium is shown in some category other than capital. To me the presumption is that a differentiation is made because there is some essential difference between stated capital and paid-in surplus. The fact that such premium is sometimes bracketed with stated capital, or the par value of capital stock, is not conclusive evidence. Railroad companies have at times bracketed bonded debt along with capital stock, but while both are sources of economic capital, no accountant considers that they are identical or even similar in nature. "The whole purpose of separating capital stock from surplus on a corporate balance sheet is to give effect to this statutory concept of a permanently impounded capital." [2]

The argument is sometimes made that premium on capital stock is to be counted as capital because it is represented by the economic capital of the enterprise, that is, the assets.[3] But if this is a valid argument, then earned surplus also

[1] In *Journal of Accountancy*, Vol. 72, p. 316 (October, 1941).

[2] Paul W. Pinkerton in *National Association of Cost Accountants' Bulletin*, Vol. 15, p. 1256 (July, 1934). See also the opinion of the French authority, Rodolphe Rousseau, *Sociétés par Actions* (Paris, 1910), p. 80.

[3] Cf. F. H. Hurdman, *op. cit.*, p. 583.

should be so grouped. Both represent a proprietary interest in an excess over the stated capital. Both are represented by assets which are being used for the benefit of the corporation.

A striking instance is found in the Chemical National Bank of New York. Some years ago this showed capital stock $300,000, surplus $6,000,000. Without inquiring as to how much of this $6,000,000 may have been contributed as premium, certainly much of it must have been made up out of earnings. No one can maintain that the Chemical National Bank was carrying on its enormous business on a capital of merely $300,000. The $6,000,000 was as much a basis for the activities of that bank as the $300,000, and it was later in large part carried to capital stock. In this and in numberless less extreme cases, earnings which represented economic capital were, at least indirectly, contributed by the stockholders and, at least for the present, retained in the business. Unless this too is to be counted as accounting capital, premium should not be called capital merely because it is represented by assets used in the business.

One reason for treating premium as distinct from capital is to provide against the disrepute attached to the impairment of stated capital. Stated capital is spoken of as a buffer to absorb losses, so that unless the total losses exceed the amount of the stated capital, the creditors cannot lose anything; similarly paid-in surplus may be looked upon as a buffer to absorb losses so that unless the total losses exceed the amount of the paid-in surplus, there will be no impairment of stated capital.

Opposing the creation of paid-in surplus as a buffer element for this purpose, Paton says: "The weakness of this position should be apparent. If losses . . . are suffered, the hardship to stockholders is not minimized by the practice of setting up the proceeds of the capital stock when issued in two sections, one of which is viewed as a form of surplus."[1] This is true but not significant. The creditors are not better protected but they are notified in advance that they cannot definitely count on the entire contribution by the stockholder, but only on the amount shown as stated capital.

It is contended by some that premium received on capital stock is neither capital nor surplus but a *tertium quid*, of an ill-determined and nondescript character. Thus Marple says the accountant "should not combine stock premiums with legal or stated capital [on the basis of] statutes and decisions limiting legal capital to the par of all shares issued. He should not enter such premiums in earned surplus because they represent contributed and not earned capital. Clearly they should be accounted for under a specific heading such as Premium on Capital Stock or Paid-in Surplus."[2]

Charges to Surplus

What items are properly to be charged to surplus, rather than to the current income account, is a matter on which accountants vehemently disagree. The problem is further complicated by a difference being drawn between Capital Surplus and Earned Surplus. In the following discussion those are debarred who consider that the Capital Surplus is really Capital and not Surplus. Obviously Capital, as a representation of a buffer fund, cannot be monkeyed with. If changes or charges are made in its amount; they must be in accordance with statutory or common law regulations. The present discussion which concerns capital surplus *qua* surplus is not concerned with the other view of capital surplus as capital.

There is a group of academic accountants who hold that all charges, representing the recognition of a lessening of

[1] *Advanced Accounting* (New York, The Macmillan Company, 1941), p. 524.

[2] *Capital Surplus and Corporate Net Worth*, p. 29.

net worth, must be charged to current income. This doctrine is most significant in relation to the discovery of errors by which the income of some previous year has been overstated. These might be due merely to clerical slips, as for instance the unintentional failure to record an accrued expense. Or they may be due to a mistaken policy regarding bad debts, or a miscalculation of depreciation. These all resulted in an overstatement of income in some preceding period, the effect on the balance sheet being that the balance of the Earned Surplus account is overstated. One theory is that when any particular item is misstated, the obvious thing is to correct that item. Thus, if, for instance, an item has been charged to B, which should have been charged to A, the accounts of both A and B are incorrect. The only thing to do is to correct the double error by debiting A and crediting B. Similarly, if in 1940 only $1,000 was charged to Income through Depreciation Expense and credited to Allowance for Depreciation when the proper amount was $2,000, two accounts in the balance sheet are incorrect. The Earned Surplus is $1,000 too large; the Allowance for Depreciation account is too small by the same amount. These errors could be immediately remedied by debiting Earned Surplus and crediting Allowance for Depreciation $1,000. This is direct and simple. Should not the same procedure be followed as in the case of the two personal accounts of A and B? But no (say many accountants), an error was made in the income account of 1940 (and therefore in the Earned Surplus Account). We will correct it by making an equal and countervailing error in income account of 1942, the year when the error was first discovered. The income of 1940 was overstated by $1,000; we will offset that by understating the income of 1942 and then all will be even Steven.

Perhaps the clearest enunciation of this dictum (should it be called "this theory" or, as some have done, "this corollary of a fundamental axiom") is found in the *Tentative*

Statement of Accounting Principles. This states, "The income statement for any given period should reflect all revenues properly given accounting recognition and all costs written off during the period, regardless of whether or not they are the results of operations in that period: . . ." [1]

The same idea was stated long before by Sir Arthur Lowes Dickinson.[2] It is also supported by George O. May [3] in his lecture on this Foundation, and by Robert H. Montgomery.[4]

The argument in favor of this procedure is simple, whether or not it is considered conclusive. It is twofold. First, one may wish to ascertain the total income for a series of years, and this can easily be done, if the correction is made in the manner suggested, by listing the amounts of income shown in each year and adding them together. Thus the cancellation of the overstatement for 1940 by the understatement for 1942 will give a correct total.

The other argument is more significant. The income for 1940 was overstated and perhaps the dividends of that year were based on that figure. If the correct showing of the income for 1942 is made and the previous error charged to Earned Surplus, the entire amount of 1942 income may be available for dividends as well as the previously overstated income of 1940. There might even be a temptation to continue year after year to neglect debits to income, and in each successive year to charge them to Earned Surplus. Thus there would be created a false impression of the profits of the enterprise which would continue as long as the Earned Surplus balance holds out.

The confusion and possible misleading of the investor, caused by charging to surplus all items not specifically re-

[1] *Accounting Review*, Vol. 11, p. 189 (June, 1936).

[2] Arthur Lowes Dickinson, *Accounting Practice and Procedure* (New York, The Ronald Press Company, 1914), p. 66.

[3] *Journal of Accountancy*, Vol. 63, p. 355 (May, 1937).

[4] *Auditing Theory and Practice* (6th ed., New York, The Ronald Press Company, 1940), p. 412.

lated to the current year, has been presented by Professor W. A. Hosmer in connection with the accounts of the United States Steel Corporation.[1]

However, "It is probably true that the majority of accountants believe in using the Surplus Account, regardless of whether it is made a part of the profit and loss statement, as the means of correcting prior period errors when the amounts involved are material." [2]

And this practice is favored by Gilman as follows: "When the loss represents an obvious correction of errors made in prior periods, it is thoroughly logical to make adjustment through the surplus account on the ground that the prior period errors have already affected previous profit and loss statements and that such errors at the time of their correction are reflected by the surplus accounts." [3] It is also favored by R. P. Marple,[4] C. B. Couchman,[5] and C. H. Langer.[6]

Similarly Victor Stempf says: "Charges and credits applicable to prior years which would tend to distort current year's net result should be carried to earned surplus." [7]

Moreover the authoritative Securities and Exchange Commission has stated that the writing off of losses which, if currently recognized, would have been chargeable to income should be made by a charge against earned surplus.[8]

[1] *Accounting Review*, Vol. 13, p. 31 (March, 1938); *Business and Modern Society* (Cambridge, Harvard University Press, 1938), p. 113.

[2] Stephen Gilman, *Accounting Concepts of Profit* (New York, The Ronald Press Company, 1939), p. 145.

[3] *Ibid.*, p. 532.

[4] *Op. cit.*, p. 114.

[5] *The Balance-Sheet* (New York, American Institute Publishing Company, 1924), p. 199.

[6] *Accounting Principles and Procedure* (Chicago, Walton Publishing Company, 1931), Lecture 25, Sec. 10.

[7] *Accounting Review*, Vol. 13, p. 61 (March, 1938).

[8] *Accounting Series*, Release 1 (April 1, 1937).

Organization Expenses

A problem arises in regard to the treatment of organization expenses. These are sometimes looked on askance, and varying recommendations are made as to how they can be eliminated from the balance sheet. Marple recommends that they should be charged against paid-in surplus.[1] Montgomery recommended a gradual writing off against income in a limited number of years not to exceed five, but in a later edition of his work he recommends that they should be charged off as incurred.[2] The German Commercial Code of 1897 forbids their inclusion in the balance sheet,[3] although that probably prohibited their showing as a separate item, still allowing them to be included in the value of the capital assets.

In my opinion, however, it is entirely logical to treat the organization expenses as one of the capital expenditures.[4] It is impossible for the corporation to become established and begin operations not only until it has acquired plant, machinery, and cash but these must be held by an incorporated company. The expenses of organizing the corporation are similar to the cost of the scaffold erected during the course of construction of a building. Even though the scaffold is torn down, its cost and even the cost of removal are a legitimate part of the cost of constructing the building. The organization expenses presumably apply as long as the corporation exists and there is no logical reason either for charg-

[1] *Op. cit.*, p. 47.

[2] *Auditing Theory and Practice*, 1912 edition, p. 281, and 5th ed., 1934, p. 299.

[3] H. G. B. Sec. 261.4. See also comments on this by H. Rehm, "*Bilanzen der Aktiengesellschaften*" (Munich, 1903), pp. 262 ff.

[4] See W. A. Paton, in American Institute of Accountants, *Papers on Accounting Principles and Procedure presented at the Fifty-first Annual Meeting, 1938* (New York, The Institute, 1939), p. 27. "Such costs (organization expenses) measured in terms of cash are just as surely and properly a part of the total capital involved in the enterprise as the cost of plant assets."

ing them off immediately as incurred or of any rapid charging off as suggested by Montgomery.

There are those, however, who like to present what is called a "pretty balance sheet," [1] and these consider such an item as organization expenses a blemish. Probably the consensus of accountants is in favor of charging them against current income if written off gradually, against earned surplus if charged off in total and in case there is no earned surplus to allow a charge against paid-in surplus.

Operating Deficits

A somewhat similar problem arises in connection with operating deficits. It is generally recommended that they be charged against earned surplus, but if there is no credit to that account there is a difference of opinion as to whether a deficit may legitimately be charged to capital surplus. I have elsewhere [2] discussed this problem and it suffices here to call attention to the fact that this procedure is approved by W. H. Bell,[3] R. B. Kester,[4] and R. H. Montgomery.[5] It may be noted that in Germany the compulsory reserve, made up primarily of premium on capital stock, was distinctly provided as a means for writing off deficits and the stockholder had the right to compel this procedure.[6]

If it is considered legitimate to levy an assessment on the stockholders, against which an operating deficit may be charged, it is clearly inconsistent to say that the deficit may

[1] The chairman of the Tube Investment Company reported to the Stockholders that the accounts showed only so much of the profits as will make a pretty balance sheet. See *Accountant*, Vol. 93, p. 812 (December 14, 1935).

[2] *Accounting Review*, Vol. 9, p. 267 (September, 1934).

[3] *Accountant's Reports* (New York, The Ronald Press Company, 1921), p. 63.

[4] *Advanced Accounting* (3d ed., New York, The Ronald Press Company, 1933), p. 527.

[5] *Auditing Theory and Practice*, 4th ed., 1927, p. 330.

[6] H. V. Simon, *Die Bilanzen der Aktiengesellschaften* (3d ed., Berlin, 1899), p. 242.

not be charged against a capital surplus created by a premium on stock issues. There is little, if any, difference between an additional contribution by the stockholders after the loss has occurred (i.e., an assessment) and a contribution made beforehand (i.e., premium on the stock) to provide in advance for just the same event.

Write-Downs

In the case of writing down of some asset the first procedure should be to charge it against earned surplus if there be such; if not to charge it against capital surplus,[1] if there be such; and as a last resort to cancel it against a surplus created by a reduction of capital, the latter being carried out in accordance with the statutory provisions of the state of incorporation. It is to be noted that the reduction of capital does not create a surplus as compared with the amount originally contributed. It is, however, a paid-in surplus as compared with the reduced capital. This is clear in case all of the reduction surplus is not wiped out by charging to it the amount written off. Thus, if a corporation with $100,000 capital stock writes off an asset at $8,000, the deficit thus created might be removed by a 10% reduction in the capital stock, reducing that item to $90,000, and creating a reduction surplus of $10,000. After charging the $8,000 to Reduction Surplus, there would remain $2,000 credit in that

[1] "The earned surplus [should be] charged for the full amount of the downward revaluation of fixed property, since such decrease in value in effect represents an accumulation of depreciation over the years which, if it were recognized at the time, would have been charged to the then current income. . . . It should be clearly borne in mind, however, that the total amount of the earned surplus should be written off completely before the capital surplus may be used to absorb any such fixed asset write-down." B. B. Greidinger, *Accounting Requirements of the Securities and Exchange Commission* (New York, The Ronald Press Company, 1939), p. 302.

Montgomery makes an almost exactly similar statement but does not attribute the decline to depreciation, saying "the reduction in value represents a loss just as surely as if the assets were sold." *Auditing Theory and Practice*, 5th ed., 1934, p. 415.

account. As the stockholders now hold only $90,000 of capital stock, and there are assets now valued at $92,000, the sum of $2,000 in excess of the capital stock would be a surplus distributable to the stockholders in case of liquidation.

The situation is similar to that already discussed, when part of the capital stock is purchased at less than its book value. The reduction of the capital stock in order to cover a write-off may be considered as a purchase at zero. In either case the reduction or retirement surplus while representing contributed capital is a surplus which would inure to the holders of the diminished stock at least in the event of liquidation.

The disagreement regarding writing down goodwill is even more marked. Some say it should not be done at all. Montgomery suggests it may be charged against current income or earned surplus.[1] Arthur Anderson in a written statement says if done "merely as a gesture of conservatism . . . it seems proper to charge such a write-off against paid-in surplus." And L. R. Dicksee says it should be shown, at least in partnership accounts, as a reduction of capital.[2] The oft-quoted and dogmatically minded Tentative Statement would charge everything (and that includes the write-off of goodwill) to the current income. There is, of course, the proviso that it must not distort the showing of the current income, as if the charging of any item which does not belong in a given account does not distort it.

I have a personal friend who gave a very elaborate reception at a San Francisco hotel. He received a bill which was even larger than the large amount he expected to be charged. Examination showed that the bookkeeper in making out the bill inadvertently added in the number of the room, 1571. Would the proponents of the Tentative Statement say: "Don't add in the room number if it distorts the total"? Or would the prohibition be universal without the modifying

[1] *Auditing Theory and Practice*, 6th ed., 1940, p. 498.

[2] *Goodwill and Its Treatment in Accounts* (London, 1906), p. 82.

proviso as to the distortion involved? Would the inclusion of the room number ever fail to distort the total?

These five views regarding the treatment of write-downs pretty nearly run the entire gamut. So far as I know there is no one who suggests charging write-downs to either real estate or sinking fund reserve.

Summary

I assert that capital, capital stock, or stated capital, as an accounting term, represents so much of the stockholders' contribution as is understood to be an inviolable buffer to protect creditors and possibly other stockholders, and ordinarily is not to be paid back to them.

Surplus, as an accounting term, represents any excess of proprietorship over capital as just defined.

Capital and surplus should be kept distinct.

A distinction should also be maintained between earned surplus and capital surplus although both "are alike surplus."

Despite conflicting opinion I hold that premium on capital stock is surplus, not capital.

Corrections of errors are best made through a surplus account, which may be attached to the income statement.

Organization expenses are logically to be capitalized.

Operating deficits should be charged to earned surplus until that is exhausted. If earned surplus is insufficient, a charge to capital surplus is proper.

Write-offs, when other surpluses are insufficient, may be charged to reduction surplus, subject to statutory regulations.

II

DIVIDENDS

TWO RULES have been laid down limiting the amount of dividends which may be paid by a corporation. According to the first rule, dividends may be paid only "out of profits." The phraseology is somewhat unhappy as one cannot pay out of an abstract term such as profits but only out of the cash box or the bank account. If one had the bad taste to pose as a purist, the phrase would be "dividends may be paid only to an amount not exceeding profits."

The second rule is that they may be paid out of the excess of net assets over capital, or as it is more commonly and less felicitously expressed, out of the excess of assets over liabilities, including capital.

These two formulas are sometimes confused, as by Dickinson who said: "Dividends can be paid only out of profits, i.e., out of the net increase in the original investment after deducting from the assets all present debts and making provision for future or contingent claims reduced to their present value." [1]

This implies that all increase in net assets is profit, a consideration acceptable to economists,[2] but obviously subject to debate by accountants.

Dividends and Profits

The rule as to profits is sometimes modified to allow dividends to be paid out of the earnings of the current accounting period despite an impairment of capital. This has been

[1] *Accounting Practice and Procedure*, p. 72.

[2] Alfred Marshall, *Principles of Economics* (8th ed., London, Macmillan and Co., 1922), p. 74.

made prominent in recent years, especially since the decision in the Verner case.[1] The idea, however, is of much longer standing, for it seems to be implied, if not specifically stated, as far back as the New York Act of 1825.[2] In this, as in most problems arising in accounting, there are conflicting opinions. Mr. Justice Petersen in an interesting decision stated that "such a dividend is not paid out of paid-up capital. If it were, the paid-up capital would be still further reduced by the payment. In fact the assets representing the paid-up capital remain the same or of the same value as before the payment of the dividend." [3]

Curiously the exactly opposite argument was made in an American case, the court stating: "The earned profits, therefore, reduced the impairment, and the declaration of the dividend again impaired the capital to the extent of the dividend declared." [4]

W. W. Cook, a high authority on corporations if not on accounting, says: "The fact that in a year prior to the declaration of the dividend, some portion of the capital has been lost and has not since been made good affords no ground for restraining the payment of a dividend out of the profits subsequently earned." [5] On the other hand, there is the statement of F. H. Hurdman: "It would appear to be sound economically that, the capital having been diminished by losses, profits should be withheld from distribution as dividends until the loss has been made good, in order that the original status of the stockholder may be restored." [6]

Dicksee said, in regard to the dictum that capital deficits should be reimbursed before dividends are declared: "There

[1] [1894] 2 Ch. 239.

[2] Donald Kehl, *Corporate Dividends*, p. 50.

[3] *Ammonia Soda Company* v. *Chamberlain* [1918], 1 Ch. 266, 273.

[4] *Branch* v. *Kaiser, et al.*, 140 Atl. 500 (1928).

[5] *A Treatise on the Law of Corporations* (8th ed., New York, Baker Voorhis Company, 1923), Vol. II, p. 1905.

[6] *International Congress on Accounting Proceedings, 1929*, p. 587.

can be little doubt as to the inherent soundness of this contention. But there is all the difference in the world between that which is economically unsound and that which is illegal *per se*."[1]

Mr. Justice Petersen, in the case cited above, expressed the same idea more trenchantly: "It may be a precept of prudence and yet be far removed from the sphere of the categorical imperative."[2]

In this country accountants have considered that impaired capital must be made good before dividends may be paid,[3] and this is rather generally implied in corporation laws of the several states. A marked exception exists in the California Corporation Law[4] which allows a dividend to be paid out of recent earnings even though there is a more than offsetting impairment of capital.

If one disregards legal regulations and views the problem in its accounting aspect, the argument seems against recognizing profit despite previous deficit. Certainly it may be argued that if a corporation has incurred a deficit of $10,000 and in the next accounting period makes a gain of $1,000, it is not correct to say there has been any net profit. The corporation has $9,000 less net assets than at the beginning. Surely there are no net earnings. Whether a dividend is permissible is a matter determined by statute. But to interpret a dividend, paid when there is an operating deficit, as a distribution of profits is an accounting absurdity. And, as has frequently been pointed out, a continuing policy of so doing, in a business with alternating periods of prosperity and depression, might conceivably result in a gradual elimination of all the contributed capital while dividends had been paid, say in alternating years, throughout the decadence and destruction of the enterprise.

[1] L. R. Dicksee, *Auditing* (13th ed., London, 1924), p. 318.

[2] *Ammonia Soda Co.* v. *Chamberlain* [1918], 1 Ch. 275.

[3] L. L. Briggs, *Accounting Review*, Vol. 9, p. 236 (September, 1934).

[4] Civil Code, § 346(2).

A problem somewhat similar to that relating to operating deficits arises in connection with watered stock, the initial assets in such a case being less than the par value of the stock.

Successful operations in the first year would increase the assets above the amount with which the business began, but these still might be far less than the par value of the watered stock. Under the profits rule it has been held that dividends may be paid out of the year's earnings.[1] If dividends are permitted only when net assets exceed the capital, must they exceed the par value without considering the water? It seems reasonable that the creditors should rely on the stated amount, and some courts have held that a dividend is unlawful until the water is squeezed out. But it is clear that a payment from the earnings of the year is not paid out of the contributed capital.

Another problem relates to a gain which has been received from the sale of some of the capital assets. Does such an increase in net wealth constitute profit, or does it mean an increase in capital? Only if it is regarded as profit could it be used as a basis for a declaration of a dividend, if the first rule stated above is held to apply. A number of accountants have held that such a gain should not be included in the income account,[2] but on the high authority of Montgomery it is as much profit as is that arising from the ordinary sale of merchandise.[3] The same opinion is held by W. A. Paton.[4]

The provision found in several statutes that the dividend is limited to profits arising from the business, or as expressed by A. S. Dewing, "through the regular and orderly movement of the business,"[5] causes additional perplexity. Does it exclude income from outside securities, held by a manu-

[1] *Goodnow* v. *American Writing Paper Co.*, 73 N. J. Eq. 692 (1908).

[2] George O. May in *Journal of Accountancy*, Vol. 63, p. 361 (May, 1937).

[3] *Auditing Theory and Practice*, 5th ed., 1934, p. 412.

[4] *Advanced Accounting*, p. 451.

[5] *The Financial Policy of Corporations* (rev. ed., New York, The Ronald Press Company, 1926), p. 494.

factory? Are incidental and subsidiary operations included? Or, are we to go to the length of accepting a startling statement once made by Roy B. Kester (of which he doubtless has repented) that a levied assessment "is of course a *real* profit as distinguished from a *book* profit." [1]

Dividends When Capital Is Unimpaired

The second formula, as expressed by Kehl, is: "The broadest and most unambiguous rule against the payment of dividends from capital is that recently adopted by modern statutes providing in so many words that dividends may not be paid when the corporation's assets are, or after payment will be, less than its liabilities including capital stock." [2]

Again arises the question as to what is the definition of capital. Is it in this case limited to the par, or stated, value of the capital stock; or does it include premium or other contributions of the stockholders? The nature of premium, as representing perhaps capital, or on the other hand, surplus, has already been discussed in its general aspects. The question is of vital significance in relation to dividends under the excess assets rule. Certainly, premium is not profit, and is not available for dividends under the first rule, but if it is neither capital nor profits, it is, under the excess assets rule, distributable as dividends.

Again there is the tiresome uniformity of disagreement on this matter, perhaps more vehement than on any other problem of accounting. Statutes vary in different states, but accountants, as indeed is proper, set themselves up as higher authority than the makers of statutes. On the one hand, Montgomery says, paying a dividend out of so-called capital surplus "comes close to moral turpitude." [3] And Paton

[1] *Accounting* (2d ed., New York, The Ronald Press Company, 1925), Vol. II, p. 441.

[2] *Op. cit.*, p. 42.

[3] *Auditing Theory and Practice*, 5th ed., p. 443 and p. 411.

chimes in with equal fervor, saying that "such a dividend deserves the general condemnation accorded by accountants" and that "it is deplorable that this is given legal sanction." [1] But on the other hand, Werntz, somewhat oblivious to the statements of Montgomery and Paton, declares: "No one will dispute the arguments that may be advanced in favor of distributions from paid-in surplus under some circumstances." [2] And Marple at least mitigates the harsh condemnation, saying: "If the common stockholder in making his capital contribution knows that a part of the amount paid in by him is to be treated as surplus and knows that such surplus is intended for use as dividends on preferred stock until such time as earnings can be used, there is less objection to this procedure." [3]

This statement, however, is deficient in referring only to the stockholders' understanding. Equally or more important is the understanding of creditors as to what they may count upon as an inviolable buffer against losses. And while some seem to think that doubtful or improper actions may be sanctified by action of the stockholders, the *Journal of Accountancy* considers a dividend out of paid-in surplus as a transformation of capital into earned surplus which cannot be made by "the resolution of either the stockholders or the board." [4]

What can your perplexed speaker, who hails from the western fringes of civilization and is neither a C. P. A. nor enveloped by the aura of eastern culture, do in such a controversy between experts? The good slogan, *experto crede*, is unavailing, for which expert is to be believed? And surely one would shrink from seeming to uphold an act savoring of "moral turpitude." Perhaps it will suffice to say that the

[1] *Advanced Accounting*, p. 567 and p. 524.
[2] *In Journal of Accountancy*, Vol. 72, p. 316 (October, 1941).
[3] *Capital Surplus and Corporate Net Worth*, p. 30.
[4] See Editorial in Vol. 64, p. 63 (July, 1937).

matter turns on two interpretations of accounting principles: Is the legitimacy of a dividend dependent on the existence of profit? If so, the payment of such a dividend is inexorably ruled out, for premium is obviously not profit. If, on the other hand, it is held that a dividend is legitimate provided the net assets exceed the capital, the decision turns on whether premium is really capital or surplus. This has already been discussed. The decision is in your hands.

Appreciation

In addition to the problem as to premium, there is the much-debated question in regard to appreciation of assets. Before discussion of the legitimacy of basing a dividend on unrealized appreciation, the more general problem of its treatment in accounts is necessary.

Three problems arise:

1. Is appreciation to be recorded in the accounts?
2. If recorded, is it to be represented as Capital, or as Surplus?
3. If considered Surplus, in which subclass of Surplus is it to appear?

Among those opposing any record of appreciation are S. Gundelfinger who states, "We deny that a given object can have a value to its owner in excess of cost."[1] Despite the fact that the essay containing this sentence received a prize, the denial transcends the bounds of reason, for it does not merely object to booking an increase, but denies the possibility of its existence. If taken literally, it is absurd.

The symposium on appreciation prepared at the University of Illinois contains the following: "The price at which the actual transaction takes place is the measure at that time of the value of the property. That is the only way value finds expression in realities. All else is conjecture and opinion.

[1] *Journal of Accountancy*, Vol. 37, p. 342 (May, 1924).

. . . Before the act takes place . . . value is fluid, perhaps gaseous were better, its dimensions are indeterminate, its very existence perhaps a mirage. At that stage value is no fit subject for entry in the accounts; in fact, there is no 'value' as yet, one only thinks there *may be*. Until tested in the market, there is only surmise. Otherwise the situation would be like asking $20,000 for a house from a prospective buyer, and then setting that figure up as its value, because he said he would 'think it over,' although he never returned." [1] C. B. Couchman says: "The mark-up has no more real tangibility than the thinnest of thin air." [2] W. D. Cranstoun says: "There is no justification for adjusting the books of account to reflect an unrealized increase in asset values." [3]

H. C. Greer says: "Revaluations . . . do violence to every proper conception of the function of accounts in recording the history of a business enterprise." [4] Parenthetically, is it not part of the history of a business that advantageous purchases resulted in the enterprise having assets worth more than they cost? Is it not part of the history of, say, the Astors that their early purchases of New York real estate have increased in value over their original cost? It may be proper to exclude from accounts such "recording of history," but surely it is an important part of history.

The *Yale Law Journal* (I regret not to quote from the *Harvard Law Review*) speaks of the showing of unrealized appreciation surplus as an "available dodge" which cannot be justified.[5] More authoritative has been the attitude of the Securities and Exchange Commission which has steadfastly opposed the showing of appreciated values in the balance

[1] *Accounting Review*, Vol. 5, p. 30 (March, 1930).
[2] *The Balance-Sheet*, p. 127.
[3] *Journal of Accountancy*, Vol. 65, p. 70 (January, 1938).
[4] In *Journal of Accountancy*, Vol. 65, p. 291 (April, 1938).
[5] Vol. 50, p. 314 (December, 1940).

sheet. In a somewhat inconclusive ruling the SEC required a company, which on the basis of an independent appraisal had marked up company property above its actual cost, to "amend its balance sheet" and "show the fixed assets at cost." [1] A more extreme instance is found in a case where a dividend was paid in whiskey, at its cost price, the stockholders being allowed to return the whiskey at the higher market value in payment for additional stock. Despite the fact that the payment for the stock was colorably an independent transaction, the Commission required the registrant to alter the return, showing the merchandise at its original cost, not at the price at which it was accepted in payment for the stock.[2]

Such a consensus seems overwhelmingly conclusive, and probably it is seconded by almost all of you. But there is a good motto, "*Audi alteram partem.*"

As a previous Dickinson lecturer, W. A. Paton, said years ago, in a text in which he was at least jointly implicated: "The fact that there is this array of opinion opposed to the practice of accounting for appreciation might be considered as *prima facie* evidence that there is very good reason for this doctrine, and hence that any argument against it might well be abandoned at the outset. This, however, would be an unwarranted conclusion. It may be that the minority opinion is right." More specifically, the same text reads on a later page, "Ignoring the appreciation of unsold assets . . . is essentially as misleading a practice as the charging of capital outlays to expense." [3]

The very one who has been honored by the establishment of this Foundation has stated: "Over a period of years changes in value due to rise or fall in prices may be suf-

[1] Accounting Series, Release 8 (May 20, 1938).

[2] *Accounting Review*, Vol. 12, p. 309 (September, 1937).

[3] W. A. Paton and R. A. Stevenson, *Principles of Accounting* (New York, The Macmillan Company, 1918), pp. 454, 469.

ficiently permanent to render it unfair to one business to maintain original cost values as compared with another whose assets have been created at widely varying costs."[1] The Bank of Montreal, whose premises appeared in its balance sheet at $600,000, decided they were later worth over $9,000,000, and modestly marked them up to only $4,000,000. And under the bank law such increased value was accepted as basis for the issue of circulation.[2] Kester admits that for certain purposes "it may be wise and proper to show the true value of the assets."[3] P. D. Leake testified that an increase in the value of consols held may be recognized, "whether or not the consols are about to be sold at the end of the year."[4]

In the important case *Ammonia Soda Company* v. *Chamberlain*[5] the court sanctioned the marking up of the company's property, enabling it thus to wipe out a previous operating deficit. This, however, was due to discovery rather than to a distinct rise in price, but it was nevertheless a showing of a value decidedly greater than the cost of the property.

The Illinois document states that to list at cost "is the only way value finds expression in realities. All else is conjecture and opinion."[6] Montgomery, in controversion, says, "Balance sheet valuations at cost ignore the practical, and substitute historical and sentimental measures of value."[7]

It may be worth while to note that the Illinois document is the fulmination of unfledged University students of accounting, while the contrary view comes from the pen of an

[1] A. L. Dickinson, *Accounting Practice and Procedure*, p. 80.

[2] *Journal Institute of Bankers*, Vol. 33, p. 2 (January, 1912).

[3] *Advanced Accounting*, 3d ed., 1933, p. 520.

[4] Great Britain, Royal Commission on the Income Tax (1919–1920), *Minutes of Evidence*, par. 3605.

[5] [1918], 1 Ch. 266.

[6] *Accounting Review*, Vol. 5, p. 30 (March, 1930).

[7] *Journal of Accountancy*, Vol. 44, p. 257 (October, 1927).

experienced and eminent practitioner. I do not venture to say which statement should carry more weight.

"It is generally legal to use unrealized appreciation surplus as a basis for stock dividends."[1] It is immaterial for the discussion of the moment that this generally implies the prohibition of a cash dividend. All that is here brought forth is a rebuttal to the statement that appreciation is never to be booked.

In discussing the nature of accounting, one cannot be entirely neglectful of such writers as Professor Fritz Schmidt, putative head of the so-called Frankfurt School of Accounting, Mr. R. S. Edwards of the British Accounting Research Association, and Professor Canning of Stanford University, all of whom favor present value, rather than cost.[3] Furthermore, it is neither axiomatic nor even true that in everyday practice accountants refrain from marking up assets. The irrefutable proof is found in the probably universally sanctioned treatment of a discounted note receivable.

If a noninterest-bearing note of $1,000 due in six months is discounted for $970, I think no accountant denies the propriety of inventorying the note three months later at $985. Here there is no new asset, there is no element of an additional claim, as might possibly be urged in regard to coupon bonds, or an interest-bearing note. The only promise was to pay $1,000, say on April 1. To mark it up from $970 to $985 is indisputably the showing that the particular asset is worth $15 more than when first acquired.

It is immaterial that there is a specific contract and hence a difference between the note and a certificate of stock. If it is legitimate to recognize the increase in value due to the approaching maturity, there needs be some specific reason

[1] H. D. Kerrigan in *Accounting Review*, Vol. 12, p. 248 (September, 1937).

[2] Fritz Schmidt, *Die Organische Tageswertbilanz* (Leipzig, 1929); John B. Canning, *The Economics of Accountancy* (New York, The Ronald Press Company, 1929); Ronald S. Edwards, "Nature and Measurement of Income," *Accountant*, Vol. 99 *passim* (1938).

given for not recognizing some other increase in value, caused by industrial or market conditions. With the billions of discounted war bonds held by the public, the gradual appreciation, as time marches on, is not a matter of insignificant importance.

If the argument were sound (which it is not) that the appreciation of the discounted note may be recognized because it contains a definite promise, the element which justifies appreciation should be certainty of value, not its legal character. But is it certain that the note on December 31 is really worth $985? Does one know that it will be surely paid April 1? Does one know that the maker will not then be bankrupt and unable or unwilling to pay the note?

Recognition of Appreciation

There are other instances in which good accounting practice does recognize appreciation of assets. This is done in regard to meat products, where inventory value is based on selling-price modified by certain deductions, in malting operations,[1] in long-term contracts such as shipbuilding,[2] and in certain jurisdictions in regard to securities, or even commodities publicly quoted in exchanges.

The Washington statute,[3] regulating banks and trust companies, requires the written consent of the supervisor of banking to the valuing of any of their assets above cost. This clearly is an intimation that showing appreciation is legitimate but providing a safeguard to assure that the valuation is justified by the fact.

A curious and to me illogical distinction is sometimes

[1] *Hutchinson* v. *Curtiss*, 92 N. Y. S. 70 (1904). But increases in number and weight were disallowed in *Hill* v. *International Products Co.*, 220 N. Y. Supp. 711 (1925).

[2] Sweeney may be right in saying: "Here, as frequently happens in accounting practice, consistency is sacrificed for expediency." *Accounting Review*, Vol. 8, p. 334 (December, 1933).

[3] Rem. Rev. Stat. § 3240.

drawn between an increase in present value of an asset which has not changed in amount, e.g., real estate, and an increase in value accompanying an increase in a material asset, as in the case of the growth of a stand of timber. This introduces into accounting a crassly materialistic concept alien to the nature of our blessed science. Accounting is not at all, or only incidentally and in subsidiary records, concerned with weight or superficies or number, but only with values, i.e., the number of monetary units attributed to the item. Particularly strange is the willingness to recognize an increase in the value of growing timber by those who are strenuous adherents to the dictum that accounting, as is the saying, is concerned with costs, not with values. The stand of timber had a definite initial cost. That cost may legitimately be augmented by expenses incurred in connection with the growth of the trees. This is not a case of appreciation in the sense here used, but merely an additional investment, allocating to the timber the value of the cash expended in its care. But if the marketable timber has increased in amount, it is inconsistent to show an increase in value if accounting is concerned only with costs, and illogical to argue that the increase in market value, due to increased bulk, is different from an increase due to an increased demand for paper pulp.

Furthermore, some who sanction recognizing appreciation in the case of growing timber adduce as an argument against marking up a static asset — that the price may go down. By the same token there is no assurance that, when the timber is cut, it will sell at the estimated price. That price may easily decline to an extent more than offsetting the increase in board feet. And if an increase in price of real estate may decline, so too might the increase in material quantity decline because of a forest fire, or a plague of hoof and mouth disease.

Somewhat similar is the situation where an added value is due to discovery, as in the case of a new vein of ore, or additional oil supply. Surely advocates of the theory that cost is the basis of all accounting, a statement which most of you probably support, must perform intellectual gymnastics to argue that the cost of a given mining property has changed because unanticipated resources are discovered. The cost is what it was. The present value of the property may be greater than its cost, because of the discovery of additional resources, or because of the emergence of additional demand, and the higher price of the material caused perhaps by the outbreak of war and the need for steel and oil. Accounting, I repeat, is not concerned with material units — tons of ore, or barrels of oil — but with values, value being interpreted as an expression in monetary terms, either of the cost value or of the present market value, depending on whether one adheres to one or the other school of accounting theory.

Perhaps futilely I beg you not to misunderstand me. I am not here arguing in favor of showing appreciation of plant, nor am I arguing against showing an increased value, due to timber growth or similar increases in material assets. I am merely arguing that it is not consistent to object to showing appreciation, say of real estate, and to allow it merely because the assets are greater in size, as the trees, or in number in case of the increase of a flock. Perhaps, however, as Mr. Bonthron has said, "When the accountants are governed entirely by logic, their usefulness will be at an end."

Several arguments adduced against showing appreciation are easily refuted. That appreciation should not be recorded because "that which has gone up may come down" is a statement frequently made but entirely inconclusive. If a block of stock is bought at 90 and later an identical block is bought at par, it may be proper, certainly it is consistent, if cost is all that accounting records, to carry them at 90 and par, respectively. But it is not consistent to give as a reason for not marking up the first block, that the price may fall, and not to apply the same rule to the block bought at par.

If there is reason for expecting the stock to decline to 85, both blocks, if one does not rigorously adhere to the cost basis, may logically be marked down. But both should be treated alike, either kept at cost, or alike marked down.

Nor is it a valid objection to showing appreciation, that it is merely an estimate. It has been said that nine-tenths of all balance-sheet values are estimates. The perhaps unfortunately accepted rule of cost or market is equally an estimate of the lower market price, and what are allowances for bad debts and the annual depreciation charge but estimates?

Perhaps the strongest argument against showing appreciation is that "it savors of nonconservatism." This may be a valid objection on purely pragmatic grounds, in view of the human tendency to overvalue one's possessions, to think wishfully as to one's success in gaining profits, save when confronting the income tax return.

But conservatism, like "present value," has too many connotations. Professor Yntema says, "In the formulation of business policies conservatism may be an excellent fault; but the deliberate statement of values below undisputed market prices is a practice scarcely defensible if the function of the balance sheet is to exhibit values." [1]

Professor Kester expresses the opinion that "conservatism [is] a principle very greatly overworked." [2] Isaac Goldberg, in his posthumous work *The Wonder of Words*, calls attention to the indefiniteness of the word "conservative" as used in politics. In accounting, too, it is a weasel word. It originally meant one who wishes to preserve existing order. In accounting, it may mean cleaving to an old expression of value, i.e., the original cost. He quotes from a popular speaker, conservatism is "a beautiful word, full of meaning. Once it denoted those who hold to that which is good, but now it is

[1] *Publications of the American Association of University Instructors in Accounting* (December, 1925), p. 20.

[2] *Advanced Accounting*, 3d ed., 1933, p. 105.

used as a shibboleth by those who believe that income tax is too high and that a thing which has been a convention for a long time is inherently good." Probably in accounting its derived meaning is: Any procedure which tends to show a lower rather than a higher value of assets, less rather than more profits. Conservatism is, on the whole, commendable. But as has often been pointed out, that which tends to show less profit in one year frequently results in an overstatement of profits in the following year. The earlier conservatism results in a later nonconservatism.[1]

"Take it any way you like [says an oft-quoted accountant] the so-called conservatism of the accountant hides understated values which it can never harm any one to know or hides overstated values which it would be useful to know." [2] An interesting pronouncement but one which can scarcely be called a conservative statement.

If it is granted, despite Mr. Gundelfinger and the Illinois report, that an object can increase in value, and agreeing with Kester,[3] Dickinson,[4] Haskins & Sells,[5] Robert E. Healy,[6] James O. McKinsey and Howard S. Noble,[7] and J. R. Wildman,[8] that at times it may be excusable to show such increase in the accounts, the question arises as to what the corresponding credit should be.

[1] Cf. W. J. Graham and W. G. Katz, *Accounting in Law Practice* (Chicago, Callaghan & Company, 1932), p. 210. E. Schmalenbach, *Dynamische Bilanz* (Leipzig, 1933), p. 111.

[2] R. H. Montgomery, in *Journal of Accountancy*, Vol. 44, p. 25.

[3] *Advanced Accounting*, 3d ed., 1933, p. 357.

[4] *Accounting Practice & Procedure*, pp. 81–82.

[5] *Bulletin*, Vol. 11, p. 74 (October, 1928).

[6] *Accounting Review*, Vol. 13, p. 6 (March, 1938).

[7] *Accounting Principles* (Cincinnati, South-Western Publishing Company, 1939), p. 480.

[8] *Accounting Review*, Vol. 5, p. 34 (March, 1930).

The Account to Be Credited

Attention was called in the previous lecture to the doctrine that a distinction is to be made between income and an increase in capital. The opinion was there expressed that appreciation in ordinary commercial accounting is not to be treated as is the growth of the corpus of an estate, although that has been implicitly supported, long since, by Mr. Justice Lopes in *Lee* v. *Neuchatel Asphalte Co. Lim.*,[1] and more recently by H. D. Kerrigan.[2]

It is true that at times accounting, perhaps unfortunately, recognizes capital losses as disassociated from income. But the leading decision [3] and the more recent statutory provisions are more concerned in what may legally be paid out as dividends than with the essential nature of what took place. And the adoption of the rule as originally laid down has led to the startling legal *obiter dictum* that the plant of an iron works constitutes circulating rather than fixed assets.[4]

It has been said that, as far back as 1915, the opinion was currently held that writing up plant values "results in a surplus which, however incapable it may be of being distributed, is still a surplus."

Another accountant says that appreciation may legitimately be credited to surplus account provided "such increase is permanent." [5] This attributes to the accountant a prescience which he should be loath to claim. Mr. Justice Lopes said that the auditor, while he may be a watch-dog, need not be a blood-hound. To that may be added that, while he should be an historian, he need not be a crystal-gazer.[6]

[1] 41 Ch. Div. 1, 26 (1889).

[2] *Accounting Review*, Vol. 12, p. 248 (September, 1937).

[3] *Verner* v. *General and Commercial Investment Trust, Limited* [1894] 2 Ch. 239.

[4] *Bond* v. *Barrow Haematite Steel Co.* [1902] 1 Ch. 363.

[5] R. J. Bennett, *Corporation Accounting* (New York, 1916), p. 336.

[6] Cf. A. C. Kelly, in *Journal of Accountancy*, Vol. 60, p. 52 (July, 1935).

Some insist that the credit should be to Capital Surplus, with a probable emphasis on the capital implication,[1] but one who is your professor of accounting, and by that very token needs no honorific adjective, objects to this nomenclature but apparently recognizes appreciation as the kind of surplus called "appraisal surplus." [2] This I judge, to use the phrase quoted above, "is still surplus."

A third view is that when appreciation is recognized the effect is an increase in "neither capital nor surplus"; [3] not surplus but a "temporary" suspense or adjustment account.[4] The credit according to Broad [5] should be carried as a "reserve for revaluation," thus approximating the familiar Reserve for Depreciation (note that Montgomery, Paton, Cole, and I persist in calling this an Allowance, not a Reserve). The balance sheet then says on one side that the asset is worth more than its cost; on the other side it says: "No, it ain't"; one side says there has been appreciation, the other side says there has not. It recognizes appreciation, but does so with its fingers crossed.

There remains the question as to the subdivision of surplus to which it should be credited. The more fundamental division of surplus is into Capital Surplus and Earned Surplus, both considered as essentially surplus. The recommendations of those who would credit Capital Surplus, but who in reality mean a credit to capital rather than to surplus, may here be waived.

There is general agreement that the credit should not be to Earned Surplus. An almost unique exception is the concession to the superprescient and prophetic accountant

[1] McKinsey and Noble, *Accounting Principles*, p. 480. See also W. A. Paton in *Journal of Accountancy*, Vol. 65, p. 288 (April, 1938).

[2] T. H. Sanders, in *Accountant*, Vol. 100, p. 577 (April 29, 1939).

[3] F. H. Hurdman, in *International Congress on Accounting Proceedings, 1929*, p. 590.

[4] R. P. Marple, *Capital Surplus and Corporate Net Wealth*, p. 126.

[5] *Journal of Accountancy*, Vol. 66, p. 226 (October, 1938).

mentioned above, who foresees that the increase will be permanent.

"Earned" is another term difficult to define; so much so that a proposal has been made [1] to discontinue the use of the phrase "earned surplus" in accounting jargon. Earned seems to imply a quasi-ethical content. Can one say that the profit of a given corporation is necessarily earned, even though it arises from its customary operations? Is the larger profit made on merchandise because of an unexpected rise in market price earned in any real sense any more than the so-called "unearned increment" derived from real estate?

There is some tendency to identify "earned" and "realized" when applied to income or surplus. But this is erroneous. Accrued interest is "earned" but not realized. There are many instances of realized income, which would or would not be included in earned income depending on the definition of earned.

Some accountants suggest that when appreciation is first recorded it represents capital surplus, but by a strange metamorphosis when the asset is sold it becomes earned surplus.[2] Can the Ethiopian change his skin, or the leopard his spots? Probably those who advocate this accounting transformation are confusing realization and earning.

Not only do accountants differ one from another but disagree with themselves. Thus in the fourth edition of a well-known *magnum opus* the author includes "accretions arising from reappraisals" in capital surplus. But in the fifth edition he says it "should be shown as a separate item on the balance sheet and not buried in either earned or capital surplus," [3] thus giving the lie to the scurrilous remark that "an accountant never changes his opinion."

[1] S. J. Broad, *Journal of Accountancy*, Vol. 65, p. 283 (April, 1938).

[2] See in opposition to this, Marple, *op. cit.*, pp. 116 and 118.

[3] Montgomery, *Auditing Theory and Practice*, 4th ed., 1927, p. 329; 5th ed., 1934, p. 101.

In order to avoid any misconception, the preferable procedure is to show the increase in net worth in a special subdivision of surplus which may well bear the descriptive title Surplus Arising from the Revaluation of Assets,[1] or more simply, Revaluation Surplus,[2] or Appraisal Surplus.[3] The reader of the balance sheet is by this warned that the item does not represent ordinary earnings, but is left uninstructed as to whether it approximates premium on stock.[4] He should infer, as S. J. Broad says, "it represents an increment and thus has the nature of profit, rather than of capital."[5]

The conclusion is that appreciation may be recognized, with the obvious understanding that the appreciation must be genuine, objectively verified, and not arbitrarily done in order to make a "pretty balance sheet."

As to the propriety of basing dividends on unrealized appreciation, very positive opinions have been expressed on both sides of this question. One of these is a categorical statement, "It is fundamental that a cash dividend cannot be paid out of unrealized appreciation in value."[6] A similar attitude is taken by other accountants, although both in accounting literature and in statutory provisions a distinction is made allowing a *stock* dividend based upon unrealized appreciation, while prohibiting a *cash* dividend. Kehl, however, considered that "it is as objectionable to increase the corporation's capitalization upon the basis of uncertain asset values as it is to pay dividends out of such illusory funds."[7] But Wisconsin has a provision which authorizes both cash

[1] Montgomery, *Auditing*, 5th ed., 1934, p. 101.

[2] McKinsey and Noble, *Accounting Principles*, p. 480.

[3] T. H. Sanders, in *Accountant*, Vol. 100, p. 577. He specifically objects to using Capital Surplus in this case.

[4] But Kaplan and Reaugh in *Yale Law Journal*, Vol. 48, p. 966 (April, 1939), speak of revaluation surplus as an "offspring of illicit affairs."

[5] *Journal of Accountancy*, Vol. 66, p. 219 (October, 1938).

[6] C. H. Langer, *Accounting Principles and Procedure, Advanced Accounting*, Vol. I, Lecture 20, p. 5.

[7] *Corporation Dividends*, p. 102.

and stock dividends based on an increase in the value of corporation property,[1] and Minnesota allows them in so far as it relates to securites of readily ascertainable value.[2] And some hold that when the statute provides that dividends may be paid to the extent that the value of assets exceeds the sum of capital and liabilities, this requires an estimate of the then value of the assets and virtually means a re-appraisal of all assets each time a dividend is declared.

Dividends Out of Capital

It is not even a universal rule that dividends may not be paid out of actual capital. There are three exceptions in accepted practice: (1) The generally accepted, and in California specifically legalized, practice in the case of wasting assets. (2) Payment of dividends out of reduction surplus. This is not universally approved, being strongly condemned by Marple.[3] (3) Dividends during Construction. This is distinctly authorized by the British Companies' Act of 1929 (Sec. 54), and a similar provision is found in the German Commercial Code of 1897 (Sec. 215). In these cases, the provision that dividends "paid in lieu of interest during construction" may be capitalized by charging them to cost of construction seems to imply that they are not paid out of capital. It is clear, however, that the only funds which the corporation has are those which were contributed as capital.

It is generally required that when dividends are paid from any source other than profits, full information be given to the stockholders. The reason for such a provision is obvious,

[1] Wis. Stat. (1937) § 182:19.

[2] Mason Supp. 1938, Sec. 7492–21.

[3] *Capital Surplus and Corporate Net Worth*, p. 105. "Since the capital surplus obtained in this way was a part of the stockholders' original contributions, it should no more be returned to them in the form of ordinary dividends than should other types of capital surplus. To use such surplus for dividend purposes is to mislead stockholders, who think of dividends as distributions of earnings."

but one may object to the statement, frequently made by accountants, that dividends from any source other than profits mislead the stockholder. Thus Marple seems to assume that dividends paid from capital are paid without knowledge that capital is being reduced. Or they are made "without informing the stockholders."[1] The objection to such dividends is not that the dividend is improper, but that the directors have failed to give the requisite notice. Marple's assumption that due notice is not given is somewhat gratuitous. If it sometimes is true, the remedy is not necessarily prohibition of the dividend but insistence on ample notification.

It is occasionally stated that dividends in this or that case may not be paid "without the approval of the stockholders." That may be merely a matter of statute law or the bylaws of the corporation. Such a provision may be satisfactory to the lawyer, but the accountant should be on his guard. If a dividend is improper from the point of view of accounting principles, it is not justified by the action of the stockholders any more than by the action of the directors. If the idea implicit in all corporation organization is that the contributed capital has been set up as a protection to creditors, no organ of the corporation, either directors or stockholders, is justified in making a one-sided abrogation of the implied contract. It may be that statutes authorize this to be done, but in that case all that the accountant can say is that the statute is faulty. The authorization of so important an interference with the interests of the creditors should require the sanction of some state authority, either by a commissioner of corporations, or by a court having proper jurisdiction. These rather than one of the parties to the contract should decide whether any inequitable act would be performed by the payment of such a dividend.

[1] *Op. cit.*, pp. 6 and 16.

Dividends Declared

It is well recognized that a dividend once declared constitutes a liability. A cash dividend when once declared may not, except in extraordinary circumstances, be revoked or cancelled by the directors, but this restriction does not hold in regard to the payment of a stock dividend. It is possible, but by no means a frequent occurrence, for the directors to vote a large amount as dividends, providing that the payment of this sum is to be spread over some period extending beyond the current one. Some accountants imply that in such a case the directors may cancel the long deferred installments at any time before they become definitely payable. This does not seem reasonable. If the declared dividend is paid by scrip or bonds maturing after the current fiscal period, it could hardly be maintained that the payment of the scrip could be prevented by action of the directors.[1] From the accounting point of view there is no material difference between a written promise to pay a dividend eighteen months later, and a book entry to the effect that such a dividend is to be paid in cash. In either case the actual payment of cash is not a payment of the dividend but rather a payment of a debt, and the refusal to pay a debt cannot properly be made by the debtor.

Other Restrictions on Dividends

In addition to the general rule that dividends may be paid only out of profit, or the other formula that they may not be paid out of capital, there are some other statutory restrictions which would apply even to cases permitted under one or the other of these rules. One such restriction is that a

[1] See Paton, *Advanced Accounting*, p. 565. "Dividends in the form of short-term scrip or notes, with or without interest, are essentially 'deferred' dividends, and the use of the long-term notes or bonds of the declaring company means a postponement of the actual distribution of corporate assets for the life of the security issued."

dividend even though otherwise permissible may not be paid if it would injuriously affect the position of preferred stockholders.[1] Another such restriction is that the dividend may not be paid if insolvency threatens or would be imminent if the dividend is paid.[2]

A less justifiable regulation prohibits the payment of a dividend if thereby the assets are reduced below some specified percentage of the liabilities. Thus in California the dividend is prohibited (when made from a reduction surplus) unless after the payment the assets "at their fair present value will at least equal one and one-quarter times its debts and liabilities."[3] If the creditors lent $100,000 to a corporation with $200,000 capital, presumably the loan was made with the understanding that the "buffer fund" amounted to twice the amount of the loan. It does not seem fair to allow the margin to be reduced to $25,000.

The payment of an otherwise legitimate dividend may also be prevented by contractual restrictions, as for instance that a certain amount of the profit shall be set aside for a sinking fund, or that a stated ratio of current assets to current liabilities must be maintained.

Another question is: Should the dividends be charged to earned surplus or to the current income? Paton[4] has said that the former practice is objectionable, but on the other hand the much bruited *Tentative Statement* says that dividends should be charged against surplus.[5] There is some advantage certainly in showing the relation between the

[1] J. C. Bonbright, *Valuation of Property* (New York, McGraw-Hill Book Company, 1937), Vol. 2, p. 915.

[2] "No dividends shall be declared when there is reasonable ground for believing that thereupon the corporation's debts and liabilities would exceed its assets, or that it would be unable to meet its debts and liabilities as they mature." *California Corporation Act*, as amended 1933, Sec. 346 (3).

[3] *Corporation Act*, as amended 1933, Sec. 348b.

[4] In *Journal of Accountancy*, Vol. 57, p. 128 (February, 1934).

[5] *Accounting Review*, Vol. 11, p. 191 (June, 1936).

amount of net profit for the current fiscal period and the amount paid as dividends. This is most clearly brought out if the dividends are charged to current income which in some cases would result in a debit balance of income being carried to earned surplus.

Finally, attention may be called to Mr. May's pregnant statement: "The third possible basis seems to me to be a recognition of the economic fact that a dividend, whether paid in cash or stock, is not a real source of gain to a stockholder; the real source of gain to him is the earning of a profit by the corporation in which he holds stock." [1]

[1] G. O. May, *Twenty-Five Years of Accounting Responsibility* (New York, American Institute Publishing Company, 1936), Vol. II, p. 389.

PROBLEMS IN REPORTING CORPORATION INCOME

George D. Bailey

HARVARD BUSINESS REVIEW

September 1948 — *Vol. XXVI No. 5*

PROBLEMS IN REPORTING CORPORATION INCOME

BY GEORGE D. BAILEY

BY AND large, the present reporting of corporation activity and corporation income is not satisfactory. It is not satisfactory either to the corporations or to the public. The corporations are trying to find better ways of telling about themselves so that there will be a better understanding of corporate workings and a better understanding of corporate profits. The public still finds the information inadequate and unconvincing — insufficient for its purposes. This is not good; and if the condition is allowed to continue, it could constitute a serious threat to our American system of free enterprise. This is a strong statement, but I do not think it exaggerates.

I make this statement with full knowledge of the progress that has been made during the last few months in presenting reports to the public and in interpreting each corporation's activity to its stockholders. The recent reports emphasize that many corporations do appreciate the necessity for improvement in reporting. But there is still much to be done.

It is my purpose here to examine the problems involved in adequate reporting of corporation activity and to set forth the basic accounting requirements for measuring corporate progress year by year. In a subsequent article I shall discuss in greater detail the refinements of the principles applicable to the presentation of corporate earnings.

Problems of Adequate Reporting

Why is adequate corporate reporting so important? Corporations are the foundation of our national business activity — almost, one might say, the chosen vehicles for carrying on the nation's business. The corporate form of organization has proved to be the effective one for large business units, for expanded operations, for nationwide

EDITORS' NOTE: This article was originally presented as part of the 1948 Dickinson Lectures before the Harvard University Graduate School of Business Administration. An article in the November 1948 BUSINESS REVIEW will complete the publication of Mr. Bailey's discussion.

activity. Business, with a capital B, is almost synonymous with corporations. It is through corporations that a large percentage of the people in this nation participate in the profit system and that mass production and mass distribution of goods are possible. So pervasive are the influences of corporations that society as a whole has a stake in the proper functioning of the corporate system, and all segments of society have an interest in how corporations carry out their responsibilities. But society, that is, the public, can only judge the effectiveness of corporations by getting reports of corporation activity that contain adequate information as to how corporations are conducting themselves.

So necessary is it to have adequate data on the functioning of corporations that, if corporations do not provide this information, there is sure to be a demand that the government provide it, that the government take over the responsibility of interpreting to the public the progress of corporations, both singly and in mass. I think there can be little question that, if a governmental bureau or agency has to take over the responsibility for corporate reporting, there will be a serious restriction upon the development of our American system of free enterprise. The task of improving present reporting should be one for the corporations themselves, and I believe that they can do it without government order.

Quantity and Quality of Corporate Reporting. The problem of adequate reporting on corporate activity is one of both quantity and quality. There must be enough corporations reporting on their own activity to provide a satisfactory cross section of business. These reports must be individual, not group or mass reports. The corporation system will need to be judged on the basis of how individual companies work.

So far as the quantity of reports is concerned, most of the large and important corporations publish reports now, as do a substantial number of the smaller ones, because of requirements of stock exchanges and other governmental rules and regulations. In addition, a very considerable number also publish reports entirely of their own volition. These groups include most of the companies with any important public security holdings. The number of corporations which issue reports is constantly increasing as time and events require the sale of securities. Altogether, the number now reporting, along with accretions to be expected, furnish an adequate quantity of corporate reports for public use, and there is no need to extend the number by including corporations which have not invited public participation in their ownership. I think the quantity of reporting may be considered reasonably adequate.

It is the quality of the reporting that is unsatisfactory. I do not think such a statement needs much argument to support it. A great deal has been written on the subject in recent months. For instance, Dr. Claude Robinson, President of Opinion Research Corporation, recently said there is evidence not only that the financial journalism of industry is not understood but, even more important, that it is not trusted. Another unpublished public opinion poll showed a surprisingly large percentage of disbelief in financial reports. Labor representatives and radicals of one kind or another are constantly attacking the validity of corporate reporting; and while much of labor's criticism is intemperate and exaggerated, more and more attacks are being presented in a reasonable and dispassionate manner that undoubtedly has some effect.

Many businessmen, too, have expressed themselves as believing that the conventional methods of presenting financial figures are not useful in this period of disturbed conditions. Even the expert analysts — or perhaps I should say particularly the experts — are not happy with the information being received. And, unfortunately, I need to submit no proof that the accounting basis of financial reporting presents difficulties for the average reader, if indeed it does not do so for the trained accountant.

Profits are not understood, generally, nor the relation of prices to profits, nor the effect of volume on profits, nor the risks. Nor is it generally understood that corporations must provide for reasonable growth from within themselves, that they must renew themselves from their own operations and protect their positions by expanding from within as the demand requires it. Nor is it realized that earnings of the corporation are not the same as the return to stockholders, that there is a difference between earnings per share and distributable dividends per share if the corporations are to be kept healthy and able to carry on the country's business. Nor is it clear that the stockholder, the security holder, is about the only participant in the corporate activity who is considered in terms of dollars instead of purchasing power, whose income (in the form of dividends) has not been adjusted for the changing value of the dollar; that a dividend increase of 25% over 1941 is, generally, a smaller "take" from the corporation than has been obtained by all those elements whose return has followed the changing value of the dollar.

Profits are the lifeblood of a corporation. They must be large enough to provide adequate inventories and facilities and tools; they must provide a return to security holders; and they must provide a reserve fund in good times against the needs of bad times. Business cannot exist without profits; our economy cannot exist without sound business. Profits must be something for all to be proud of; they should not be suspect. The job of defining profits and explaining their nature and uses is only now being undertaken.

It is strange, in a way, that criticism of corporate reporting should be getting more articulate and misunderstanding more evident in the very period when corporate reporting has been making considerable progress and improving in many ways. Apparently the need for understanding has increased in recent years even more rapidly, probably because more people want to use corporate reports and want to understand them, and some of those people have become vocal in their criticism when they have found reports inadequate.

So far as progress and improvement are concerned, corporation reports certainly are more elaborate and more attractive; they have more pictures and more charts; and occasionally they attempt to apply simple language to figures. But, on the whole, the emphasis has been on getting more people to read the reports, to have more people understand a little about the corporation, rather than on giving more significant information to those capable of using it. The adaptation of corporate reports to the objective of educating the public is no doubt necessary; at least, those skilled in public relations appear to think so. The "new look" in reports, however, has not added materially to the information given to those who have been making a purposeful effort to study and analyze reports and to use them in forming serious judgments.

I think it is not too much to say that most reports are pitched at too low a level of reader intelligence. So far the low level has received much attention; but equally important is what is provided for the high level of reader intelligence, and it is with the latter area that I propose to deal in this and the subsequent article.

The core of the problem is in adequate financial reporting — in satisfactory financial statements — and at the heart of that is the reporting upon annual income or earnings. If there can be useful, satisfactory, and adequate reporting of earnings, we shall, I think, have found the answer to the main problem. Not that statements of income alone will suffice; certainly other financial statements will be required, such as *Assets and Liabilities,* and even more will interpretation and analysis from the corporations themselves be required. But presentation of earnings remains the key.

Unfortunately, there are many difficulties in the way of adequate reporting of earnings. Some of these problems I propose to treat in some detail.

Need for Public Education. The first problem is how to increase the number of people who can be expected to understand corporate reports so that there can be an informed public to deal with the information; to see that a purposeful minority does not mislead; to see that corporations do live up to their responsibilities and, if they do, that they have full opportunity to function. That means that there must be a great increase in the number of stockholders who can understand reports and in the number of others who can correctly interpret and appraise corporate reports from the standpoint of the public. Just as in other phases of a free society, an informed public is the best assurance against abuses from within and subversive attacks from without. For the maximum usefulness of the corporate system, a definite program of education is called for.

The task looks difficult at times, particularly when letters from stockholders to a corporation are read at the time of its annual meeting, or when the lack of attendance at annual stockholders' meetings is considered. One could not be blamed for thinking that stockholders have little understanding of, and perhaps even less interest in, anything but dividends and executive salaries. There is, however, encouragement in the increasing number of stockholders, or stockholders' representatives, who have made intelligent analyses and who ask searching questions at annual meetings. The increasing number of such people justifies a belief that there may develop in our society an adequate group of people who understand corporate reporting. The colleges have done much in the development of such a group and can do much more. The responsibility for increasing public knowledge is largely theirs.

Two facts, the increase in the number of those going to college and the even greater increase in the percentage of those who are interested in learning of business economics, suggest that the colleges in their formal programs can contribute more and more to business understanding. Education in accounting is spreading rapidly, but if the goal is to be achieved, more and more people must understand the underlying principles governing the presentation of financial statements.

I think perhaps the greatest contribution of the colleges to this end has been in removing accounting and financial reporting from the realm of the impossibly mysterious to that of the possibly understandable. It has not been many years since accounting was regarded as an esoteric science which all but accountants should leave alone. In the past, it was quite usual for otherwise intelligent business or professional men to admit unashamedly that accounting was beyond them. What is more, they were satisfied to remain in that state of ignorance. Parenthetically, I might state that the trouble was with the accountants and their own confusion just about as much as it was with the laymen, and that as accountants have been resolving their confusion, laymen have been less resigned to their lack of understanding. At any rate, great progress has been made in taking accounting from the realm of the esoteric and putting it in the place of an understandable art.

Formal education in accounting needs to be extended, not only among those who are taking courses in business but to others. More people must know a little about corporate financial statements, if only to know enough not to be afraid of them. I am not advocating making expert analysts of thousands of men and women, but I am advocating enough education so that thousands can understand and use the reports of expert analysts. We do need, badly, some kind of adult education on this subject. It ought to be as much a part of the educational program as a course in civics, economics, or history.

This adult education can come about in many ways: by formal group work with others in the extension courses given by so many universities; by improved literature available for study by individuals; but beyond these, and perhaps more practicable in this age where men and women will not read very much, by the explanations which can be given in corporate reports themselves to aid the reader in interpreting the financial statements included therein.

This program, however, will require a better understanding of accounting by public relations experts and those who are advising corporations on how to publish financial data. The public relations group is a crucial one in the dissemination of adequate information on financial statements, and it needs to be adequately grounded in a knowledge of accounting and other business problems. There is evidence that this group has come some distance in such understanding, and self-interest can, I believe, be counted on to extend it.

In addition, there should be better reporting of corporate income and financial affairs in the newspapers and business magazines. Increased interpretation and analysis would be helpful, but what is urgently needed now is just plain understanding of the net income for the year. The difficulty is not only that the coverage of corporate reports is inadequate but that sometimes it is downright misleading. I am not critical of the newspapers or of the financial editors. There are definite limitations upon them, particularly the fact that space must be apportioned. But it would help tremendously in the public understanding of corporations if more of the explanations which are readily available in corporate reports were retailed by the press. Wider dissemination of the news contained in the reports is badly needed. A comparison of one figure of income with that of the previous year is just not adequate reporting; even worse, the figure in the paper is sometimes not the net income shown by the financial reports.

That there is not better understanding of financial reports in the newspaper offices is, I think, as much a criticism of accountants and of corporations as of the press. It is hard to imagine how a financial editor could have any confidence in analyzing statements when he has found, day after day, so great a variety of practice in the stating of income. As accounting develops more standards, or more criteria, and reduces the variety of practice, perhaps then a financial editor can write with more assurance. But, nevertheless, the time has come when it is quite necessary for financial editors to have a better understanding of the principles of financial statements and the philosophy of corporation income if the newspapers are to publish the news of corporation earnings and to discuss and report upon the progress of corporations.

I hope the colleges and universities will take the lead. Their faculties are experts in education. On an undergraduate or even graduate level the task is not too difficult; all that is needed is an acceleration of the present trends. But I want to suggest that the colleges and universities, particularly those with large schools or colleges of business administration undertake more responsibility for adult education in the field of published financial reports, both to see that literature is available — such as some readable books emphasizing the understanding rather than the techniques of accounting — and to see that seminars or group opportunities for discussion are provided. Perhaps there could be refresher courses for financial editors or public relations people or investors, or for accountants for that matter. And, further, perhaps the colleges could help to start annual forums or short courses specializing in corporate reporting.

If we can look forward to a wider interest in and a better understanding of corporate reports, as I believe we can, then we can profitably proceed to an examination of the financial data that can and should be presented to this higher level of intelligence.

Problems of Presentation

In a consideration of the proper presentation of corporate earnings, there are again several different problems to be examined, such as the identity of those to whom the reports are to be directed, what is needed in the way of information to make them useful, the form and manner of presentation, which accounting practices and concepts can be most useful, and the adequacy or inadequacy of the orthodox methods of accounting.

If it were not for the present disturbed economic conditions, the accountants might feel pretty complacent about the tremendous amount of progress made in improving the accounting principles used for financial reporting over the last few years. But the current stresses and strains have shown some weakness in the ability of accounting, as it has so far been developed, to report adequately on corporate activity; so the whole system is under challenge. Moreover, the point is that although accounting as it has been developing over recent years — and for want of a better word we can call this orthodox accounting — has been doing an increasingly valuable job, it is now in a position to do an even better one. A review of what has been developing will indicate what can be expected of orthodox accounting.

Purpose of Corporation Reports. The first step is to determine who are to be reached by corporate reporting and then to find out what is useful for them.

Confusion of thought has arisen because of the great increase in the number and size of the segments of society that are interested in corporate reports. Historically, reports by corporations were reports to stockholders or security holders, and they were primarily reports on what had happened in the way of the accumulated results from operations. With most companies there was great care not to overstate the results of the accumulations. In effect, it seems to me, as I look back on it, that the unformulated thought was to report as if to a stockholder who was a permanent participant in the enterprise and who needed to know only whether the investment appeared safe and the dividend policy reasonably secure. It was as if the reporting were quantitative and not qualitative. Each corporation thus reported in its own way and for itself alone, without regard to others.

Accounting thought, generally, was that within reason any principle of reporting was all right as long as it was consistently applied and produced conservative value amounts for the showing of resources and liabilities. At first conservatism and then conservatism and consistency were the cardinal virtues; and, on the whole, they seemed useful, perhaps even adequate, for the needs and abilities of the times. It took the business abuses of the 1920's and the violent dislocations of the depression period of 1929 to 1932 to show that much more was needed.

At the end of the 1920's and on through the 1930's new groups wanted to form judgments on corporate progress. Instead of being reported to as a permanent investor, the stockholder wanted to be reported to as if he might be temporary. He wanted reliable information to help him judge whether he should sell his holdings or buy more. Then, because corporations used the security markets, it became recognized that they had obligations arising from such use to provide information for possible new stockholders. The community interest began to be apparent, evidenced on a local level by the vital interest a town or city might have in its dominant industry.

Then in the 1930's sharpened bargaining developed among those who had a stake in the fruits of a corporation's activity, among stockholders, labor, management, suppliers, and customers, sometimes with bargaining power so heavily weighted by government regulation or intervention in favor of certain groups that it destroyed the proper balance between them that might have come from adequate information and a freer play of the economic forces. And, in addition, the public reliance on corporations for promotion of business gave everyone an interest in corporate activity. All these groups wanted information from corporate reports which would be useful for their varied purposes. In such a setting the old concepts of consistency and conservatism alone were inadequate.

Content of Financial Statements. In spite of the wide variety of interest among those concerned with corporate reports, basically there is not so much difference in what they need from corporate reporting. If all the needs of the stockholder or investor are satisfied, then the published statements will be useful for the others. What does the stockholder need — and what should he have?

The stockholder is entitled, first, to a frank report of stewardship, a report on what happened, and an accounting of what the management did with the tools and facilities, the goodwill and going business entrusted to it. But he should have all this in a way which permits him to form a sound judgment about how well that management is performing and whether the management should be rewarded or not be kept at all. For this the stockholder needs qualitative information instead of only quantitative. For this he must have comparative data, to judge the corporation not in the vacuum of its own performance for one year but in comparison with the preceding year and in comparison with other corporations and their progress from year to year. There must be information to permit the stockholder to form judgments not on how much but on how good. If that information is furnished, the public, as well as the stockholders, will be getting the information needed.

Those qualitative data, or comparative data, require one basic thing: the sharpest possible determination of the earnings of the corporation for each year's operation, prepared on the basis of certain generally accepted standards for all business so that the progress of each corporation will be measured by the same measuring stick.

Accountants have been doing a great deal of work in this direction, and current — perhaps I should say new — accounting principles are proving very useful in sharpening the presentation of income.

Extent of Information. There seems to be pretty general agreement on the extent of the information which is desirable in financial statements. The Securities and Exchange Commission and other regulatory bodies have been dealing with this question for a number of years, as have the accountants, and certain minimum requirements appear to be generally accepted. These minimum data, properly sharpened, will give adequate information on the progress of the corporation year by year. Any great elaboration of detail might well raise more questions than it would answer.

I think such a philosophy is sound. It does not seem to be desirable to extend disclosure in financial statements to information on the details of operating management. For instance, while it is highly desirable for corporations to publish annually the amount of sales, seldom is it necessary or desirable to break those sales down into the sales of the various products; there is even less desirability of allocating the various costs and expenses and profits to specific lines of product. There is other information which, on the surface, may seem desirable but which experience has shown to be so susceptible of misleading inferences that its publication is not helpful to anyone.

Classification of Expenses. While there is no noticeable demand for more detailed information in the presentation of each year's earnings, there are two recent developments which should be encouraged. Income reporting has been based on certain breakdowns of costs and expenses which in many cases have little to recommend them except historical familiarity. In certain lines of business, such as retail and wholesale trade, finance, transportation, utilities, and others, the classifications are useful and comparable; for manufacturing companies the historical breakdowns leave much to be desired. Separation of depreciation and amortization, income taxes, bonus and pension plans, nonrecurring and unusual items is desirable and useful; but the basic division into cost of sales, on the one hand, and selling, general, and administrative expenses, on the other hand, which provides only a surface comparison with the preceding year, seems to me to be unsatisfactory.

Some corporations have not been satisfied to report merely one figure for cost of sales and one for commercial expenses. Lately there has been considerable experimenting with the presentation of a division of expenses and costs by natural classifications, such as labor, cost of materials and services bought, cost of the use of and maintenance of tools and facilities, depreciation, taxes, amounts provided as estimated future costs incident to production already completed, and other similar classes.

The United States Steel Corporation was a pioneer in the change in classifications, and its lead has been followed by other important corporations, some of which base their entire report of operations upon natural classifications while others submit the new classifications as a supplement to the historically more orthodox form.

The presentation of costs and expenses in this way would add to the comparability of figures, one year with another and one company with another. In addition, if the method were widely followed, the aggregate of the information would be useful in showing trends and shifts of balance among the various interests and could have some useful over-all economic and statistical importance. For instance, if all the steel-making companies were to follow the lead of the United States Steel Corporation, and if other large companies producing basic materials were to do likewise, cumulative information with respect to changes in the divisions of the fruits of business might be discernible.

Further experimentation is necessary. For instance, the groupings into so few natural classifications may not be adequate; the groupings may be too general, and some breakdowns may prove to be necessary. In general, however, I think the development is to be commended, and the use of such classifications should be more widely adopted.

Single-Step Presentation. Another recent development has been a trend toward what has become known as the single-step form of income presentation. The orthodox, or historical, form of presentation is to break up the determination of net income into several steps, variously labeled gross profit, operating profit, profit before taxes, profit before special charges, and, finally, net profit, or perhaps not even such a title as net profit. Some years ago accountants began to challenge the significance of the special totals and to wonder why some items of cost or expenses appeared to outrank others, as if there were an option about some of the costs. It seemed desirable to some to reduce confusion by showing only one profit, to avoid meaningless subtotals, and to show all costs and expenses as necessary elements to be deducted together before determining the profit for the year.

There should be little argument about the desirability of reducing the confusion and concentrating attention on one figure of profit, yet the idea has been slow to take hold, has not been actively advocated by many accountants, and even has been actively opposed by the Securities and Exchange Commission because it did not require a showing of profit before taxes. To my mind, there is little to be gained, outside of mathematical or statistical convenience, in showing such a figure as profit before taxes; and the misuse which has been made of such so-called profit figures is evidence of their undesirability. By all means let there be a showing of the amount of income taxes, but let the report on the operations of the company emphasize the only profit — the net earnings for the year. The number of companies doing just that is increasing, and there is reason to hope that the trend will accelerate.

Semantics. Closely related to improvements in the form of presentation of the results of operations is the problem of improvements in the wording used. In the attempt to remove accounting from the realm of the esoteric, greater attention should be paid to using words which have meaning to a layman as well as to an expert. There is a wide area for improvement, and the necessity for improvement is being recognized. Many corporations have actually changed from some of the old familiar accounting terms. While the accountant moves slowly and while to him, as to others, familiar things are comfortable, enough has been done already to indicate that a general change may come quite rapidly.

Some changes have already received approval from accountants and from others, and more will undoubtedly be accepted. Right now much credit would seem to be due to the United States Steel Corporation and the Caterpillar Tractor Company for starting the movement.

First came a change from a *Profit and Loss Statement* to a *Statement of Income* or a *Statement of Earnings.* I think I prefer the latter. *Earnings* sounds like something that comes from work, and that is just how it has come. *Earnings* is a good word with good connotations.

Then there is *Surplus.* The word has a special meaning in accounting but certainly has connotations to the lay reader not always in line with the accounting meaning. To most, *Surplus* means something over and above needs, so in corporate statements no one can blame a reader for thinking that *Surplus* may be an amount unneeded. To make matters worse, accounting has set up an *Earned Surplus* and a *Capital Surplus.* The words have no logic even for accountants and do not provide for an automatic classification. So now we are seeing the term *Earned Surplus* replaced occasionally by the term *Earnings* (or *Income*) *Retained for Use in the Business,* a phrase that certainly is easier for a reader to understand than was its predecessor. Likewise, *Capital Surplus* is becoming *Capital Paid in by Stockholders in Excess of Amount Assigned to Capital Stock.* Even *Capital Stock and Surplus,* a major classification, is becoming *Stockholders' Investment.*

Then there is improvement in the term *Net Current Assets,* surely a term of art. This is being replaced in some cases by the term *Working Capital,* which at least sounds less formidable. Even the term *Balance Sheet* is being replaced by titles such as *Statement of Resources and Liabilities,* or *Assets and Liabilities.*

Perhaps more than any other, the word *Reserves* needs attention; it has so many conflicting meanings, often in the same statement. In England it is suggested that amounts set up for specific needs should be called *Provisions* and that the term *Reserve* should be used only where there is no specific need.

Other changes in wording could aid in the understanding of the earnings presentation and of financial statements in general. Experimentation in this field should be continued, and the changes already made should have a thorough trial. I think that some of them have already done something to clear up confusion and to provide sharper self-definition. And, as evidence of the desirability of change, I myself shall henceforth refer to the results of operations of a corporation as *Earnings* instead of using several different terms more or less interchangeably as I have heretofore.

I add a plea to the teachers of accounting to give special attention to this problem of semantics, a study in which many of them were pioneers.

Determination of Earnings

All the foregoing are important problems, but all come to naught if the accounting determination of the results of the year is not adequate or satisfactory. We have agreed, I trust, that the information needed by stockholders and others about the operations must be information which sets forth as sharply as possible the earnings for each year; that it must be submitted in accordance with generally recognized standards in order that it may be comparable with the past and future; and that it must be as useful as possible for comparison with other companies. Variations of basic accounting principles need to be reduced to a minimum.

Before I go much farther, I should say more about what I have called comparability with other corporations. I was asked recently how it was possible to compare the results of operations of one corporation with those of another when corporations do business in such a great variety of ways, with such a wide difference in products, and under such different conditions. The mere fact that one corporation makes more money than another, or has more stability of earnings, or shows more earnings per dollar of sales or dollar of investment, means little in judging the efficiency of the corporation. Even a comparison of companies doing the same kind and only the same kind of business in the same way is likely to be misleading because of the variety of the business conditions, such as location, accumulated goodwill, lack of immediate strong competition, and so on.

When the products are different and the methods of doing business are different, comparative results for one year alone are even less useful in judging efficiency. And a multiplication of standard forms and terminology will not overcome the inherent differences. But it is possible for us to get some help if we can measure the progress of one company from year to year with the progress of another company from year to year. In fact, it is only by such comparisons that the knowledge of the operating results of each company becomes truly useful. It is only in this way that the stockholder can know not only how much but how good.

When we understand the desirability of being able to compare one year with another and one company with another, we can understand the necessity for a sharp determination of earnings for each year and a minimum variety of accounting principles.

Basic Accounting Requirements. In order to reach the goal of a sharp measurement of progress year by year and company by company, there are three basic accounting requirements: (1) There must be a minimum of arbitrary shifting of items of income or expense from one year to another. (2) There must be a minimum of extraneous or arbitrary items that distort the showing of the results of operations.

And (3) earnings must be clearly etched against the backdrop of the economic conditions of the year.

It is in these three areas that there has been the greatest need for a reduction in variety of accounting practices and for criteria to guide practice. It is here that differences of thought and practice have been the cause of the greatest confusion in reporting corporate earnings and in understanding them. In recent years accounting concepts in these areas have been sharpened and accounting principles have been more clearly stated. The full effect of what has been done will not be apparent until corporate reports on 1947 earnings can be analyzed and compared, and perhaps not fully apparent until there is a second year of reporting under the new refinements.

The most significant work which has been done in recent years in the statement of accounting principles has been that of the American Institute of Accountants through its Committee on Accounting Procedure. This committee consists of 21 members and is composed of accountants, in public practice or in teaching, who represent different geographical and professional points of view. The committee has been working for nine years and has had the help of an able research staff. It issues opinions from time to time, called Accounting Research Bulletins, and it is these which have dealt with points where variety of practice has interfered most seriously with achieving the three goals I have mentioned. The committee has no authority except the prestige of its members and the soundness of its positions, but these have been sufficient to give its bulletins great weight.

The committee is not the only group dealing with these problems. Other associations of accountants are making contributions. Individuals, by articles and books, are helping to clarify thinking and often preparing the way for progress. Governmental agencies and commissions are dealing more and more with accounting. Progress is not due to any one group or agency. The Institute's Committee on Accounting Procedure has, within the past four years, issued ten bulletins, which, taken together, can be appraised in retrospect as having pointed the way to portrayal of earnings of corporations which will satisfy the basic requirements that I have been discussing. I do not propose to deal extensively with the committee or its recent bulletins; I have done that elsewhere (*Journal of Accountancy*, January, 1948). I do need to refer briefly to some of these bulletins, however, in order to show that great progress has been made in establishing standards and in sharpening the concept of net earnings.

Accounting Research Bulletins. The first of this series of recent bulletins was Bulletin 23, on *income taxes*, issued in December 1944. It said, in effect, that special items excluded from the earnings statement should carry with them the applicable tax effect. In other words, where an item of importance was excluded from the statement of earnings because it distorted the year's results, the tax effect was to be excluded also. The same idea applied to the use of reserves to absorb charges. It has been taking a long time for this principle to be generally adopted, but I think the position has greater validity today than at any time since 1944.

A natural extension of Bulletin 23 appeared in Bulletin 26, dealing with *the use of war reserves.* The use of such reserves or their return to earnings was to be dealt with net of the related income tax. More than that, however, the bulletin attempted to minimize the variety of practice in the use of the war reserves and their treatment. It took the position that amounts of the reserves which were to be brought back into the earnings statement or used to relieve earnings should be limited to the amount of the net effect on earnings of certain restricted classes of expenses or costs growing out of war production or activity.

Bulletin 28 dealt with *contingency reserves.* Here, in the past, had been the most commonly used method for shifting income from one year to another with or without much justification or need. The practice had been condemned generally for several years, but this bulletin was an unequivocal statement against the setting up or using of general-purpose contingency reserves to affect earnings.

Bulletin 29 suggested *practices of pricing inventories.* The aim was to reduce the variety of practice and decrease the effect of practices which had merely shifted income from good years to bad ones, or vice versa.

Bulletin 31 dealt with *reserves for future losses not inherent in the assets on hand,* designed only to protect against economic changes of future years. This bulletin, by recommending against such reserves, went a long way to make possible a statement of earnings that would be sharply etched against the backdrop of the economic conditions of the year rather than having some cushion within itself (usually entirely arbitrary) against those economic conditions.

All these bulletins were directed to reducing variety of practice and thus increasing comparability. But they are bound to have an important effect in another direction, namely, removing one of the causes for doubt of the integrity of accounting and accountants. It had long been obvious that an important basis for criticism had been in the use of reserves — for contingencies, for postwar adjustments, for future decline in inventory prices. First there was no consistency in the provision of the reserves. One company would provide a reserve; another company similarly situated provided no reserve. There seemed to be no criteria for determining the amount, though there were cynics who said it all depended on the amount of the earnings. Yet independent accountants approved the report of earnings in identical language in all these varying cases.

When it came to the use of the reserves, a similar variety of practice was discernible. Sometimes the reserves were used; sometimes not. Sometimes they were returned to income in full or in part; sometimes not. Again, accountants stated that each of these separate practices was in accordance with generally accepted accounting principles. It was little wonder that there were those who said that the determination of net earnings was too much a matter of management desire.

The ban on general-purpose contingency reserves, the recommendation against reserves out of earnings which cushioned the influence of the economic background of the year, and the setting up of criteria for the use of reserves, all of which took place in 1947, should have removed much ground for criticism, and the reports on corporation earnings for 1947 should be more usefully comparable.

Effects of Rising Prices. But in addition to the areas of confusion of prior years, 1947 raised a new point of confusion all its own. The impact of the change in the value of the dollar hit corporation reporting in full force in 1947. Demands were being made that accounting reflect directly some of the effects of that disturbance on the measurement of earnings. Particularly was it said that earnings including inventory profits arising from orthodox accounting were not real and that depreciation charges based on cost were a snare and a delusion. Many and varied were the methods tentatively tried out during 1947 to meet these new demands. Just when arbitrary reserves seemed to have been banned in income reporting, a new set of reserves, infinitely more difficult to measure and much more subject to individual discretion, began to crop up.

Orthodox accounting spoke up for orthodoxy — for the use of cost for depreciation instead of the use of current values. Whether the Institute's committee was wrong remains to be seen; indeed, it did not itself dismiss the new idea forever. The chief point in its bulletin on this subject is, I think, in the stated desire of the committee not to encourage such a tremendous variety of practice as would have existed had the use of current replacement costs for depreciation been approved, and thus undo all that the committee had done to sharpen the determination of income and increase confidence in the integrity of corporate reporting.

This controversy was essentially a conflict between the economic concepts of income, albeit somewhat vaguely delineated, and accounting concepts; it was not settled by the bulletin, except on one point and temporarily. That conflict is the most important problem before accountants and others involved in improving the reporting of corporate earnings. The whole problem of concepts of income, with the implications for presentation of earnings, will be discussed in detail in my subsequent article.

CONCEPTS OF INCOME

George D. Bailey

CONCEPTS OF INCOME

BY GEORGE D. BAILEY

THERE is today a great deal of concern with the measurement and meaning of profits. In an article in the September Number of the HARVARD BUSINESS REVIEW entitled "Problems in Reporting Corporation Income," I dealt with the sharpening of the accounting concepts of income, the reduction of variety of practice in certain important areas, and the way in which the bulletins of the Committee on Accounting Procedure of the American Institute of Accountants have been moving to result in greater usefulness of earnings statements. We are justified in a hope that such progress will do much to increase confidence in the integrity of accounts and accountants. In this article I shall take up another subject on which the work of the committee has been important: the refinements of the principles applicable to presentation of earnings.

Accordingly, I should like to treat two major questions: (1) the desirability of a presentation which focuses attention on the earnings of the particular year — the "exclusive" concept; (2) whether the further step should be taken of trying to reflect the impact of changing conditions, so as to secure a better interpretation of the year's earnings.

Focusing on the Year's Earnings

In addition to sharpening the determination of earnings, orthodox accounting has done something in the way of sharpening the methods of presentation of the net earnings for the year. This is a much more important problem than appears from the mere statement of it. It involves the question of whether the statement of net earnings for the year shall be pointed to a figure showing the results of operations for the year, or whether the statement primarily is to be the channel and the only channel whereby all items of income get into the accumulated earnings of the company.

As I have stated the problem, there would not seem to be much room for controversy; obviously, the figure of earnings for the year is the important item. In the historical development, which I explained earlier, the difference between the accumulated results at the close of one year and at the close of the next year has become progressively less and less adequate for current needs in appraising the progress of a company. As we saw, the accumulated results of all years were of quantitative and not of qualitative usefulness. Yet the argument as to which is the proper emphasis still persists; and because it does, I propose to deal with the controversy at some length.

Let me state again what that controversy is: whether it is better (1) to have all items which are treated in the accounting of a year considered as part of the determination of earnings for the year, and to have items get to accumulated earnings only through the *Statement of Earnings* — the all-inclusive concept; or (2) to have the earnings re-

EDITOR'S NOTE: This article completes the publication of Mr. Bailey's 1948 Dickinson Lectures before the Harvard Graduate School of Business Administration.

ported for the year freed of important large items which have nothing to do with the operations for that year and to apply those items directly to the accumulated earnings of all years. The second theory completely rejects the necessity of bookkeeping all items through the yearly earnings statement.

I hope it even sounds a little silly to mention the possibility that the bookkeeping techniques could override a sharp determination of earnings. If it does sound that way, the reason is in part the use of the word *Earnings* instead of the term *Profit and Loss Statement* and in part, I trust, the cumulative effect of the arguments for the necessity of a sharp determination of earnings as developed and presented in these two articles. I regard the all-inclusive argument as a dangerous doctrine and believe its persistence has had a strong deterrent effect on progress toward a sharp determination of earnings. The problem, in my opinion, should no longer be which theory to accept but how to establish criteria and standards to make the exclusive theory most useful.

Of course, the problem cannot be quite so simple as I have made it out to be. There have been serious difficulties with the exclusive concept and sound criticisms of the way it has sometimes been applied in practice. Nevertheless, to revert to the all-inclusive theory merely because the exclusive theory could not be completely policed would be to accept what I believe to be a limitation on progress toward a meaningful presentation of earnings. Perhaps a further glance at historical developments will clarify this point.

Historical Abuses. In all fairness, it must be noted that the all-inclusive argument got its start in abuses in income reporting. In the decade of the 1920's companies were selling securities and diffusing ownership — and reporting to the public during some quite hectic financial periods. The old idea that it was proper to exclude many kinds of items from the showing of income took a good deal of abuse. This was an era when items classed as nonrecurring were excluded from earnings, when the direct charges to *Surplus* were sometimes difficult to find among the several statements, when exclusions were mostly charges that would have reduced reported earnings, and when historical records of earnings as well as current statements were all affected by the nonrecurring theory. It was an era of reconstructed earnings, of what the earnings would have been *if* the effect of items not likely to recur in subsequent years were eliminated. Then came the collapse of the stock market, the depression, and the adjustment of security values — and the examination of financial and accounting policies of the period.

It was apparent that the nonrecurring theory, the reconstructed earnings theory, was wrong. Business always operated with mistakes, incurred unexpected costs or losses. Each year there was a different set of nonrecurring items. It was apparent that earnings could not be reconstructed to indicate the next year's earnings or earning power. They could only be sharpened to show more clearly what had happened. Then later the depression developed heavy and unexpected losses which corporations sought to have excluded in reporting income. So, when public offering of securities began again, there was a Securities and Exchange Commission and a memory of abuses in the reporting of earnings. The cure at the time seemed to be the all-inclusive concept. Put everything in the earnings statement, and let the reader decide what should be excluded. There was to be no more of this nonrecurring argument. Corporations, so it was said, were not to be trusted to deal objectively with exclusions to sharpen income, and the accountants were not to be required to police them.

Of course, that did not work. The pendulum had swung too far. Items continued to be excluded, not because they were nonrecurring but rather because they were not related to the year's operations. Although no reconstruction of earnings was acceptable on an "if" basis, and although for financing purposes earnings had to be reported upon the all-inclusive basis for several years, it was frequently necessary and advisable to reconstruct the past earnings in order to allocate completed transactions back to the right year. The doctrine of exclusion to avoid misleading inferences again began to have more respectability. So in the late 1930's once more the necessities of a sharp determination of earnings became dominant, though still somewhat suspect.

Then the impact of the war brought on many adjustments, either provisions for the fears of the future or corrections of past reserves, tentative accounting for current uncertainties, and subsequent settlements thereof. This situation led to a new rash of exclusions and, because the accounting profession had not established adequate criteria, brought also a wide variety of practice on inclusions or exclusions. Some accountants thought that perhaps, after all, the all-inclusive theory, with all its weakness, might be an improvement. Particularly did this doubt appear to be recurrent with the staff of the Securities and Exchange Commission.

Approval of Exclusion Theory. During the last decade, the Committee on Accounting Procedure of the American Institute of Accountants has accepted the theory of exclusion from earnings of items which would result in distortion or possible misleading inferences. It has done so cautiously, because of the historical background, but it has done so very definitely nonetheless. In several of the years the committee reexamined its position — and regularly reaffirmed it.

After the war the committee found itself in a position where it must do something with the problem — either accept the all-inclusive theory or establish some criteria for the exclusions. Fortunately for corporate reporting it did the latter. In its Bulletin No. 32, the committee reaffirmed its position in favor of excluding some items, in some circumstances, from the determination of earnings for the year to be reported to stockholders and to the public. For the first time, the committee proposed criteria and standards for exclusion, and, instead of a position which was permissive only, took one which recommended exclusion subject to these standards.

In the meantime the American Accounting Association has consistently advocated the all-inclusive theory as the only one. It has taken the position that everything was to go to *Surplus* by way of the earnings statement; that the reader could do better for himself in judging the relevancy of the special items than any insider could do for him. The Association presented this thesis in 1937, reaffirmed it in 1940, and only recently has again reaffirmed it. The Association, representing the academic world, is sincere and objective, beyond question, and its position can be referred to by those who prefer the easier way, because it is easier beyond doubt for corporations, for accountants, for government regulatory bodies, and for the SEC to have everything treated before determining an income figure (obviously not earnings) than it is to assume the difficult responsibility of excluding extraordinary and material transactions not related to the year's operations, a task involving accounting knowledge, integrity, and independence of the highest order. Certainly the acceptance of the all-inclusive theory would make for an easier, even though not a more useful, profession of accounting.

The SEC too has shown some disinclination to accept the position of the Committee on Accounting Procedure – at least as expressed in Bulletin No. 32. The SEC staff clearly is not happy with the bulletin, and no doubt it does make operations as a government bureau more difficult. But financial statements cannot be poured into a mold, and accounting questions cannot always be based on fixed rules. This matter of exclusions from income, even within the criteria, still involves judgment. Apparently, the Commission has recognized the impracticability or unwisdom of an all-inclusive rule, but it does not agree to accept the judgment of the corporations and the accountants. Accordingly, with the approval of the Commission, its Chief Accountant has issued a letter which says, in effect, that he does not like the extent of the freedom for judgment allowed under the criteria, and proposes to substitute his judgment and that of his staff or the Commission's judgment as to the propriety of exclusions, whenever that may be deemed necessary.

But before we cry that this is contrary to free corporate reporting, let us wait and see how the Commission will operate. Perhaps the powers implied in that letter will be helpful in giving to the bulletin the authority necessary to prevent abuse. It is unthinkable that the SEC will not do all it can to assist in the sharpest possible showing of earnings for the year. This is a good place to point out that there has been a very high degree of cooperation between the SEC and the Committee on Accounting Procedure, and that the areas of disagreement are not numerous; in fact the Commission by its acceptance of the positions set forth in most of the other bulletins of the committee has given to them an authority which otherwise could not have been so quickly attained. The disagreements are really few in number and are influenced, I think, by the necessities of running a government agency or bureau.

Certainly Bulletin No. 32 deserves to have influence. Without dealing here with the details of the bulletin, I can say that the criteria it sets up are directed to a sharp presentation of earnings for the year and the exclusion of extraneous bookkeeping, windfall, or other nonoperating events. This leaves to the corporation and its certifying accountants the responsibility for the sharp determination, which I submit is just where that responsibility belongs. If they cannot handle it, after a fair opportunity to do so, then will be time enough for fixed governmental rules or controls.

Presentation of Excluded Items. The propriety of exclusions is only one phase of the problem. Another is how to show the excluded items. The recovery of a tax claim for a distant prior year is important information, even if it has nothing to do with the earnings of the current year. The loss on the indicate that accounting was an obsolete tool.

Of course, orthodox accounting had served adequately during periods when there was a reasonably stable price level. Changes in the price levels, as long as they were gradual, had little effect, and economic income was not so far from accounting income as to require definition and consideration. The surprising thing is that there was so little examination of the nature of corporate income in those earlier periods when prices did change violently. I think the answer lies in the fact that not so much was expected of accounting. There were too many hazy concepts anyway, and emphasis in accounting was, to a large extent, still on the balance sheet and not on earnings. In these years of 1947 and 1948, however, the inflationary effect of prices on profits is combined with a very high level of business activity, so that earnings expressed in dollars are frequently unusually high. Because these earnings are being criticized by some, it has become necessary, almost for the first time, that the true nature of profits be understood.

Different Kinds of Income. We need to know more about the nature of business income and to find out what concept of income — whether it be an economic concept or some other kind — is most useful for corporate reporting. If we do find out, the findings must have the support of all elements of our society that are interested in corporate income because overwhelming sponsorship will be necessary if the findings are to be generally accepted. Such a study is not one to be made by accountants alone, although the accounting profession has a primary responsibility to see it through.

Fortunately, Mr. George O. May, retired senior partner of Price, Waterhouse & Co., the firm which made possible the Dickinson lectures on which these articles are based, saw the need for such a study some years ago. Largely as a result of his efforts, a research group has been formed under the responsibility and direction of the American Institute of Accountants, with grants by the Institute and the Rockefeller Foundation, to develop definitions of terms commonly used in accounting, consistent with the meanings of the same terms as they are used in law, economics, statistics, and other areas of the social sciences. The most significant of these terms will, I am sure, be those related to corporation income. Thus the study should distinguish between the various concepts of corporate income, and perhaps by this process it will suggest the most useful of them for our current social needs. This project is world wide and fundamental, and, like all such projects, it may take some time to conclude. It will not settle accounting for accountants or economics for economists, but it should be of help to both. In the meantime, the more preliminary discussion, the better.

I have been thinking lately that one of the troubles with financial reporting is that the statements are a mixture of concepts — a mixture that prevents or obscures logical development. There are four basic concepts interwoven into one fabric of reporting of earnings: (1) accounting, (2) tax, (3) legal, and (4) economic. Let us look at each of these, as briefly and as generally as possible.

The accounting concept has been frequently defined as a matching of costs against related revenues. This definition is not quite true because the process is limited by the necessity for prudent deferment of costs already expended against revenues yet to be determined. Business uncertainties being what they are, prudence has proved to be necessary. It is this prudence which is responsible for the cost or market theory for inventories, the immediate absorption of the costs of advertising or selling, the practice of immediately charging off experimental and development expense, and many other similar items. Within the limits of prudence, progess has been toward a sharper and sharper matching of costs and revenues. It follows that the balance sheet is a statement of costs, and not values, except where prudence requires adjustment of costs for anticipated losses.

The tax laws have set up an entirely different concept of income, perhaps roughly differentiated from the accounting concept by tests of final determination as well as by certain almost whimsical departures caused by court decisions, statutes, or government policy. Accounting has found its way around most of these, but some anomalies are still noticeable. For instance, the preference of the tax authorities for straight-line depreciation has almost driven out other useful methods (such as the application of high depreciation to the early years of use of the facilities, which relates costs to anticipated usefulness instead of anticipated years of life) because many corporations have desired to have their books agree with the tax bases of depreciation. Lately there has been greater recognition by the Bureau of Internal Revenue of various methods of depreciation, but the administrative limitations have been such as to discourage their use. Another illustration is the requirement that the use of LIFO for stating inventories for tax purposes is contingent upon its use for corporate reports to the public.

The legal concept of income is hardly a concept at all, but a structure created by statute and court decisions. Nevertheless, it has had its influence. The capital stock structure is displayed in accordance with the respective state laws and shows all stockholders' investment in accordance with state laws. There is pressure to show legally distributable accumulations of earnings regardless of the practical possibility of distribution; to show earnings in accordance with the needs of debentures, bonus contracts, and so on. Particularly there has been an attempt to tie bonus income into accounting income and, where they conflict, to sacrifice accounting determinations.

Finally, there are the economic concepts of income. I am not going to attempt to define in detail just what the economic concepts of income of a corporation are. That is something which is the province of economists and something that may be expected to come out of the research study I have referred to. I am going to assume, however, that an economic concept of income for a corporation includes matching current replacement costs against sales income. It will be seen that as long as price levels remain reasonably constant, the economic concept, to this extent, does not differ materially from the accounting concept; it is only as price levels change materially that the differences become large and important. And that is what has happened.

Profits and earnings determined on cost must be retained for reinvestment in inventories and for reinvestment in plant facilities, both at higher prices. Thus, since there is no increase in goods, there is no real income. But there may be other factors in determining real income in addition to those of inventory and plant. To arrive at economic income it may be necessary to deal with long-term debt. And further, it may be necessary to consider the expansion required in working capital and facilities for a business to maintain its relative position or serve the demands upon it, as well as merely to maintain the status quo.

The research group referred to can, I believe, be expected to produce some practical definitions and concepts of economic corporate income. Whether it can provide agreement on the methods of measurement of that income is something else. If it does, can such a measurement be stated in relation to the monetary unit with enough definiteness to make it wholly useful as a measure of reporting on corporate income? I hope so.

Avoiding Too Much Variety. Nevertheless, perhaps the most useful procedure may be to work first toward a sound, logical, and sharp determination of income and earnings based on the accounting concept, freed from distracting influences of the other concepts. Then there can be a separate or additional presentation of the effects of economic forces, or the showing of tax or legal earnings, where necessary. If we have one concept to use as a starting point, we will have a minimum of variety of practice between companies, and accountants can present a sharp determination of income for use in judging the progress of corporations. Upon this foundation can be applied economic concepts to translate the accounting income to economic income as soon as some agreement can be reached as to what to apply and how to measure it. For we cannot afford to go back to a great variety of practice and a great variety of measurement of the one figure of net income if we wish to preserve and increase confidence in financial reporting and in professional accountants.

The problems of freeing reporting from distractions caused by the tax or legal theories are not too difficult – or perhaps I should say are not difficult to specify. Take, first, the tax concept. Accounting as such has done rather well in refusing to accept tax accounting as its basis. It has reduced the disturbance between the two concepts by agreeing that provisions or reserves may be net of taxes and that tax effects may be related to special items, as in Bulletin No. 23 and Bulletin No. 26 of the Committee on Accounting Procedure. But there are some changes that ought to be made in the tax laws to reduce the problems: (1) Provisions for depreciation should be greatly liberalized. (2) The requirement that LIFO must be the basis used for all reporting should be eliminated; it is a policing requirement that is not needed. (3) Reserves or provisions for future costs should be permitted when a reasonable estimate is possible. These and a few other changes in the tax rules would remove the interference of the tax laws with adequate reporting.

The necessity for this reconcilement is receiving recognition, and there is hope for success. There really is no need for government to base its taxes on an excessively strict annual determination. It should make little difference in which year it collects a tax on income. It does make a great deal of difference that it should not tax unrealized income. The best way to tax corporate income is, of course, when it reaches or should reach the stockholder. At that time income is in a shape in which the tax can be paid. But that has many problems and is a long time off. The next best hope is to have taxable income related to economic income. Thus, government should not tax inventory profits except on the basis of current replacement costs (a revised LIFO), and it should not tax income which should be assigned to replacement of facilities at higher levels than cost, to mention but two illustrations. If tax income can be related to economic income directly rather than through the medium of an accounting statement, all three concepts would be better served — tax, economic, and accounting.

The problem with respect to the legal concept is not very difficult either. Accounting has considered its own logic and its own concepts as of greater importance than statutory permissions or requirements. It has adopted the consolidated statement of earnings for a parent and its subsidiary companies, in spite of the lack of legal support; it has its own concepts for distinguishing between earnings and capital; and, finally, it has emphasized fairness of presentation of earnings to avoid misleading inferences instead of a legal concept of earnings, as in Bulletin No. 32. There are other points where conflict may be eliminated, but they are not important to the present discussion.

The problem with respect to eliminating economic concepts from current reporting is largely that of dealing with LIFO, since the use of reserves to cushion the impact of economic forces has been almost entirely eliminated. It is not a very difficult problem because it means only the determination of earnings in the orthodox way — that is, by the method most applicable to the actual flow of goods into and out of inventory — and then applying the effects of the LIFO calculations for inventory.

There would still remain at least three important difficulties with respect to LIFO for inventories. The first would require the development of some general and logical theories, related to accounting and not taxes, on the treatment of replacement reserves and on the need for such reserves. This ought not to be difficult. The second is a need for some criteria as to when LIFO is really the best matching of costs for a particular business (an almost orthodox use). This is a long-time project, but it need not be resolved at once. The third question would be whether to advocate LIFO for use by all companies. With some agreement in these fields, the income statements would be useful not only before the application of LIFO but after that application as well.

Dealing with Economic Forces. The above suggestion leaves unsolved the problem of how to deal with the impact of economic forces. Business and accounting are faced with a decision on whether to accept the economic concept much more broadly as the best means of reporting and interpreting corporate income, or whether to give it up to the extent it is now used. The present situation is not at all satisfactory.

The problem is really a business choice, because accounting can adapt itself to either. Accounting can easily accept and reflect any one concept which will be generally applied by business and which will have support of economists and statisticians, as well as business, provided there can be general criteria against which to test judgment both in the application of the concept and its measurement, and provided further that the new concept will be applied in an orderly way and over a long period of years. But neither accounting nor business can afford a policy designed for one year only, or for years of high profits only, or to be applied at the whim of a company. The new concept must be one which will be more useful than our present one.

If it were possible to eliminate LIFO from the determination of the first or orthodox method of determining earnings, and then to add LIFO calculations for inventory for all corporations and adjustments for current costs of replacement for all corporations, we would have both a useful figure for comparisons, along the lines accounting has been developing, and a figure for those who need an appraisal of economic income. In the meantime it would be helpful to current reporting if those companies using LIFO were first to make a showing of income on the orthodox basis and then to make the final determination by adding the LIFO adjustment as a separate item.

While the problem is primarily one of earnings or income, there are related problems as well. It is one thing to put into effect a sort of LIFO on plant facilities; it is quite another to do so without integrating it into the accounts as a whole. Perhaps equally important as earnings is the showing of capital or stockholders' investment at current levels. Earnings should be related to current prices, and dividends also should be so related. To restrict earnings to a return on original cost is to invite the destruction of our system. Thus, it may be a necessary part of the use of current costs to have the balance sheet show current costs.

This sounds like the use of appraisals, but the suggestions so far being made deal mostly with adjustments of cost through index figures rather than through consideration of all the other matters that influence fair value. But it seems to me almost necessary that any change of concept on earnings carry forward into the balance sheet. This thought is not original with me, of course; it is being actively advocated both in this country and in England. Its use would show clearly the replacement problems for industry; there would be generally acceptable index figures for use; and there could be changes from year to year if there continue to be violent fluctuations in our economy. Earnings, for instance, could then be stated in percentage of return on investment at current values and not on old book values which mean little.

Conclusion

I keep coming back to the point that this in large part is a business problem. Accountants should not take an inflexible, "Maginot Line" attitude. If public usefulness requires a change, they should be ready to change. But accountants can ask that responsible business make up its mind as to what it wants. If responsible business is willing to say that the orthodox methods of accounting determination of earnings are wrong and that corporate earnings are properly reported only on economic concepts, this year and future years, good times and bad, then accountants can develop theories and methods with some assurance of practical application.

To the extent that the current argument in behalf of economic concepts is expedient and pragmatic, business may well hesitate to take such a position; but if the argument stems from a sincere conviction that the present method of reporting earnings is wrong, then such a pronouncement can be forthcoming. Accounting has stood against permitting a great variety of methods of treatment and measurement and against the use of devices to modify high earnings, but I do not think it will stand against an agreement by responsible business and other elements of our society on what is most useful.

There is much work to be done in improving the reporting of corporate earnings, even though a great deal has already been done during the last few years. A realization of that necessity by the various interested groups, and cooperation between them, should accomplish much more in the immediate future. It is a task for all those interested in preserving our corporate system and one in which I hope the profession of accountancy will lead.

COST FACTORS IN PRICE-MAKING

Howard Clark Greer

Harvard Business Review

Vol. XXX · Number 4 · July–August 1952

Cost Factors in Price-Making

By Howard Clark Greer

PRICE-MAKING is one of management's most important tasks. The success or failure of an enterprise may depend on the ability of its management to select the right prices for its goods.

This is a difficult and delicate operation. The successful price-maker needs a knowledge of economics, an understanding of markets, a familiarity with distribution techniques, and a grasp of the relevant cost facts. This last aspect of the problem is the particular subject of this discussion.

The attempt here is to describe the price-making function as the writer has come to know it, through a quarter-century of close association with such activities, as an accountant, analyst, adviser, executive, and director, serving numerous business enterprises in a variety of industries. The discussion is based on observation and interpretation of what actually takes place in the price-making process. Accordingly the conclusions are derived from practical experience rather than abstract reasoning.

How does a manager go about the job of establishing a price? What conditions confront him? What considerations influence him? What facts does he require? In particular, what cost information is significant, and what bearing will it have on his decisions?

Part I: In a Free Economy

These questions may be answered first in terms of what happens under a free price system. The problems of establishing prices in a controlled economy require separate consideration and will be treated in Part II of this discussion, in the next issue of the Review.

The Price-Cost-Volume Equation

An understanding of prices requires some understanding of costs. Prices and costs are indissolubly connected. Each affects the other. Both prices and costs, in turn, affect volume. Accordingly, the three factors of price, cost, and volume are fundamental to virtually every business activity, every business decision.

The interrelation of these factors is a subject of great confusion and misunderstanding, in business as well as out of it. Because certain influences are commonly significant, it often is assumed that they are universally controlling.

Editors' Note: This article is based on the first of the author's Dickinson Lectures (1952) before the Harvard Graduate School of Business Administration. An article in the September–October Harvard Business Review will complete the publication of Mr. Greer's discussion of "Cost Factors in Price-Making."

Because simple conclusions are craved, interpretations are oversimplified and become misleading. Thus laymen come to believe that they can comprehend price-cost problems which actually baffle the experts.

For example, it is commonly asserted that costs control prices – that the businessman computes his costs, adds a profit, and establishes a price. Acceptance of this postulate leads to assumptions that prices are controlled by producers, that every cost change will be reflected in a price adjustment, that profit margins are optional with sellers, that inflation stems from cost increases, and so on.

Conversely, it is sometimes contended that costs must be governed by prices – that the producer can pay out for materials, wages, taxes, rents, and other costs only what he can collect from his customers, less a reasonable return on the capital employed. This leads to beliefs that consumers may be exploiting producers, forcing down wages and commodity prices, destroying investments, and so on.

It is not that simple. Costs do influence prices, but seldom control them (in the sense of exercising the final, exclusive dominance over their precise level and variation). Prices do influence costs, but cannot regulate them (in the sense of forcing adjustments of specific amount in any particular component). Both costs and prices influence the volume of goods that will be produced and distributed, and it may be volume that is affected when the cost-price relationship changes.

The fact is that prices and costs are in a continuous process of becoming adjusted to each other, with neither in absolute control. When costs rise, there is a tendency for prices to be raised, provided the conditions which produced the cost increase will also warrant a price increase. In many cases, however, a higher cost (e.g., one due to shrinking volume and higher overhead) cannot be "passed on" to the buyer. Likewise, product price reductions put pressure on cost elements like raw material values, wage rates, and taxes, but some of these are rigid and inflexible charges which yield to pressure very little and very slowly, if at all.

The third factor in the equation, and the one most likely to fluctuate, is the volume of business done. For most products there is no single, uniform, invariable price. Rather there is a range of prices within which some sales can be effected. A limited amount of business can be done at the top of the range, a larger amount at the bottom. The question is how much sales volume can be generated, and how much production stimulated, at any particular price level.

Price-Maker's Choice. What the price-maker must do, when considering the proper adjustment to a change in either the strength of demand or the level of costs, is to decide how much of the gain or loss should be reflected in margins and how much in volume. The combined reaction of all the individual price-makers in an industry determines the change for the industry as a whole.

For example, if demand is strong, sellers may elect to raise prices (widening unit margins) or to seek increased volume (possibly lowering costs and raising total margins). If demand weakens, sellers may choose to cut prices (in an effort to maintain volume, even at lower unit margins) or to "hold the line" and let sales decline (in the hope that maintained unit margins may offset shrinking volume).

Similarly, if costs rise, sellers may attempt to raise prices proportionately (at the risk of curtailing volume if demand is not likewise rising), or may "absorb" the increases (on the theory that lower volume might raise costs even more than higher wage or material costs). If costs decline, sellers may reduce prices to get more business (figuring they can afford it) or may try to reflect the savings in wider margins (accepting current volume as adequate).

Thus the precise effect of a cost change on prices cannot be predicted with assurance. The reaction of sellers will vary with the circumstances. If the cost increase occurs during a generally rising level of wages and consumer incomes, prices are quite likely to be advanced, because a strong level of demand is indicated. If the cost increase occurs in a period of shrinking volume and heavier unit fixed charges, prices are unlikely to be adjusted upward – in fact they are more likely to be reduced.

It is most certainly *not* true, as so often contended, that all cost increases bring about commensurate price increases, or even that costs are the chief element in market-level advances. Growing demand does more to raise prices than do advancing costs. The inflationary effect of wage advances is to give people more money to spend rather than to make products cost more. Prices do not go up and down, and cannot be put up and down, simply because costs have risen or fallen. Many other factors influence the result.

Ceilings and Floors. One reason why prices are not immediately, or necessarily, responsive to cost changes is that for most products there is a fairly wide range within which prices may be established with moderately satisfactory results. There usually is no single, inevitable, "right" price, which cannot be either higher or lower. There is likely to be a top and a bottom for permissible quotations, but often these limits are quite far apart.

This being the case, a cost increase or decrease may not necessitate an immediate price adjustment. An increase can perhaps be absorbed, a decrease retained as profit. Costs change constantly, and prices may have to be quoted for a whole season at a time. When an adjustment is postponed, it may ultimately prove unnecessary.

It is noteworthy that price ceilings are established by consumer demand and the absence of competitive pressure, while only price floors are created by production and distribution costs. If the product is scarce and in strong demand, the price may be pushed up far above the highest conceivable cost. If the product is plentiful and has acceptable substitutes, the price may be driven down close to the out-of-pocket cost of the most efficient producer.

Obviously a cost change is not necessarily a price influence unless prices are already so close to costs that there is no room for absorption. In all other cases the result is speculative, depending on numerous factors, a few of which are mentioned later.

Product-Type Influences

Some of the confusion about price-cost relationships arises from lack of understanding of the price characteristics of products of different types. The controlling factors in the establishment of a price vary according to the nature of the article priced. Attempts at generalization breed confusion, since the principles applicable to one group of products are not necessarily significant in other groups.

A few illustrations may help to clarify this point.

Basic Commodities. This group consists of the primary raw materials obtained from field, forest, mine, and ocean (such as grains, livestock, timber, and petroleum), and the products resulting from their initial processing (like flour, meat, lumber, and oil). While the volume of such products is immense, the number of enterprises in these industries is relatively small, and the nature of their pricing problems is unfamiliar to the average citizen, and even to most businessmen.

For all such products the controlling factor in price determination is the size of the supply and the state of the demand. Except as it influences supply (often remotely and indirectly), cost is not a factor in the short-run price movements affecting such products. They sell for what buyers will pay, irrespective of what they may have cost.

Meat furnishes a good example. The supply is regulated by the amount of livestock produced for market, often determined by producer decisions made a year in advance. The demand is a function of consumer incomes. The product is perishable and therefore must be moved promptly. The composite meat price is the total of the family meat budgets of all households in the country divided by the total quantity of meat available for sale.

The cost to any producer, processor, or dealer has no bearing whatever on the price he will be able to obtain. He is completely at the mercy of his customers. They pay what they wish, and he must accept it. What he offers for his raw materials may be based on what he thinks he can resell them for in processed form; but once he has made his purchase, he is helpless against the decisions of his clientele.

This compulsion of demand-fixed selling prices in controlling costs is more widespread than is generally recognized, though in many lines of activity the effects are obscure, complex, and delayed. With basic commodities the effects are prompt and unmistakable. When flour sales are poor, the price of wheat goes down. When textiles are dull, cotton declines. When gasoline moves slowly, petroleum slumps.

In such industries cost calculations work backward. The seller subtracts his expenses from his obtainable selling prices to determine what he can afford to pay for his raw materials. The collective ability of raw material processors in any such industry to guess right and figure accurately determines the amount of profit they can obtain. The important factor is the margin which the markets afford. All other influences are secondary.

By-Products and Joint Products. Many basic commodities, when processed, yield one major product and several by-products, or a number of joint products. Livestock, for example, produces meat, skins, fibers, greases, and pharmaceuticals. Petroleum is converted into gasoline, fuel oil, and a myriad of basic chemicals. Cotton supplies fiber, oil, meal, and livestock feed.

The ineffectiveness of costs in influencing prices is even more clearly evident where by-products or joint products are concerned. Cattle costs have no bearing on hide prices, and what is paid for cotton has no influence on what can be charged for cottonseed oil. For the individual items in a group of joint products (like ham, bacon, chops, and lard), no true cost can be determined. The price of lard, for example, has varied over the years from double to half the cost of the live hogs from which it was produced.

What *is* true is that the combined price of all the products has a strong and direct effect on the price which will be paid for the raw material. Processors of agricultural commodities make frequent calculations of total prospective realizations, minus probable processing and marketing expenses, to determine what material cost can be incurred with some promise of a profit. The collective result of such calculations is a market influence of no mean proportions. It is not solely controlling, but highly important.

It is noteworthy that in such industries the burden of processing-expense increases tends to fall first on the raw material producer, not on the product purchaser. Higher milling costs are more likely to depress the price of wheat than to raise the price of flour. High transportation costs may hold down raw material values rather than put up product prices. The cost of the box is more important to strawberry growers than to shortcake eaters.

Processed Commodities. When secondary processing occurs, costs (in the form of conversion expenses) begin to be a greater factor in price determination. Here the processor normally has some choice about doing the conversion job. When there is a market for the commodity he owns, he is unlikely to incur the expense of converting it into something different unless the finished product can be sold at a price which will cover the basic commodity value plus at least the out-of-pocket expenses involved.

Thus, in setting the price on a processed commodity, the manufacturer begins to work forward as well as backward in his cost-price calculations. He reflects the *raw-material market plus processing expense* in his asking price for the finished product, while at the same time he considers the *product price less processing expense* in appraising the raw material market.

When the two markets get out of relationship, as they often do, it suggests that a corrective change may be in prospect, or that an abnormal competitive condition exists, or that the public demand for the article has become exceptionally strong (or weak), or that some other unusual element is present in his situation. Deciding which of these conditions prevails is the essence of successful management in enterprises of this type.

Since most commodity-processing industries are highly competitive, with margins narrow and market fluctuations severe, knowledge of processing-cost data is an indispensable element in the development of sound price-making policies. Often a sequence of processing operations is involved, with the product salable at various stages of completion. Allocation of joint costs among the processes becomes an important factor. The influence of volume is a vital one.

Under normal conditions each stage in the processing will produce an increase in value equal to the conversion cost plus some margin of profit. Manufacturers thus naturally seek to extend their processing as far as possible. Flour millers go into the breakfast-food and bake-mix business; meat packers make sausage and canned meats; cotton oil processors become producers of packaged shortenings; steelmakers turn out rails, pipe, and wire — even fences, bridges, and houses. The price influence of these "integrated operations" is important and particularly difficult for an outsider to comprehend.

Alternative Uses and Sources. Many raw materials have several alternative uses. Animal and vegetable oils, for example, may be processed into edible products (lard, shortening, margarine, salad dressing) or into inedible products (soap, paint, lubricants, cosmetics). Conversely, many needs can be met from alternative sources. Meat, for example, may be replaced on the menu by fish, poultry, eggs, or cheese; for many purposes, metal and wood are interchangeable with glass or plastic.

The availability of substitute outlets and sources is an important influence on prices. Nothing can be purchased for less than it will bring if diverted to its next most valuable use. Nothing can be sold for more than the price of its most acceptable alternate. Gasoline will bring not less than fuel oil, not more than benzene. Rough lumber must command more than firewood, less than finished flooring.

A whole series of prices may be influenced in this way. In the packing business, for example, it is said that the price of grease may affect the price of pork chops, since lard is a substitute for grease, salt pork for lard, bacon for salt pork, ham for bacon, and pork chops for ham. All meats affect each other; cheap beefsteak may mean lower ham prices, high veal chops strengthen lamp chops, and so on.

In transportation the effects of such competition are striking. Barges compete with pipelines, railroads with barges, trucks with railroads, airplanes with trucks. The cost of the service is less significant in its price than the availability of an alternative facility. High cost of an unsatisfactory service will not necessarily raise its price, though it may ultimately eliminate it from competition. The bus and the private automobile put the electric interurban out of business. Labor and materials flow into trucks and planes if freight cars cost too much to be a profitable investment.

For the past generation most agricultural by-products have been under pressure from synthetic substitutes of chemical origin. Petroleum products crowd the inedible oils of animal and vegetable derivation; rubber and plastics push leather aside; man-made fibers elbow cotton and wool in the textile field; oil and gas have ousted coal from its monopoly of the fuel business; and asphalt roofing has made the wood shingle obsolete.

Fabricated Articles. Somewhat different conditions prevail in the broad field of fabricated articles, such as automobiles, appliances, furniture, clothing, personal goods, and industrial equipment. Because of the huge number and wide variety of such items, they tend to be regarded as typifying price formation in all lines of business, which is an unfortunate misapprehension. These products do, however, furnish the most numerous (and therefore the most impressive) examples of price-making activity, and call for extremely careful attention.

With all such products, cost becomes an important factor in price determination. These goods do not exist in nature, merely awaiting cultivation or extraction; they come into being only as created by man to satisfy an apparent need. Since man expects a compensation proportionate to his efforts and risks, he normally will undertake production only if reasonably assured of an adequate return. He must know his costs and their probable relation to his potential selling prices before he devotes his capital and his energies to the undertaking.

This condition exists, however, only at the initiation of the venture. Once facilities are provided, an organization created, and a trade established, the venture becomes subject to all the hazards of competitors' activities, public preference, and cost fluctuations that beset commodity processing or any other form of commercial endeavor. The first price may recover the first cost, but it does not follow that subsequent prices will reflect subsequent costs. Cheaper, more attractive merchandise may appear. Advances in material costs, or wage levels, or tax rates, or promotional services may raise costs faster than values rise. Continuing profit is far from assured.

On the other hand, the value created may be far in excess of the *cost plus normal return on investment*. New discoveries in fields such as chemicals and drugs may provide goods which sell (initially at least) for double or treble their cost. A brand name may create more profit than a brand-new factory. A trade-mark may sell for more than a transit system.

Again it becomes apparent that costs affect prices but seldom control them. For fabricated articles, cost may establish a floor, never a ceiling. Wide profit margins stimulate increased production and attract competitors. More goods and more sellers tend to lower prices until margins shrink to normal or less. Demand, however, is still the most significant factor in determining the price.

Individual Projects. At the far extreme from the basic commodity stands the individual project – the once-and-for-all, not-to-be-repeated job of constructing an object or performing a service on a special contract, unique in its characteristics, beginning and ending with itself.

Here, and here alone, cost normally becomes the solely controlling factor in the establishment of the price. Since no labor, materials, or facilities are committed to the job in advance, it is evident that no one is likely to acquire and supply them unless he feels sure of getting his money back. Since other contractors are normally awaiting the same opportunity, it is unlikely that anyone can include an abnormal profit in his bid without losing the business to some competitor who is willing to work for less.

Unusual conditions (such as labor and material shortages), peculiar circumstances, or extraordinary demand may stretch or shrink the normal margins, and exceptional efficiency or good fortune may lower costs; but on the whole the selling price of construction, investigation, development, and promotion tends to be related very closely to the costs incurred. It is unfortunate that this well-known fact should lead to the conclusion that the same principle applies to the sale of goods and services of other kinds.

Cost Influences

For those industries in which cost calculations form at least the primary basis for determining what prices should be charged (i.e., will be profitable), what cost data are useful and how are they employed?

Here again the answer is far from simple. The "cost" of a product is not some single precisely calculable figure. Cost is a composite of numerous elements – some direct and some imputed, some fixed and some variable, some provable and some theoretical. No two cost-finding procedures are identical, and no one procedure will produce continuously identical results.

Thus cost-finding for pricing purposes is necessarily the assemblage of a variety of cost facts, which can be combined in a variety of ways to produce a variety of answers. The price-maker can use them only as a guide and a point of reference. In constructing his price list, he will apply cost facts more or less conscientiously according to his philosophy and his circumstances.

Every seller would prefer a price list in which the price of each item fully covers the total computed cost of that item. Such a list would consist of "safe" prices, involving no risks of loss if adequate volume is obtained.

In practice, however, it is often found that not all items will carry full overhead. Competition may limit the obtainable price for certain products. Staple items, turning over rapidly, may justify narrow margins. Overhead analysis may indicate that apportionments have been faulty, with some products bearing more than a fair share. It may be even argued that available prices should dictate the overhead distribution. Should by-products carry full costs? The variations are endless.

Price lists ultimately may be forced into patterns established by competition. The question then becomes one of how much cost is recovered by any given price. The slim-margin items are tolerated; the wide-profit numbers are actively pushed. Price-cost relationships must be constantly checked, as a basis of production and sales policy, even when prices themselves seem immune to the influences of cost computations.

Cost Components. Price-making, of course, is not wholly (or even mainly) the job of establishing general price levels or constructing price lists. Almost every seller is constantly confronted with individual selling opportunities requiring him to arrive at a quotation for a particular piece of business involving some one item, or order, or quantity, or customer. Here the knottiest cost-price problems occur.

The normal condition is one in which the seller is anxious to make the sale. In ordinary times, thanks to this country's enormous natural resources and productive capacity, business is conducted in a so-called "buyers' market." The seller must be the aggressor; he must go after the business. To get it he must match, or better, competitors' prices. How low can he afford to go?

This raises the broad and important question of what elements of cost are significant in establishing prices for individual transactions where more volume is needed, competition is severe, and close figuring is essential. The right answer depends on a full knowledge of the components of costs, a shrewd appraisal of the probable effect of the decision, and a generous portion of ordinary good luck.

In the typical enterprise the total of the costs assignable to an individual product or sale comprises cost elements of several types, usually including the following:

1. Costs which are directly connected with that one product or sale and which occur if that product is made or that sale consummated and not otherwise — so-called *direct* costs.
2. Costs which are related to the total volume of business done, but not specifically to any individual fraction of that total — sometimes referred to as *variable overhead* costs.
3. Costs which are predetermined and constant. irrespective of individual transactions and even of all transactions combined — commonly known as *fixed overhead* costs.

The first group is made up of such elements as materials and direct labor; the second, of costs of such services as maintenance, power, communications, travel, and operating supplies; the third, of such facility and organization costs as insurance, taxes, depreciation, advertising and executive salaries. How much of each of these costs must be reflected in an acceptable selling price?

The orthodox answer is that every price should cover the full cost of the article, including not only direct out-of-pocket costs but a full apportionment of fairly allocated variable and fixed overhead. It is argued that unless each sale returns its share of such costs, all sales combined are unlikely to prove profitable. The dangers of below-cost selling are widely advertised.

The trouble with the advocated principle is the impossibility of applying it. Overhead costs relate to individual items only in theory, and the amount properly assignable to some one unit of goods or services is never precisely measurable. Even when the philosophy of cost apportionment can go unchallenged, the size of the overhead burden per unit cannot be determined unless the number of units is known. Getting or losing a particular order may in itself affect the cost of filling it. The manager is almost bound to assume the acceptance of his bid in figuring his overhead, even though his past experience suggests that higher average costs are probable.

Taken by itself any order is desirable if the price will cover its direct costs and contribute something to the overhead. In few cases, however, can an order be taken entirely by itself. A low price on one sale may involve low prices on others. The order which our low price takes away from a competitor may be canceled out by some other order which his low price takes away from us. Too much cheap business may crowd out more profitable orders obtainable elsewhere. The business might ultimately consist of orders which were individually desirable but collectively unremunerative.

In spite of all this, the fact remains that not all business can be obtained at exactly the same price and that some concessions from top prices are commonly necessary to meet many situations. How far such concessions can extend is an ever-present problem of price-making.

Apportionment of Joint Costs. An invaluable aid in the solution of such problems is a clear understanding of the principles underlying the apportionment among products and activities of those costs which apply jointly to many products and transactions. Which will be greater or less if a certain pricing policy is adopted, and by how much? From which classes of business can fixed-overhead costs be recovered, and at what rate?

The first task of the cost accountant confronting a pricing problem is to study all the indirect costs connected with production, distribution, and administration in an effort to determine which ones are positively affected by the amount and kind of business taken. These may then be grouped according to the *factor of variability* influencing each, and a cost *per unit of activity* may be developed.

In a factory, for example, certain costs may vary with the man-hours operated, others with machine-hours operated, others with quantities processed, and others with values invested. In a transportation system costs may vary with miles of track maintained, with locomotive-hours operated, with car-miles run, with tons hauled, or with passengers carried. In a store or warehouse costs relate to sales volume, inventory volume, space occupancy, personnel employment, promotion, supervision, and so on.

The cost data so developed are not necessarily those incorporated in product or departmental costs, assembled for bookkeeping purposes. They must consist of basic cost elements — "building blocks" from which any specific cost computation can be made to meet whatever need may arise. Even the contents of a block may have to be varied according to the circumstances. The job must be done over and over, with costs assembled in a variety of combinations, to meet the requirements of each particular situation.

Normally the calculation of total cost is a two-stage operation. The first step is to add to the known direct out-of-pocket costs an appropriate allowance for variable overhead costs of all types — the amounts by which the aggregate expense of conducting the business will be increased if this particular order, or class of orders, is obtained and filled. The second step is to add a reasonable (or perhaps the maximum obtainable) share of fixed overhead costs — those charges which will continue in substantially unchanged amount whether or not this particular business is handled. The resulting figure is the basic "sold" cost which a price must attempt to recover.

Unfortunately the distinction between variable and fixed overhead costs is often difficult to maintain. Few overhead costs are uniformly variable or wholly fixed. The principle is easy to state, often difficult to apply. While the mechanics of applying it cannot be fully described here, at least some further attention to the influence of fixed costs on prices may be in order.

Sunk Costs. Businessmen, apprehensive of price-cutting by competitors, commonly argue that every price quoted should reflect a "fair" share of all costs, including those fixed charges which result from the maintenance of an investment and an organization and which are not directly related to any individual activities in which the business may subsequently engage. Economists, however, recognize that many of these outlays create what are sometimes termed "sunk" costs, irrevocably committed to the enterprise and therefore not necessarily an element in the future price decisions of its managers.

While every manager strives mightily to price his goods so that these costs, with all others incurred, will be fully recovered, he usually recognizes that there is no fixed or determinable fraction of the total which is necessarily assignable to, or recoverable from, any individual transaction or group of transactions. While he will use as a guide some possibly arbitrary apportionment of such costs to particular units or classes of products or orders, he must remain conscious that the profitableness of a price, or a price schedule, is not adequately measured by its relationship to costs thus determined.

The reasons are obvious, though they seem often to escape both managers and cost accountants. First, the basis of apportionment is necessarily theoretical and subject to wide variations according to the theory adopted. Secondly, the unit amount of such overhead costs is more closely related to total volume than to the size of the costs themselves. Thus the determination of the fixed-cost component in a total cost involves both a theory as to apportionment and an assumption as to volume. Such a cost factor has no intrinsic veracity, stability, or dependability. It constitutes merely a guide, a measuring stick, or an objective — not a controlling element in price calculations.

The manager's task, broadly considered, is to establish a pricing program which will insure the recovery *in the aggregate* of all costs incurred, plus a maximum of return for the use of the capital employed. Sound pricing usually involves quoting for each item an amount high enough to cover its direct cost, plus its proper share of variable costs, plus its maximum contribution toward fixed overhead and profit. To determine the latter amount it is necessary to estimate the size of the volume obtainable at any level of prices, the probable influence of competition, and many other factors.

Distribution Costs. With attention long concentrated on manufacturing costs, inadequate consideration is frequently given to the expense of marketing the product after its manufacture is completed. Yet distribution accounts for a large percentage of all costs incurred and commonly has more influence on pricing policy than the bare cost of production.

Distribution may include any or all of the following activities: publicity, contact, solicitation, warehousing, display, order filling, delivery, service, credit extension, market research, and the related supervisory and administrative functions. Costs of such activities differ according to products, quantities, channels, locations, customers, and methods of sale. The cost differences vitally affect the price which will be remunerative under varying conditions.

The skillful price-maker must know accurately what cost variations are involved in the offering of goods under the widely differing conditions which may be met in a typical marketing program. One product may differ from another in frequency of sale, rate of turnover, breadth of customer demand, and so on. Unit selling cost for quantity orders is normally far less than for small transactions. Selling to wholesalers is usually much cheaper than direct-to-retailer merchandising. Distance and congestion increase delivery costs. Some customers require more service than others.

Most enterprises develop a pattern of price differentials designed to reflect these cost differences. Quantity discounts are common, and functional (i.e., customer-class) discounts apply in many fields. Delivered prices may include transportation charges. Extra service may rate a special charge.

In no field, however, are there greater temptations toward abuse of the differential cost principle or toward price-cutting of an indiscriminate character. Knowledge of the differences in distribution costs is frequently inadequate; many of the costs are "joint," or seemingly in the category of fixed overhead; the lure of the big order is ever present. The sales temperament plays a part. "If our competitor can do it, so can we" becomes a comfortable excuse for any kind of careless or damaging price-making.

This subject has had intensive study in recent years, but most businesses still have a lot to learn about it. Sound cost calculation is an invaluable aid to sound organization of the selling program. The right selection of customers and channels and the right differentials between classes of service may mean the difference between success and failure for the entire enterprise.

Prior and Current Acquisitions. A particularly perplexing price-cost problem arises from the ownership of materials or facilities acquired at prices substantially above or below those currently prevailing. Should cost calculations (and the related price quotations) be based on actual original costs or on current replacement costs? Should the advantage of the fortunate acquisition be retained by the owner or passed on to the buyer? Should resale prices originally established be maintained even though the goods can now be bought for less?

This is a highly controversial issue, fraught with supposed moral implications as well as real, practical complexities. Is a dealer a "profiteer" if he raises his prices to correspond with changes in replacement costs and sells his low-price inventory for more than he expected to get? Is he a "chiseler" if he marks down his high-cost goods when he learns that lower markets are on the way?

The moralist's response is likely to depend on which theory of price-making appeals to him. If he is a cost-recovery advocate, he may contend that higher replacement costs should not be reflected in higher selling prices till the old low-cost inventory has been sold. This theory comfortably ignores the fact that public demand is expressed in rising prices, and that there is no more justification for denying a seller the advantages of a higher level of purchasing power than there is possibility of protecting him from the penalty of shrinking incomes among his prospective customers. People have to be charged more when they can pay more, and less when they have less to spend.

Oddly enough, sellers often refuse to take advantage of the opportunities for abnormal margins resulting from fortunate acquisitions, using their favorable position instead to "undersell the market" and thus grab some business away from not-so-fortunate competitors. This causes great indignation throughout the trade. The merits and dangers of such a course must be carefully weighed by each seller in the light of his own particular circumstances.

One aspect of this problem is the competitive influence of low-cost and high-cost productive facilities, existing side by side and turning out goods for the same market. Should the owner who acquired his plant at a bargain price — either from a distressed seller or during a period of deflation — use correspondingly reduced depreciation allowances in computing his costs (and setting his prices)? Or should he incorporate in his charges a provision for replacement at current price levels?

The answer again is not properly one of morality or philosophy, but one of judgment, depending on manufacturing conditions, market demand, available trade, volume and profit objectives, and other factors. The utilization of low-cost facilities often involves high operating and maintenance costs, and an inflated depreciation provision may raise the hypothetical product cost to an irrecoverable level. On the other hand, the refusal to recognize a higher level of plant replacement costs may result in "giving away" the economic values inherent in the facilities, when higher prices and wider profit margins are essential to provide the funds needed for replacements.

"Follow the market" is normally the soundest pricing policy. Here again, as in so many other cases, the seller's own actual cost will not constitute the sole (or even an important) determinant of what should be charged. Cost is simply one factor to be considered, receiving greater or lesser weight according to the circumstances.

Incidence of Costs. Despite all the uncertainties as to how much cost can be recovered in any given price, one important fact can never be disregarded, namely, that all costs ultimately burden someone. When the buyer does not pay them, someone else must. Who that someone is depends on circumstances.

It is plainly *not* true that all costs are eventually passed on to the consumers of the products in question. Excessive costs, abnormal losses, and higher income taxes are *not* merely added to selling prices. More than one-fourth of the country's business enterprises normally lose money and thus are obviously not recovering all their costs. Even whole industries may sell their output below the cost of production.

Who takes those losses, carries those burdens?

Most of them, of course, fall on the owners of the enterprises through reduction in, or elimination of, the hoped-for profit — perhaps eventually through dissipation of their capital investment. Others, however, may also be involved.

Unprofitable sales (i.e., those not recovering the costs incurred) in due course put pressure on both volume and costs. The least remunerative business is dropped; special services are discontinued; quality may be lowered. Suppliers are pressed to reduce their quotations for materials and parts. Workers may be forced to accept lower wages, fewer "fringe" benefits. Rents are cut, by using less space or taking cheaper quarters. Tax payments are pushed down, income taxes disappear, and authorities are petitioned for lower property tax assessments.

Thus prices may put pressure on costs as often as costs exert influence on prices. In the long run, for broad segments of the economy, there must be some relationship between the two, but in individual cases it is often difficult to determine which is cause and which effect.

Trade-Position Influences

Costs, then, influence prices, but seldom control them. Costs, moreover, show wide variations according to the basis of computation, which may be altered according to the objectives of the costing process. The conclusion will differ depending on whether the perspective adopted is short-range or long-range, particular or general, aggressive or defensive, complacent or concerned. A price-cost relationship which is acceptable under one set of conditions may be wholly unattractive under another.

It is obvious, moreover, that many considerations other than current and immediate costs have a profound influence on price-making. The trade position of the enterprise is a vital factor. Some of the elements in this position deserve attention.

Competitors' Prices. Run-of-the-mill price-making probably is more strongly influenced by the known (or supposed) prices being quoted by competitors than by any other one factor. Sensitiveness to other people's prices is one of the most marked characteristics of the typical sales representatives. "We can't ask more than they do," the argument runs; "and if they can make money at such prices, so should we."

Persuaded by such flimsy arguments, many enterprises do little more than imitate or adapt their competitors' price lists or individual quotations. Many managers have a blind faith in the soundness and profitableness of a price offered by anyone whom they consider a leader in the field. Others, convinced that competitors are ignorantly or maliciously selling below cost, still feel constrained to meet the price regardless of consequences.

The interpretations of competitors' pricing policies are often unjustified. We cannot assume that any given price is adding to (or subtracting from) a competitor's profits; or that, if adopted, it will add to (or subtract from) our own. There are too many uncertainties, too many differing interpretations, to permit a clear-cut conclusion about the probable effects of a policy on either party concerned.

Competitors' prices may frequently be found unprofitable, in the sense of making less contribution to margins than we consider necessary for the success of our own enterprise. Some concerns consistently underprice their goods, and eventually go broke. On the other hand, the fact that a competitor's price is below *our* cost is far from proving that it is below *his* cost. Some people can and do produce more cheaply than others, and use their cost advantages to establish lower prices, thus either broadening the market or obtaining a larger share of it. Either condition must be presumed possible.

The price-maker's difficulty is in appraising the profitableness of any given quotation he is called on to match. Is it an unwarranted, "flash-in-the-pan," loss-leader type of price, which cannot be consistently maintained, or is it symptomatic of someone's ability to make money on a lower price level than our own cost position appears to justify? Should the lead be followed or disregarded?

While few concerns are in a position to know the details of a competitor's costs, it may be possible, from a study of one's own cost experience, to form useful hypotheses as to the facts which may underlie the other fellow's decisions. For example, it is possible to set down all the numerous components of our own calculated cost for the item in question, and then to guess at the probable elements in the competitor's figuring by seeking answers to such questions as the following:

Has he an advantage in raw material cost; and, if so, how much? Are his labor and facilities more efficient; and, if so, what is his maximum saving? What volume may he be enjoying (or seeking), and what fixed-overhead cost per unit would our factory have if operated at the same percentage of capacity? What distribution methods does he employ, and how costly are they? Is this item one of his major products, or a by-product, or a side line? How large a contribution to overhead and profit might he normally be expected to seek from such an item? What is his stock position, and what is that of the trade generally?

The answers may be conjectural, but often even a conjecture is illuminating. Furthermore, our own costs take on additional meaning when viewed in the light of what we believe other people's may be. Much as we may desire to realize a price which will compensate us for all our costs, justified or unjustified, we cannot expect our customers to pay us a premium to cover inefficiency, wastefulness, or disadvantageous position.

If we have bought our materials too high, or employ our labor carelessly, or use obsolete equipment, or fail to attain adequate volume, or spend too much on maintenance or supervision or advertising, we create no values through those expenditures — none, certainly, that a customer will recompense us for if similar goods are being produced for less by aggressive competitors who are willing to work on narrow margins to improve their volume and increase their turnover. Under such conditions an excess cost becomes a loss, not something that can be recovered in a price. When it is one thing and when the other is one of management's perennial $64 questions.

Continuity of Operations. It is significant that just as cost factors influence prices, so also do price decisions influence costs. This is so because the production volume generated by a given price is itself one of the important factors in determining what the product will cost.

This is not merely a matter of the size of the unit-overhead cost, which is strongly influenced by the over-all volume level, but it is also a question of continuity and orderliness in the scheduling of production and distribution. In most lines it is not possible to stay in business by accepting prices (making sales) only when margins look favorable. Continuous, uninterrupted activity is one of the most important elements in effective cost control.

For this reason many concerns plod patiently along through what are sometimes long-extended periods of unremunerative prices, taking business at whatever price level they may obtain, because the penalties of price reductions on business done are less than the penalties of cost increases resulting from business refused. Conversely, the enterprise which tries to protect its margins by refusing orders at substandard prices may find those margins impaired and its maintained prices no longer profitable if its production schedule is too often disturbed by interruptions.

As production has become more highly mechanized, and as labor costs have become more and more inflexible, the effect of this factor has become more pronounced. Set-up and start-up expenses for short runs become prohibitive. Guaranteed minimum weekly pay rates prevent savings from the layoff procedure once widely employed. Labor shortages and high training costs make it essential to preserve a skilled labor force, even when profitable employment for all of it cannot currently be found.

The exact cost significance of these factors can be measured only with great difficulty and considerable uncertainty. Their importance is, however, rather generally recognized, and they become a compelling influence on pricing policy.

Maintenance of Trade Position. Even more important than continuity of operations is maintenance of trade position — that is, holding one's normal share of whatever business is available. For every regular article of commerce there is an established pattern of distribution, and neither sellers nor buyers want it disturbed to their own disadvantage. Normally they will make substantial sacrifices to maintain it.

For a seller, building up trade is a costly and difficult job. He must make his goods known to potential customers through advertising, publicity, promotion, and display. He must form acquaintances, create confidence, solicit orders, and establish a method of transportation and delivery. He must pave the way for repeat orders, provide customer service, and aid in secondary distribution. Eventually he has a heavy investment in his trade position, perhaps comparable in size with his investment in plant facilities.

The position thus established is one not lightly to be abandoned, and an aggressive seller will defend it stubbornly. He is too conscious of the cost of "getting in" to let himself be easily pushed out again. To maintain his position he may have to make price concessions which appear unwarranted from a cost and profit standpoint, but this step may be cheaper in the long run than to let someone else take his place in the market and then try to win it back at some future date.

The hard choice between selling at a loss and not selling at all may be forced by several different conditions. A competitor's advantage in cost, in location, in service, or in some other factor may make his offerings more attractive and compel us to make a price concession to retain the business. Again, a competitor's willingness to sell at a loss to obtain a "first order" may make our prices look high. The customer may find his own resale margin squeezed by similar competitive factors in his own field, and may demand reductions in the prices he is paying. Substitute goods of a new type may threaten the whole fabric of our trade.

Whatever the cause may be, the effect is often to push prices disturbingly far away from the level which would prevail if current costs and desired profit margins were the only considerations in price-making.

Market-Level Equilibrium. Much of the foregoing has emphasized the pressures toward lower prices which are exerted on the seller by his desire to expand volume, broaden markets, maintain production, and protect trade. These "trade considerations," however, are by no means all on the side of price reductions. Several powerful influences work in the opposite direction.

One of these is the inherent tendency of management to lean to the "high side" in computing costs. Businessmen instinctively fear "close prices." They prefer guides which allow for possible unanticipated cost increases or other contingencies. Accountants are typically conservative. They abhor costs which may turn out to be understated. They like to "forget" possible cost savings in the hope that they will form a welcome, if unexpected, addition to profits.

More important, however, is the disinclination of the average seller to upset an established market equilibrium. Often there is a strong prevailing demand for all the goods currently being produced at prices which are reasonably remunerative to everyone concerned. Why disturb a favorable situation?

True, a lower level of prices might broaden the market, stimulate greater sales, lower costs, and widen the opportunity for profitable employment of capital in expanded plant facilities. When margins are wide and demand apparently insatiable, the pressure for increased competition becomes irresistible. But the typical situation is the one on the border line, where today's prices are barely satisfactory and any reduction seems likely to damage the profit position of the enterprise, perhaps of the entire industry.

Sellers in such cases are characteristically wary. They know that price reductions on their own part may lead to retaliatory price-cutting by others. Often they see little possibility of substantial expansion in the over-all volume of the industry and fear that lower prices will mean simply lower margins and no improvement in trade position. A sort of trade stigma may attach to a seller who "breaks the line."

The fear of the consequences of price-cutting sometimes has become so great as to encourage collaboration among sellers to maintain existing price levels through formal or informal agreements not to lower them. The foolishness, the ineffectiveness of such joint undertakings has been amply demonstrated, and for half a century they have been legally outlawed, but a wistful desire for "protection" of this sort still lingers in the minds of many businessmen.

Lacking the opportunity for outright price-fixing schemes within the law, apprehensive sellers resort to moral preachments on the evils and dangers of price reductions; and the atmosphere thus created does definitely discourage individual adjustments, thus sometimes offsetting the pressures toward lower prices which come from cost and other considerations previously mentioned.

To cut or not to cut, that is the question. There is no formula which will provide an answer. Each seller must assemble, analyze, and evaluate the available trade information, reaching a solution which seems calculated to give him the best profit possibilities for both the immediate and the long-term future. The decision is likely to be a sound one only if it is based on comprehensive factual data, among which the particulars of costs, both actual and potential, are of prime importance.

Conclusion

Costs influence prices but do not control them, except in a limited and special sense. Goods sell for what buyers think they are worth, whether this price is more or less than cost. Business must recover from its total revenues its total costs, but not every sale will show an adequate individual profit. A contribution to overhead is all that can be expected from some classes of business.

Most enterprises will go to great lengths to maintain volume, continue operations, protect trade position. Sales will be made close to cost (or even below cost) before the operation is abandoned. On the other hand, wide profit margins are eagerly accepted, actively exploited.

In a free economy no seller is "entitled" to a price which will cover his costs. He is entitled only to the price the market affords. He must learn to live on that price, or quit. He cannot burden the buyer with excess costs; he must absorb them himself.

In a free economy the buyer is king. He buys what he wants, pays what he chooses. He must offer enough to bring out the production he desires, but no more. He takes nothing not wanted, and supports no one not needed. He makes his own price controls, and it is surprising only that he should imagine anyone else could do it better.

This, it should be emphasized, is his experience in a free economy. His experience under the "protection" of government regulations is the subject of Part II of this discussion, to be published in the next issue.

THE DEVELOPMENT OF CONTEMPORARY ACCOUNTING THOUGHT

An Arno Press Collection

Baldwin, H[arry] G[len]. **Accounting for Value As Well as Original Cost** *and* Castenholz, William B. **A Solution to the Appreciation Problem.** 2 Vols. in 1. 1927/1931

Baxter, William. **Collected Papers on Accounting.** 1978

Brief, Richard P., Ed. **Selections from Encyclopaedia of Accounting, 1903.** 1978

Broaker, Frank and Richard M. Chapman. **The American Accountants' Manual.** 1897

Canning, John B. **The Economics of Accountancy.** 1929

Chatfield, Michael, Ed. **The English View of Accountant's Duties and Responsibilities.** 1978

Cole, William Morse. **The Fundamentals of Accounting.** 1921

Congress of Accountants. **Official Record of the Proceedings of the Congress of Accountants.** 1904

Cronhelm, F[rederick] W[illiam]. **Double Entry by Single.** 1818

Davidson, Sidney. **The Plant Accounting Regulations of the Federal Power Commission.** 1952

De Paula, F[rederic] R[udolf] M[ackley]. **Developments in Accounting.** 1948

Epstein, Marc Jay. **The Effect of Scientific Management on the Development of the Standard Cost System** (Doctoral Dissertation, University of Oregon, 1973). 1978

Esquerré, Paul-Joseph. **The Applied Theory of Accounts.** 1914

Fitzgerald, A[dolf] A[lexander]. **Current Accounting Trends.** 1952

Garner, S. Paul and Marilynn Hughes, Eds. **Readings on Accounting Development.** 1978

Haskins, Charles Waldo. **Business Education and Accountancy.** 1904

Hein, Leonard William. **The British Companies Acts and the Practice of Accountancy 1844-1962** (Doctoral Dissertation, University of California, Los Angeles, 1962). 1978

Hendriksen, Eldon S. **Capital Expenditures in the Steel Industry, 1900 to 1953** (Doctoral Dissertation, University of California, Berkeley, 1956). 1978

Holmes, William, Linda H. Kistler and Louis S. Corsini. **Three Centuries of Accounting in Massachusetts.** 1978

Horngren, Charles T. **Implications for Accountants of the Uses of Financial Statements by Security Analysts** (Doctoral Dissertation, University of Chicago, 1955). 1978

Horrigan, James O., Ed. **Financial Ratio Analysis—An Historical Perspective.** 1978

Jones, [Edward Thomas]. **Jones's English System of Book-keeping.** 1796

Lamden, Charles William. **The Securities and Exchange Commission** (Doctoral Dissertation, University of California, Berkeley, 1949). 1978

Langer, Russell Davis. **Accounting As A Variable in Mergers** (Doctoral Dissertation, University of California, Berkeley, 1976). 1978

Lewis, J. Slater. **The Commercial Organisation of Factories.** 1896

Littleton, A[nanias] C[harles] and B[asil] S. Yamey, Eds. **Studies in the Historv of Accounting.** 1956

Mair, John. **Book-keeping Moderniz'd.** 1793

Mann, Helen Scott. **Charles Ezra Sprague.** 1931

Marsh, C[hristopher] C[olumbus]. **The Theory and Practice of Bank Book-keeping.** 1856

Mitchell, William. **A New and Complete System of Book-keeping by an Improved Method of Double Entry.** 1796

Montgomery, Robert H. **Fifty Years of Accountancy.** 1939

Moonitz, Maurice. **The Entity Theory of Consolidated Statements.** 1951

Moonitz, Maurice, Ed. **Three Contributions to the Development of Accounting Thought.** 1978

Murray, David. **Chapters in the History of Bookkeeping, Accountancy & Commercial Arithmetic.** 1930

Nicholson, J[erome] Lee. **Cost Accounting.** 1913

Paton, William Andrew and Russell Alger Stevenson. **Principles of Accounting.** 1918

Pixley, Francis W[illiam]. **The Profession of a Chartered Accountant and Other Lectures.** 1897

Preinreich, Gabriel A. D. **The Nature of Dividends.** 1935

Previts, Gary John, Ed. **Early 20th Century Developments in American Accounting Thought.** 1978

Ronen, Joshua and George H. Sorter. **Relevant Financial Statements.** 1978

Shenkir, William G., Ed. **Carman G. Blough: His Professional Career and Accounting Thought.** 1978

Simpson, Kemper. **Economics for the Accountant.** 1921

Sneed, Florence R. **Parallelism in Two Disciplines.** (M.A. Thesis, University of Texas, Arlington, 1974). 1978

Sorter, George H. **The Boundaries of the Accounting Universe** (Doctoral Dissertation, University of Chicago, 1963). 1978

Storey, Reed K[arl]. **Matching Revenues with Costs** (Doctoral Dissertation, University of California, Berkeley, 1958). 1978

Sweeney, Henry W[hitcomb]. **Stabilized Accounting.** 1936

Van de Linde, Gérard. **Reminiscences.** 1917

Vatter, William J[oseph]. **The Fund Theory of Accounting and Its Implications for Financial Reports.** 1947

Walker, R. G. **Consolidated Statements.** 1978

Webster, Norman E., Comp. **The American Association of Public Accountants.** 1954

Wells, M. C., Ed. **American Engineers' Contributions to Cost Accounting.** 1978

Worthington, Beresford. **Professional Accountants.** 1895

Yamey, Basil S. **Essays on the History of Accounting.** 1978

Yamey, Basil S., Ed. **The Historical Development of Accounting.** 1978

Yang, J[u] M[ei]. **Goodwill and Other Intangibles.** 1927

Zeff, Stephen Addam. **A Critical Examination of the Orientation Postulate in Accounting, with Particular Attention to its Historical Development** (Doctoral Dissertation, University of Michigan, 1961). 1978

Zeff, Stephen A., Ed. **Selected Dickinson Lectures in Accounting.** 1978